IN DEFENCE OF WELFARE 2

Edited by

Liam Foster • Anne Brunton • Chris Deeming • Tina Haux

P

First published in Great Britain in 2015 by

Policy Press
University of Bristol
1-9 Old Park Hill
Bristol BS2 8BB
UK
t: +44 (0)117 954 5940
e: pp-info@bristol.ac.uk
www.policypress.co.uk

North American office:
Policy Press
c/o The University of Chicago Press
1427 East 60th Street
Chicago, IL 60637, USA
t: +1 773 702 7700
f: +1 773-702-9756
e:sales@press.uchicago.edu
www.press.uchicago.edu

Transferred to Digital Print 2016

Special SPA report to accompany SPA pdf available at:
http://www.social-policy.org.uk/what-we-do/publications/in-defence-of-welfare-2/

British Library Cataloguing in Publication Data
A catalogue record for this book is available from the British Library.
Library of Congress Cataloging-in-Publication Data
A catalog record for this book has been requested.

ISBN 978-1-4473-2792-9 paperback

Cover design by Policy Press
Front cover: image kindly supplied by Matteo Pescarin
Printed and bound by CPI Group (UK) Ltd, Croydon, CR0 4YY
Policy Press uses environmentally responsible print partners

CONTENTS

LOOKING AHEAD

Introduction

Nick Ellison, Chair, Social Policy Association, University of York
nick.ellison@york.ac.uk

We live, as ever, in interesting times. With a General Election imminent, the UK Social Policy Association has decided to repeat its successful publication *In Defence of Welfare*, published for the 2010 election with a follow-up volume, *IDOW 2*. The intention is to publish *IDOW* in the run-up to successive future elections as a means of marking the 'moment' and drawing attention to developments (or the lack of them) in social policy over the presiding government's term of office. What is in this current volume? Nearly fifty short pieces from a diverse range of social policy academics and commentators – senior academics, those just starting out on their academic careers, policy makers and journalists – that concentrate on one aspect or other of 'welfare' over the past five years. The overriding tone is critical, whether the focus is on growing inequalities of income and wealth, the nature of welfare reform and the impact of 'austerity' on the worst off sections of the UK, migration and immigration or the vagaries of the changing labour market. Taken together, these contributions amount to a sustained attack on a government that has displayed little understanding of what it means to be 'disadvantaged' (a word that barely conveys the social and financial exigencies to which many people have been exposed in recent years) – a government that has quite clearly and systematically favoured the demands of the powerful and better off over the needs of the poorest sections of society.

It is not difficult to understand why this particular kind of favouritism should be the case. 'Twas ever thus, many would say. Fatalism of this kind, however, is not what is required – and not what characterises the views expressed in this volume. What *is* required is a sustained critique of embedded neo-liberal assumptions that privilege wealth creation over distribution, private over social investment, tax cuts over public spending and, consequently, inequality over equality. Looked at through a social, as opposed to economic, lens, what the Coalition Government has done is to place the demands of an economic deficit over those of a growing *social* deficit. Better, apparently, to stick to the line that the most wealthy must be allowed to continue their pursuits unhindered, in the interests of protecting liberal capitalism, rather than address the obvious weaknesses of a system so starkly exposed by the banking scandal and ensuing economic crisis – and reform the system itself. Greater attention to the social deficit – the social and individual consequences of, *inter alia*, extensive benefit cuts, increasing conditionality, low wages, cuts to local government services, 'efficiency savings' in health and social care, and cuts to legal aid – would produce a more equitable balance between the needs of people and the (supposed) 'needs' of the economy.

To move in this direction – to embed the economic within the social rather than vice versa – is not an easy path to choose because it brings critics face-to-face with the serried ranks of politicians and economists who persistently proclaim that there is no alternative to deficit reduction and the austerity measures that accompany it. Their views need to be challenged. Leaving aside the question of whether the notion of the 'deficit' is essentially a social construction (it is), the constant refrain about the need to reduce it and the policies developed to achieve this aim means that it is certainly real in its effects. In the UK and elsewhere, the message has gone out that deficit reduction is the only thing that matters and, further, that the only way of achieving this goal is to cut public spending radically, while allowing private wealth creation to flourish. The result, of course, has been a failure to tackle head-on the inequalities of wealth and income that have grown in the UK over the past thirty years, the cumulative costs of which underpin many of the analyses presented in this edition of IDOW. It is for social policyists, social scientists and citizens in general, to challenge the claim that reducing the deficit should be the single most important objective of the next government. This assumption should be countered at every turn in the shape of questions that ask about the social costs of narrowly cast economic policies. Is it acceptable, for example, that suicide rates among benefit claimants are increasing in the wake of rising sanctions (penalties levelled against ESA claimants, for example, rose 470% between December 2012 and June 2014, see the *Observer*, 14th December, 2014)? Is it acceptable that people in receipt of benefits should be removed from their homes and communities because they cannot pay the 'bedroom tax'? Conversely, is it OK that wealthy individuals do not apparently face penalties when their tax avoidance and evasion strategies are exposed? Again, how reasonable is it that zero hours contracts and/or exploitative working conditions for those at the sharp end of the labour market are allowed to continue (at significant cost to taxpayers!) by a government that has continually claimed that 'work pays'?

To those who ask about alternatives to austerity, it is not difficult to argue that taxation should play a bigger part in the overall picture – there is considerable room for both higher income and property taxes, for example, in addition to the proper enforcement of the current tax regime. Social investment strategies, particularly those that target local, regional and UK-national economies, could help to regenerate areas of the UK outside London and the South East. Further, policies designed to re-empower trade unions would help to balance a labour market environment which has seen too much power accrue to large employers with inefficient and inegalitarian results. The wider point, though, is the need for balance. A future government should seek to restore the significance of the social, valuing what a focus on this dimension has to say about what it means to govern in the interests of *all* citizens. Crucially, as part of this approach, there is a real need for politicians to develop a responsible civic language that does not divide people into the simplistic categories of 'scroungers', 'benefit cheats' and 'shirkers' – or, for that matter, 'taxpayers' and 'hard working families'.

A final word of thanks to the editors of this edition of IDOW – Anne Brunton, Chris Deeming, Liam Foster and Tina Haux. Special thanks to Liam for getting the copy into final shape.

Nick Ellison
Chair, UK Social Policy Association

WHAT'S THE POINT OF WELFARE?

What is the state of economic inequality in the UK? And why does it matter?

Danny Dorling, University of Oxford
danny.dorling@ouce.ox.ac.uk

Introduction

Most discussions of economic inequality focus on income, the annual flow of monies to people – earnings, benefits, rent and interest. This one will focus on wealth. Wealth is not income. It is accumulated monies; a stock not a flow. The wealth of the rich produces their income, and the income of the rich produces their wealth. When income inequality is reduced, wealth inequality also tends to decrease, but only decades later. In the past the direct taxation of wealth has sped up this process, making everyone better-off. Today a small and very wealthy group of people prefer you not to know this.

The reported average median household wealth of the best-off tenth of all households in the UK is £1,393,900 more than the paltry median wealth of the poorest tenth. The former have, on median average, recourse to £1.4 million of household wealth each; 290 times the median average household wealth of the poorest 10%. Of what can be counted, this richest tenth hold 42% of their wealth in pension rights, 32% in property, 20% in savings and just 6% in goods (ONS, 2014a). By contrast, almost all the wealth of the poorest tenth of households is accounted for by the low value of their household goods. The gap between those at the very top and the rest has been growing rapidly. The UK *Assets and Wealth Survey* unfortunately does not sample the very rich sufficiently to accurately measure their wealth. This means that the wealth of the richest 1% of the population is mostly not included in the reported wealth of the best-off tenth in the UK.

The *Sunday Times* has reported on the very rich for many years (and in increasingly fawning terms). When the annual rankings are revealed, its magazine now profiles 'top billionaires' and their wives with *OK* magazine style photo-shoots and sycophantic write-ups. In its most recent survey it found that almost half of the richest 1,000 of families in the UK live in London. The London rich are, on average, considerably richer than the superrich living elsewhere in the UK.

Regional variations in the wealth of the super-rich are orders of magnitude greater than those found between average households. For instance, average household wealth in the South East of England was recently recorded to be £309,000, as compared to £143,000 (and falling) in the North East of England (Wearmouth, 2014).

Unlike in the case of income, hardly any households are average when it comes to wealth. Figures from the most recent ONS assets and wealth survey suggest that, again on average, Southern households have £12,300 saved in the bank compared to a household average of £2,400, in the North East. Most have far less. When it comes to wealth, the median holdings are always much lower than the mean.

Offshore wealth and tax avoidance

It only takes a few more members of the 1% to take about an extra quarter of their income through various forms of tax avoidance – registering their property as a company and so on – to return the measure of UK income inequality back to that last seen when the Titanic sank. Since wealth inequalities tend to follow income inequalities (with a lag) we can expect rising wealth inequality in the near future.

Most wealth inequality estimates assume that people pay their taxes. Estimates of the wealth of the top 1% are heavily reliant on data about taxation. Tax data on people who have died has been the main historical method of estimating wealth distributions, but it has relied on families not trying to avoid paying inheritance tax. Yet even according to that data – that is, even assuming zero tax avoidance/evasion – both wealth and income inequality in the UK are at a post-war high and have been for some time (Dorling, 2011).

Whilst many people in the top 1% pay all the tax they should pay, almost all of the very big tax dodgers will be in the 1%, and therefore the mean average income of the group as a whole will rise greatly if estimates for tax avoidance/evasion are included. In the United States there is a tax incentive to declare how much money you hold overseas. In 2012 some 290 large US corporations revealed that they collectively held around $1.6 trillion in off-shore accounts (CTJ, 2012). In the United Kingdom hardly anything is declared, but huge quantities of the wealth of UK citizens are thought to be hidden offshore.

Moving backwards

In 2013, levels of income inequality in the UK returned to those last experienced in the 1930s. But if you assume even a very low level of tax dodging, you find that we have already returned to the 1920s. Include the wealth of the super rich, and the wealthiest 10% of households in the UK now have 1,154 times the wealth of the poorest 10% (ONS, 2014b).

The UK itself operates as a tax haven for many of the world's super-rich, who usually have one of their many homes in or near London. The global super-rich are estimated to have squirreled away between £13 and £20 trillion of wealth in countries where they can avoid tax, including in the UK. In 2012, even as global income fell during the great recession, the income of the very richest rose abruptly. An additional 210 people became dollar billionaires, a club whose 1,426 members together sat on almost £4 trillion (Bowers, 2013).

To be in the global 1%, to be one of the best-off 70 million people in the world, requires wealth of at least £440,000. However, it takes 1,400 of the worst-off of this global 1% to match the wealth of the poorest billionaire (Bowers, 2013).

Wealth, health and harm

I have tried here to describe, in a nutshell, what we know about wealth inequality in the UK and where it's heading. There is huge wealth in the UK but mostly just held by a tiny proportion of residents. But why does it matter that distributional patterns now resemble those prevailing before the Second World War?

There is now substantial evidence to suggest that wealth inequality has a widespread and significant negative effect on well-being (Pickett and Wilkinson 2015). After many possible confounding factors are taken into account, people living in affluent countries with the greatest wealth inequality live, on average, four years less than those in the most equitable countries. The relationship between wealth inequality and life expectancy in affluent countries is far stronger than that found with income inequality (Dorling, 2015).

In addition, rates of infant mortality are twice as high in unequal affluent countries compared to the most equal affluent countries. The supposed benefits of holding wealth for the rich are thus outweighed by the harm suffered by the poor and the rest of the population in a country where only a few have access to wealth and many simply have debts. '(E)nsuring income security in retirement would reduce the need to accumulate private wealth and would provide households with sufficient material living conditions, and more confidence and stability, which are likely predictors of good health' (Nowatzki, 2012: 419).

Correlation is often not causation, but it is rarely pure coincidence. One instance of how economic inequality appears to be related to health is the degree of recourse to drugs. Legal and illegal drug use tends to be higher, per person, in countries with greater inequalities of wealth and hence greater incentives to escape inequitable and precarious realities. For example, the UK has some of the highest rates of cocaine use in Europe.

The UK and Russia have similar levels of income inequality where the worse-off 10% receives about 14 times less to live on a year than the best-off 1%. In both countries the rich are similarly successful. Those who are successful in amassing such an unfair share of their nation's wealth will each harm the prospects of many others in a myriad of ways. It is not possible to accumulate great wealth without causing harm. There comes a point when profit is not rewarding efficiency but Machiavellian traits. In a more equitable affluent nation, selfish behaviour is more likely to be seen for what it is and frowned upon. The population is more likely to develop safeguards against a few people securing most of the wealth. Provision of good pensions to all is likely to be far better and so the incentive to a few to try to become very wealthy to secure their own safer future is diminished. More people are more able to choose to do work and other activities that are to the benefit of their fellow citizens. There is far less truck for believing that just a few people are 'wealth creators' and that most of the rest rely on them. But very unequal countries can improve.

Denmark is an example of a country in which wealth inequalities, although very high, are reducing. Denmark has some of the highest levels of wealth inequality in the European Union, but its levels of income inequality are very low so, over time, wealth inequalities diminish. Young adults in Denmark receive a university education that is free at the point of delivery and numerous other benefits that young adults in the USA, for example, do not receive, despite similar levels of wealth inequalities in both countries. There are many other examples to suggest that substantive change is not just possible, but is underway. We are a long way from the end of history, and a global race to ever greater inequality. There are many examples of inequalities falling in parts of Europe, the Americas and Asia.

Addressing global wealth inequality

Michael Mernagh (2014) has looked at the implications of a redistribution of just one half of one percent of global wealth away from the richest 1% towards the poorest half of humanity. The richest 1% of people in the world own almost half of all its wealth, so losing half of one percent of all wealth would be hardly noticeable to them. It would, however, represent a doubling of the wealth of the poorest half of humanity. Few people believe that this is possible. How have we got to the point where even such a small positive change is near impossible to imagine?

Conclusion – The politics of wealth inequality

Regrettably, despite their unimaginable privilege, those with wealth and power tend to view even the mildest redistribution of wealth as a mortal threat and mobilise energetically to prevent it. Hundreds of millions of dollars a year are channelled to right-wing think-tanks. Usually this is done secretively to advance the views of many of those who hold the most wealth.

In the UK, wealth inequalities are high and rising, and none of the three main political parties are committed to reducing them. There are no well-funded think-tanks or lobbying organisations committed to explaining the problems caused by a tiny number of people becoming richer and richer. That work is left to global poverty charities like Oxfam, a handful of analysts shocked by their findings and a constant stream of articles reporting views from the political fringes. But there are positive signs that change may be afoot.

Public concern about greed and inequality is growing. People are not routinely asked their views on wealth, but in 2010 75% of those who responded to the annual British Social Attitudes survey said that the income gap was too large. By 2012, this figure had risen to 82%. Most importantly, only 14% agreed that the gap is 'about right'. Only 1 in 7 people think the rich deserve to be so rich and most of that minority appear to have little appreciation of just how much better-off the 1% are even when compared to those immediately below.

Two years ago Robert Shiller, the winner of the 2013 Nobel Prize in Economics, declared that '... the most important problem we are facing now, today ... is rising inequality'.

Greed is being challenged again – but we have a long way to go.

References

Bowers, S. (2013) 'Billionaires' club has welcomed 210 new members, Forbes rich list reports', *The Guardian*, 4 March, http://tinyurl.com/cq7h8cl

CTJ (2012) 'Fortune 500 Corporations Holding $1.6 Trillion in Profits Offshore', *Citizens for Tax Justice Report*, 13 December, http://tinyurl.com/kmvbkcm

Dorling, D. (2011) 'Underclass, overclass, ruling class, supernova class (chap. 8)', in A. Walker, A. Sinfield and C. Walker (eds.), *Fighting poverty, inequality and injustice*, Bristol: Policy Press, http://tinyurl.com/k6tnteh

Dorling, D. (2015) The mother of underlying causes – economic ranking and health inequality, Social Science and Medicine, http://www.dannydorling.org/?page_id=4350

Mernagh, M. (2014) 'What if the poor doubled their share of the world's wealth?', *Significance Magazine*, http://tinyurl.com/ouuk9v6

Nowatzki, N. R. (2012) 'Wealth inequality and health: a political economy perspective', *International Journal of Health Services*, 42, 3, 403-24.

ONS (2014a), Total Wealth, Wealth in Great Britain 2010-12, *Assets and Wealth Survey*, http://tinyurl.com/mt5xgfj

ONS (2014b) Breakdown of aggregate total wealth, by decile and components: Great Britain, 2006/08 – 2010/12, Assets and Wealth Survey Tables 2.3 and 2.4, with £518.9bn added from the *Sunday Times* estimates of 2014. The ratio falls to 1:1027 without that addition.

Park, A., Bryson, C., Clery, E., Curtice, J. and Phillips, M. (eds.) (2013) *British Social Attitudes: The 30th Report*, London: National Centre for Social Research, http://tinyurl.com/odezlfy

Pickett, K. E and Wilkinson, R. G. (2015) Income inequality and health: a causal review, Social Science and Medicine, http://www.sciencedirect.com/science/article/pii/S0277953614008399

Wearmouth, R. (2014) 'Revealed: how the Government has been bad for your wealth', *Newcastle Chronicle*, 1 June, http://tinyurl.com/n86f2tn

Note

A longer version of this article is available as: Dorling, D. (2014) What Everyone Needs to Know about Wealth in the UK, http://www.dannydorling.org/?page_id=4208. This version is condensed and updated.

Welfare and well-being – inextricably linked

Elke Heins, University of Edinburgh, and Chris Deeming, University of Bristol,
elke.heins@ed.ac.uk
@socpolEdinburgh

Introduction – Well-being and the measurement of social progress

Although never being intended to measure anything else than economic performance, measures of economic growth such as Gross Domestic Product (GDP) have become proxy indicators for social progress and national well-being grounded on the assumption that a growing economy will inevitably lead to societal advancement. However, there have long been doubts about the suitability of measuring a complex concept such as well-being with one economic indicator and subordinating 'the social' under 'the economic'. The many problems with this include, for example, that economic growth is partly based on the depletion of natural resources and contributes to environmental pollution thus undermining the sustainability of social and economic progress or that, as a measure of aggregate wealth, GDP does not tell us anything about the distribution of this wealth within society, or indeed the social inequalities and lived experiences of most people. These are very relevant criticisms since unequal distributions of material resources are found to be connected to important social outcomes such as poor health or high crime rates, while hurting the economy and growth rates in turn.[1]

Concerns about the suitability of GDP and similar measures of economic growth as indicators of positive societal development have become mainstream more recently, not least in the context of the 2008 crisis. Internationally, these concerns found their culmination in high profile reports such as the Report by the Commission on the Measurement of Economic Performance and Social Progress.[2] Subsequently, many countries are now taking a more holistic approach to understanding well-being and measuring social progress – including the UK where the ONS has launched its Measuring National Well-being project in addition to well-being initiatives in Scotland, and more recently, Northern Ireland.[3]

Internationally, there is growing momentum to go 'beyond GDP'. Today, well-being is commonly defined and measured as a multidimensional concept of which economic or material well-being is just one dimension, usually supplemented by dimensions and indicators that capture sustainability aspects as well as quality of life. The new measurement tools furthermore comprise both objective (e.g. average life expectancy) and subjective dimensions (e.g. self-rated health). For example, the European Commission launched an initiative to this effect and now measures 'Quality of Life' according to nine dimensions.[4] The OECD has similarly developed a new index to measure well-being holistically.[5] These new attempts to measure how countries (or other geographical units) are performing on key well-being indicators is relevant because what gets measured influences what policy makers do. If we too single-mindedly only focus on one indicator when comparing nations and assessing governments, we may overlook other important aspects of life and give the wrong advice to those in charge.

Welfare and social well-being are inextricably linked

Developments in this field matter from a welfare and social policy perspective because key well-being outcomes and welfare policies are closely linked. The media in the UK often portrays social security benefits and welfare state interventions more generally in a bad light (for example, when talking about a 'dependency culture'). However, evidence emerging from cross-national research shows that more encompassing welfare states, aiming for more social and gender equality, almost always perform better across a range of well-being measures; including objective measures such as physical and mental health, educational attainment, social mobility and social connectivity, crime and imprisonment rates (Wilkinson and Pickett, 2010), but also the self-reported measures of health, happiness and life-satisfaction (Deeming and Hayes, 2012). In summary, a well-funded and functioning welfare state, based on solidaristic principles, can play a critical role in securing societal well-being as a whole, from which everyone benefits.

Of the many functions of the 'welfare state', two are particularly prominent: the 'Robin Hood' function which operates to redistribute resources within society (i.e., between members) in order to promote social well-being (Hills, 2014); and the 'piggy bank' function, which is concerned with the redistribution of resources in order to promote individual well-being over the lifecycle (i.e., 'from cradle to grave'). These functions of the welfare state are the principal mechanisms by which the advanced economies help their citizens collectively to guard against adverse social risks, such as unemployment and poverty, but also social investment in the early years, in education and training for work (i.e., active labour market policy) that not only helps to secure greater levels of equality in society but also fosters human capital for future generations (Deeming and Smyth, 2014; Kvist, 2014). The welfare state not only impacts directly on citizen's well-being through the provision of personal services and family benefits, but also more indirectly through improving the health, wealth and social well-being of a whole nation. The welfare state through its comprehensive health, education, pensions, and care services plays a key role in securing economic growth. It provides the infrastructure to support and develop 'human capital' in the form of a healthy workforce equipped with the necessary skills demanded in the modern knowledge economy, and all of society benefits by enabling people of working age to fully participate in the labour market through the provision of care services for children and older people.

Addressing the social determinants of subjective well-being

Successive studies point to the important role that social policy plays in promoting positive well-being, but analysis of the large-scale survey data also reveals that well-being is unevenly distributed within the British population. Inequality continues to be a problem in society and this presents a clear challenge to policy-makers who need to do more to ensure more people can lead happy and fulfilling lives. We now know that well-being is socially determined in important ways (Deeming, 2013). Education helps to promote well-being, and is well-recognised as a cultivating force within society. Work is increasingly seen as the best form of welfare in the twenty-first century, and minimum income policies and wages help to promote economic security and well-being (Davis et al., 2014). A decent job and access to affordable housing matter for the achievement of many important well-being outcomes. Women are more anxious and stressed than men. Women spend longer hours in unpaid domestic work, and often combine employment and care roles. Ensuring single parent families are able to both support themselves and to care for their dependants without material disadvantage continues to be a major challenge. Structural components of ethnic disadvantage persist, despite various employment initiatives and legislation. The well-being of unemployed people from 'black and minority ethnic' (BME) groups is a concern in the UK. The interplay of factors at stake here is likely to be complex, but will include known factors such as overt and 'hidden' discrimination, expectations, stereotypes, alienation, family and economic structures. People living in poor health – which often means coping with a longstanding illness – are amongst the most vulnerable members of British society, reporting the lowest levels of well-being. People in poor health need access to good health and social care. There may be some limits on the reliability of responses to standard well-being questions at the individual level, with responses varying according to mood or the context of the survey. Nevertheless, we may expect such idiosyncrasies to average out in research with representative population samples. Further links between well-being and policy interventions will become clear as this field develops.

Conclusion – Happiness as a policy and objective of good government

Arguments about the size and role of the state have long been a source of political tension, at least in party political terms. Liberal market societies like the UK grapple to find the acceptable balance between 'excessive' and 'insufficient' government involvement in people's everyday lives. On the one hand, the classic argument usually advanced by those on the right of the political spectrum, who have long argued for small government, is – in simplified terms – that too much state intervention may impose on individual freedoms, undermine people's resilience and self-reliance – all of which might have a negative effect on population well-being. People may dislike having to pay higher taxes for more expansive social provision, and higher tax 'burdens' may mean there is less individual freedom to choose. On the other hand, people may feel dissatisfied if everyday life risks such as unemployment and sickness become understood as issues of personal failure and responsibility rather than social problems to be addressed through collective action. Although we are currently living through an era in which many welfare services are being cut, international research findings clearly show that welfare policies and well-being outcomes are inextricably linked. Research continues to offer a broad justification for the principles of social welfare in a more substantive form, at least as a means for promoting well-being and happiness in the population. Government clearly does have a responsibility to help create the underlying conditions in which all citizens can strive to enhance the quality of their lives and the fabric of society around them.

References

Davis, A., Hirsch, D. and Padley, M. (2014) *A minimum income standard for the UK in 2014*, York: JRF, a summary is available at: http://www.jrf.org.uk/sites/files/jrf/Minimum-income-standards-Summary.pdf.

Deeming, C. and Hayes, D. (2012) Worlds of welfare capitalism and well-being: a multilevel analysis, *Journal of Social Policy* 41, 4, 811-29.

Deeming, C. (2013) Addressing the social determinants of subjective well-being: the latest challenge for social policy, *Journal of Social Policy*, 42, 3, 541-65.

Deeming, C. and Smyth, P. (2015) Social investment after neoliberalism: policy paradigms and political platforms, *Journal of Social Policy*, 42, 3, 297-318.

Hills, J. (2014) *Good times, bad times: the welfare myth of them and us*, Bristol: Policy Press.

Kvist, J. (2014) A framework for social investment strategies: Integrating generational, life course and gender perspectives in the EU social investment strategy, *Comparative European Politics*, 14, 1472-4790.

Wilkinson, R. and Pickett, K. (2010) *The spirit level: why equality is better for everyone*, London: Penguin.

Notes

[1] Inequality hurts economic growth, finds OECD research http://www.oecd.org/newsroom/inequality-hurts-economic-growth.htm

[2] Report by the Commission on the Measurement of Economic Performance and Social Progress: www.stiglitz-sen-fitoussi.fr.

[3] http://www.scotland.gov.uk/About/Performance/scotPerforms

[4] http://ec.europa.eu/environment/beyond_gdp/index_en.html

[5] http://www.oecdbetterlifeindex.org/

Well-being and welfare under the UK Coalition: happiness is not enough

David Taylor, University of Brighton
d.taylor@brighton.ac.uk

> 'Senior advisors to the prime minister are drawing up a set of indicators that will include whether ... policy will increase, 'the sum total of human happiness', or make people feel miserable and unfulfilled' (Sunday Times, 13.03.2011).

Introduction

Happiness has long been of interest to politicians and policy-makers but it gained significance with the election of the UK Coalition Government in 2010. Inspired by the French Commission on the Measurement of Economic Performance and Social Progress (Stiglitz et al., 2008), the Government tasked the Office of National Statistics (ONS) with developing a set of well-being indices that would allow the measurement of 'how well we are doing as a nation' (as a counterbalance to GDP measures) and would enable comparison between the UK and other countries. The ONS eventually settled on four questions to measure subjective personal well-being related to happiness and overall life-satisfaction in the Annual Population Survey (APS) and a broader index with 41 questions from a variety of data sets that measure both subjective and objective well-being (ONS, 2014).

The ONS states, 'Developing better measures of well-being and progress is a common international goal ... Within the UK there is a commitment to developing wider measures of well-being so that government policies can be more tailored to the things that matter ... Wider and systematic consideration of well-being has the potential to lead to better decisions by government, markets and the public and as such better outcomes' (ONS, 2014).

Happiness is not enough

Debate about the meaning of subjective well-being has been dominated by positive psychology and behavioural economics in recent times with their focus on individual experience and behaviour. At the same time, popular political imagination has been preoccupied with the idea of individual happiness as a basis for national well-being.

Looking beyond happiness, positive emotions, life-satisfaction and flourishing have come to be regarded by some as the yardstick of subjective well-being. Seeking to flourish, however, is typically seen as the product of individual actions without an examination of social context. As Greco and Stenner have argued, this failure splits 'the subject from their world ... treating feelings and desires as purely internal, individual and subjective affairs ... effectively cutting people off from any of their powers that do not correspond to a limited mode of entrepreneurial subjectivity and practice' (Stenner and Greco, 2013: 106). Such approaches de-socialize the self-reporting individual and divorce subjective well-being from objective well-being – the conditions which may be necessary in order to be well.

In order to grasp national well-being, individual self-reports are aggregated up to form a larger picture – an approach which is firmly methodologically individualist and cannot grasp collective or shared senses of well-being among national or other communities. Importantly, it also says nothing about how the well-being of some stands *in relation to* the well-being of others (other than as different rates between statistical aggregates) and how it may be an outcome of the *quality of that relationship*.

Martha Nussbaum has also argued that single questions such as 'how satisfied are you with your life as a whole' ask respondents to aggregate their own feelings in unrealistic ways. 'There is no opportunity for them to answer something plausible, such as 'well, my health is good, and my work is going well, but I am very upset about the state of the economy, and one of my friends is very ill' (Nussbaum, 2012: 329).

A parallel problem with approaches influenced by positive psychology is that negative emotions are only seen as detrimental to well-being and to be overcome in favour of positive emotions. That life is a complex set of positive and negative internal emotions played out with others in social relationships is not considered. As Daniel Kahneman has recently said there is also the problem of reinterpretation of experience and emotion. How we experience our lives and how we remember those experiences are very different things. Reflections on overall life-satisfaction by the 'remembering self' may reinterpret past experiences often putting positive or negative interpretations on events which were experienced quite differently at the time by the 'experiencing self' (Kahneman, 2015). Remembering for the purposes of survey response, may take this form, but also takes place as an isolated individual act without the benefit of interpretive discussion with others, whereas experience is socially situated in relation to others, their experiences and, in this case, their well-being.

So we should be very wary of taking aggregate accounts of individually self-reported happiness or life-satisfaction as meaningful accounts of national well-being. That said, what do early findings from the ONS indicate about national well-being so conceived, and how valuable are they for social policy and for the future of welfare?

The ONS organises its 41 measures of National well-being, 'into ten 'domains' including topics such as 'Health', 'What we do' and 'Where we live'. The measures include both objective data (for example, the unemployment rate) and subjective data (for example, percentage who felt safe walking alone after dark) ... in order to compare UK well-being with European Union countries the ONS uses similar European data where available from five sources: Eurostat, the European Quality of Life Survey, Eurobarometer, the Programme for International Students Assessment (PISA) and the World Gallup Poll' (ONS, 2014).

Recent key comparative findings include:

- In 2011, 71.8% of adults aged 16 and over in the UK rated their life satisfaction as 7 or more out of 10, higher than the EU-28 average of 69.3%.
- The average rating of satisfaction with family life by people aged 16 and over in the UK in 2011 was 8.2 out of 10, higher than the EU-28 average of 7.8 out of 10.
- Over 6 in 10 people (62.7%) aged 16 and over in the UK rated their health status as very good or good in 2011, lower than the EU-28 average of 64.0%.
- In 2011, 58.4% of people aged 16 and over in the UK reported that they felt close to other people in the area where they lived, lower than the EU-28 average of 66.6%.
- A fifth (20.2%) of households in the UK in 2012 reported great difficulty or difficulty in making ends meet, lower than the estimated EU-28 average of 27.7%.
- In 2013, 79% of adults aged 15 and over in the UK scored very high, high or medium on an index of cultural practice (measuring frequency of cultural participation), higher than the EU-27 average of 66% (Source: ONS, 2014).

On a range of accounts UK respondents' rate above the EU 28 average but on some, such as health and feeling close to other people in the area, they rate below.

Looking at the four life-satisfaction measures over time in the UK there has been a slight and continued rise since 2011 in self-reported sat-

Distribution of personal well-being ratings, United Kingdom, 2011/12 – 2013/14

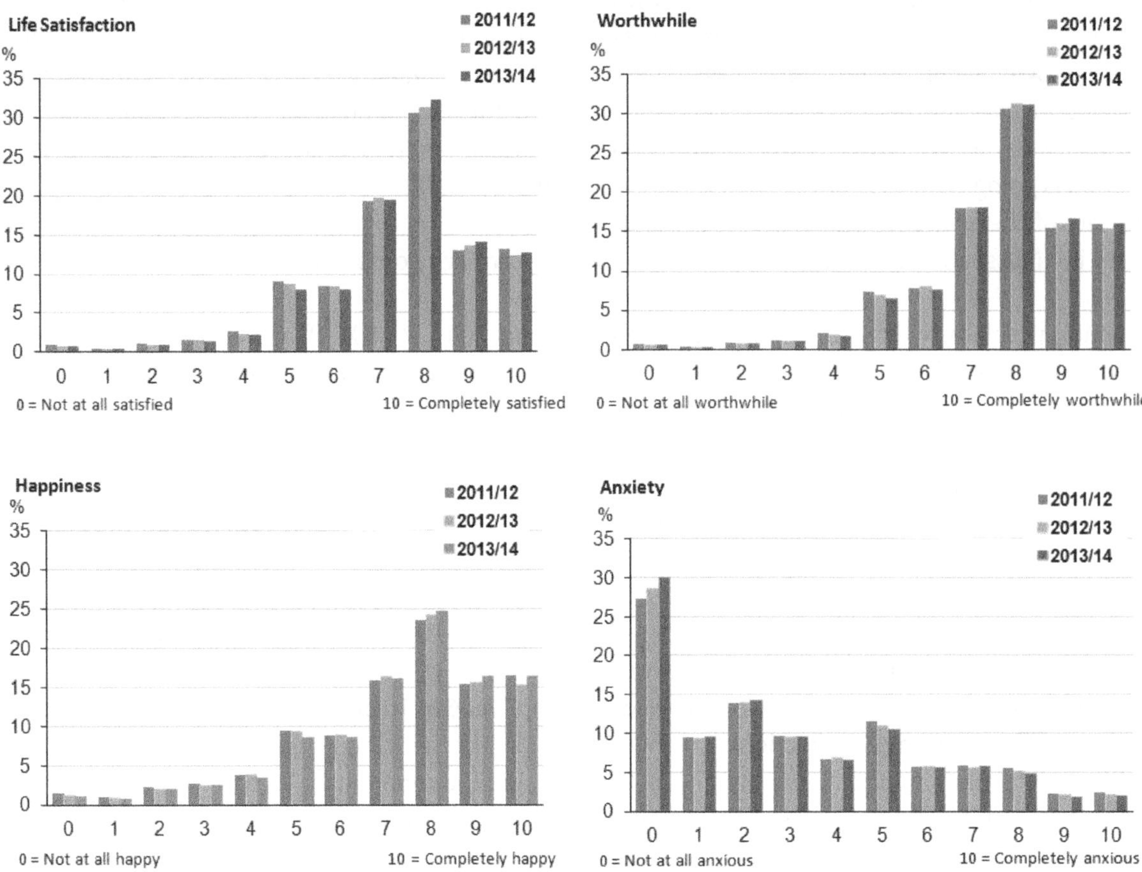

Source: Annual Population Survey (APS) – Office for National Statistics, Statistical Bulletin (2014)

isfaction and decline in reported anxiety (see tables below).

This apparent increase in life-satisfaction during a period of financial crisis, austerity and attacks on welfare provision may seem surprising and rather limited. As Deeming (2013: 543) points out, 'to date, ONS reports have largely been descriptive, showing basic cross-tabulations and average estimates of SWB for different sections of the population ... Their findings do not reveal with any degree of certainty which sections of the British population are particularly vulnerable to experiencing low levels of SWB. Yet we know from the international research literature that a range of socio-demographics can help to explain well-being'. However, we can, as Deeming attempts with more sophisticated regression analyses, show correlations between the different 'social determinants' of well-being. Deeming's analysis shows, 'that well-being is not evenly distributed within the UK. Socio-demographic characteristics such as age, gender, ethnicity, employment, household composition and tenure all matter, as does health status and self-reported indicators' (Deeming, 2013: 541).

It is far cry from here, however, to show causal links between specific policy decisions and happiness or life-satisfaction outcomes. It is an even harder to suggest that where direct links have been established they have in fact influenced policy-making to improve well-being in the way the ONS suggests they might.

Yet we already know from many sources that there are general social characteristics that are associated with collective well-being. Marmot (2010) and Wilkinson and Pickett (2009) already showed the correlation between social inequalities and worse levels of health and many other social determinants of well-being. A key issue here is that inequality is a distributional *relationship*. It is also, generated in the context of unequal power relations. This relational analysis of well-being is missing from much of the recent literature and goes to the heart of debates about how to improve social as opposed to statistically aggregate national well-being.

Conclusion

Attention to *the quality of relationships should be at the heart of policy decisions concerned with well-being*. Abse, for example, has argued for a more relational approach to family policy: 'Emotional health and the strength of people's relationships, whether these be intimate or familial or within communities is closely correlated. If governments fail to create the conditions that promote nurturing families, the capacity for healthy interpersonal relationships is harmed. This has political as well as personal consequences because good relationships are fundamental to the development of communities based on reciprocity, tolerance and cooperation' (Abse, 2014). And as the authors of *The Relational State* argue, there is a 'need for human relationships to be given greater priority as a goal of policy and in the design and operation of public services' (Cooke and Muir, 2012: 8).

The quality of personal and social relationships must be at the heart of any future social policy. Provision to meet certain objective conditions for well-being, such as income up to a certain level, is crucial, but we know that beyond a certain level it is the quality of the experience of those conditions e.g. the relative position of a person's income in relation to others or the type of employment and the quality of that employment, that has the most effect on well-being. As Deeming (2013: 561) concludes, 'The value of social policy is that it recognises the plurality of human ends and needs (not just ideas relating to 'happiness' or SWB), and as such it invokes our social values and principles for thinking about resources, material circumstances, and their distributions'.

References

Abse, S. (2014) 'Labour needs to use family policy to support and strengthen relationships', *New Statesman*, 17/04/2014. http://www.newstatesman.com/politics/2014/04/labour-needs-use-family-policy-support-and-strengthen-relationships [accessed 04/02/2015].

Cooke, G. and Muir, R. (eds.) (2012) *The Relational State: how recognising the importance of human relationship could revolutionise the role of the state,* IPPR

Deeming, C. (2013) 'Addressing the social determinants of subjective well-being: the latest challenge for social policy?' *Journal of Social Policy*, 42, 3, 541-65.

Greco, M. and Stenner, P. (2013) 'Happiness and the art of life: diagnosing the psychopolitics of well-being', *Health, Culture and Society,* 5, 1.

Kahneman, D. (2015) 'The riddle of memory versus experience', *Ted Talks*, http://www.ted.com/talks/daniel_kahneman_the_riddle_of_experience_vs_memory? [accessed 14/01/2015].

Marmot, M. (2010) *Fair society healthy lives*, UCL Institute of Health Equity.

Nussbaum, N. (2012) 'Who is the happy warrior? Philosophy, happiness research, and public policy', *International Review of Economics,* 59, 335-61.

Office for National Statistics (2014) Economic well-being – framework and indicators http://www.ons.gov.uk/ons/rel/wellbeing/economic-well-being/framework-and-indicators/art-economic-wellbeing.html [accessed 14/01/2015].

Office for National Statistics (2014) Income, expenditure and personal well-being, http://www.ons.gov.uk/ons [accessed 14/01/2015].

Office for National Statistics (2014) Personal well-being in the UK, 2013/14, http://www.ons.gov.uk/ons [accessed 14/01/2015].

Seligman, M. (2011) *Flourish – A new understanding of happiness and well-being – and how to achieve them,* London: Nicholas Brealey Publishing.

Stiglitz, J., Sen, A., and Fitoussi, J, (2008) Report of the Commission on the Measurement of Economic Performance and Social Progress, http://www.stiglitz-sen-fitoussi.fr/en/.

Wilkinson, R. and Picket, K. (2009) *The Spirit Level: why more equal rich societies almost always do better*, Penguin Books

'Ways of extending the welfare state to the poor'

Steve Crossley, Durham University
s.j.crossley@durham.ac.uk
@akindoftrouble

Introduction

The Chancellor of the Exchequer recently declared that Britain can no longer afford the cost of the welfare state and has promised to make it fairer for those who need it, as well as for those who pay for it. As the 2015 general election approaches, differences between the main political parties on the issue of what used to be called 'social security' mainly amount to how much to cut and when. Long-term economic security and the end of a something for nothing culture are the order of the day with 'scroungerphobia' (Deacon, 1978: 124) making an unwelcome return. The idea of a more expansive system of protection for people at the margins of our society does not attract much discussion at present. And yet, some parts of the welfare state are actually becoming more inclusive and relaxed. Policies such as a reduction in the highest rate of income tax, increased childcare allowances, a proposal to cut inheritance tax and the development of 'social investment bonds' represent a more inclusive approach to welfare provision, especially for higher earners. This article argues that, far from being too generous to people reliant on benefits for their income, the welfare system, understood in a broad sense, does not adequately include or protect them and suggests that as well as 'defending' welfare, we should be exploring 'ways of extending the welfare state to the poor' (Titmuss, 1965: 20).

Excluded from state support?

The Coalition Government have made no secret of their desire to reform the welfare state. The introduction of Universal Credit, for example, has been a central part of these reforms, although the results to date have not matched the rhetoric with only very small numbers of people claiming Universal Credit. Much has also been made of increases in the threshold at which people start paying tax, although announcements about low-paid people being 'taken out of the tax system altogether' unfortunately ignores the role of VAT and doesn't do a great deal to help those people who are not in work, for whatever reason.

Part of the reason for these reforms is the return of what has previously been called 'scroungerphobia' – the fear that there are people 'milking the state' for as much as they can and choosing to live on benefits as part of a lifestyle choice. Politicians of all colours have sought to pit 'hard-working families' against 'troubled families', the Chancellor has talked of people on benefits sleeping in behind 'closed curtains', whilst Iain Duncan Smith has expressed fears that there are 'entire communities' where no one has worked. This desire to end a 'something for nothing culture' (which has never been proven to exist), coupled with the 'need' to cut the deficit, has led to a number of welfare reforms targeting some of the poorest people in our society.

The unprecedented rise in the numbers of people using food banks has been linked to the increased use of sanctions and delays in the processing of benefits. The child benefit rate has risen by around just 20p per child in the last four years and there has been recent discussion about capping child benefit at two children, even though families with three or more children are at greater risk of poverty than smaller families. Large families have been hit particularly badly the Coalition's tax and welfare reforms although it is lone parents who have fared worst (De Agostini et al., 2014).

A strong political and media focus on stopping benefit fraud unfortunately disguises the fact that large numbers of benefits go unclaimed by people who are perfectly entitled to receive them. Recent analysis of labour market figures suggest that around 50% of unemployed people are not claiming Jobseekers Allowance (JSA) (CESI, 2014). The figure for young unemployed people not claiming JSA has risen by more than 20 percentage points since October 2012, when the current JSA sanctions regime began. The last release of information about non take-up of benefits suggested that in 2009-10, between £7.52 billion and £12.31 billion was left unclaimed (DWP, 2012). In comparison, the latest fraud estimates for the benefits system suggest that around £1.2 billion was lost to fraud in 2013-14, lower still than the amount underpaid as a result of administrative errors (DWP, 2014). A recent prepaid card pilot was announced, which will restrict where people out of work can spend their benefits and what they can buy with them. The increased stigma attached to being reliant upon benefits as a result of the reforms and accompanying rhetoric, is hardly likely to encourage more people to claim state support that they are entitled to.

The examples above – and there are many more which can't be covered here – suggest that state support for many people who lead precarious lives on low and/or insecure incomes is becoming either increasingly difficult to obtain or people do not believe it is worth the hassle associated with applying for it. When support is secured, it is often insufficient to enable them to achieve an adequate standard of living.

A more inclusive approach ...

State support in relation to higher earners generally receives less attention, but when we do look upwards, we can see that the state is becoming more inclusive and benevolent to certain groups of people. By way of example, in the 2012 Budget, George Osborne announced that he was cutting the tax rate for higher earners from 50% to 45%. At the same time, he announced an extension of a planned cut in corporation tax, from 26% to 22% over a three-year period and there is now an increasing awareness of the extent of a wider 'corporate welfare state' in the UK, which has been estimated to be worth around £85 billion (Chakrabortty, 2014).

A recent report found that 'Two-earner households, and those with elderly members, were the most favourably treated' group by the current government's tax and benefit policies (De Agostini et al., 2014: 23). One such policy aimed directly at this group came in the 2014 Budget, when nearly two million families where both parents work became eligible for up to £2,000 per child towards childcare coasts. Families where both parents are in work are one of the population groups least likely to be living in poverty. The same report noted that pensioners, another group with relatively low levels of poverty when comparted to the wider population, also did comparatively well from the government's fiscal policies. The 'triple lock' that applies to pensions has seen pensioner's incomes rise much faster than earnings, at a time of wage stagnation and changes to the way benefits are uprated annually.

The government's Help to Buy scheme provides another example of how the state is intervening to support people who are often excluded from discussions about the welfare state. The scheme offers interest free loans of up to £120,000 for five years for anyone purchasing newly built homes. This is at a time when, as well as the introduction of the infamous 'bedroom tax', the number of people identified as homeless is rising and increasing numbers of people, including families with children, are being placed in temporary bed and breakfast accommodation due to housing shortages.

Changes to the way public services are being delivered also offer opportunities for private sector organisations and 'high-net worth individuals' to benefit from the 'welfare state'. The introduction of market mechanism into the NHS, mirroring the situation in education and 'welfare-to-work' programmes, has seen an increase in private, profit-making healthcare companies providing services for the NHS. The introduction of social investment bonds means that people or organisations are able to invest in new models of public services aimed at some of the most disadvantaged members of our society. Iain Duncan Smith hopes that 'new investors – private sector companies, high-net individuals, and venture capitalists ... groups who might never before have seen themselves as part of the solution for change' will be attracted by a Social Investment Tax Relief which will help the 'growing social investment market' and 'incentivise anyone with savings to put their money into social investment' (Duncan Smith, 2013).

Conclusion

There are, of course, more reforms which are affecting more – and different – groups of people, but it is not possible to cover them all here. The intention is to highlight that the dominant portrayal of the current 'welfare state' as being too generous and encouraging welfare dependency is wholly inaccurate. The reality for those on the lowest and most precarious incomes in the UK is that the current system of state support often falls short of helping them and does not go far enough. Increased conditionality, tougher sanctions and unhelpful political and media rhetoric do not suggest an inclusive approach to supporting people experiencing disadvantages. If, however one takes an alternative and expanded view of the welfare state and examines welfare reforms for those on higher incomes, it is difficult to view them as anything other than increasingly generous. John Hills recently remarked in his book *Good Times and Bad Times*, in relation to welfare spending in the UK, that 'If anyone has got too expensive, it has, in fact, been the rich' (Hills, 2014: 45). It is in this context, then, that, as well as defending welfare, we should be arguing, as Richard Titmuss did fifty years ago, for the extension of the welfare state to support the poorest and most marginalised people in our society. A system of social security which appeared designed to support, rather than punish, poor people would be a good place to start.

References

CESI (2014) Labour Market Live, Centre for Economic and Social Inclusion e-briefing 12 November 2014, http://us5.campaign-archive2.com/?u=c32612be25d976fb2af6c77edandid=c16ecc2714 [accessed 4 January 2015].

Chakrabortty, A. (2014) *Cut benefits? Yes, let's start with our £85bn corporate welfare handout*, http://www.theguardian.com/commentisfree/2014/oct/06/benefits-corporate-welfare-research-public-money-businesses [accessed 4 January 2015].

De Agostini, P., Hills, J. and Sutherland, H. (2014) Were we really all in it together? The distributional effects of the UK Coalition government's tax-benefit policy changes, Social Policy in a cold climate Working Paper 10, LSE, http://sticerd.lse.ac.uk/dps/case/spcc/wp10.pdf [accessed 4 Jan 2015].

Deacon, A. (1978) The scrounging controversy: public attitudes towards the unemployed in contemporary Britain, *Social and Economic Administration*, 12, 2, 120-35.

Duncan Smith, I. (2013) *Social Justice 2nd annual conference speech*, https://www.gov.uk/government/speeches/social-justice-2nd-annual-conference [accessed 2 January 2015].

DWP (2012) Income related benefits: estimates of take-up in 2009-10, https://www.gov.uk/government/uploads/system/uploads/attachment_data/file/222914/tkup_first_release_0910.pdf [accessed 4 January 2015].

DWP (2014) Fraud and error in the benefit system 2013/14 estimates, https://www.gov.uk/government/uploads/system/uploads/attachment_data/file/371459/Statistical_Release.pdf [accessed 4 January 2015].

Hills, J. (2014) *Good times and bad times: the welfare myth of them and us*, Bristol: Policy Press.

Titmuss, R. (1965) The role of redistribution in social policy, *Social Security Bulletin*, June 1965.

Rhetoric and reality: exploring lived experiences of welfare reform under the Coalition

Ruth Patrick, University of Leeds
r.patrick@leeds.ac.uk
@ruthpatrick0

Introduction

Over the past five years, the Westminster Coalition Government has placed marked policy emphasis on efforts to radically reform welfare, promising to bring about the most significant reshaping of the British welfare state since the Beveridge Report. Back in 2011, Secretary of State for the Department of Work and Pensions, Iain Duncan Smith, outlined his vision for welfare reform:

'We will make sure it pays more to be in work than it does to sit on benefits. And because of that, we can say that if there's work you can do, we expect you to do it – or no more benefits. Work that pays. Benefits with conditions. The two halves of the equation: fairness for the jobseeker, fairness for the taxpayer' (Duncan Smith, 2011).

While there are real questions about how far the Coalition approach in fact represents a radical departure, or instead shows marked continuity with its New Labour predecessors, there is no doubt that the Coalition Government have succeeded in ushering in substantial welfare reform. With a continued emphasis on a supposed need to end 'welfare dependency' and return 'responsibility' to the benefits system, welfare reforms have sought to create a new 'contract' between the state and the citizen. In particular, attention has focused on out-of-work benefit claimants who are judged to require support but ultimately compulsion to make the shift from 'welfare dependency' to 'independence' in the paid labour market. Policy tools of welfare conditionality and benefit sanctions have been liberally applied, while a wide range of accompanying reforms have seen restrictions in eligibility for, and reductions in the real value of, many working-age benefits.

The 'strivers' and 'shirkers' narrative

These reforms have been accompanied by a rhetoric that often seems to vilify out-of-work claimants, who are characterised as passive and inactive and displaying problematic behaviours. Claimants 'sleeping off a life on benefits' (Osborne, 2012) are compared with 'hard working families', with divisions between 'shirkers' and 'strivers' a contemporary reworking of long standing distinctions between 'undeserving' and 'deserving' populations.

This rhetoric has material value in providing a justificaiton for the Government's reforms, as well as seeming to fit with a hardening of public attitudes towards welfare and benefit claimants in general (Hall et al., 2014). However, there are real questions about the extent of its (mis)match with everyday lived experiences. In an attempt to forefront these experiences, and draw a contrast with dominant narratives on welfare, small-scale research was conducted into the lived experiences of welfare reform. The research project tracked a small group of out-of-work benefit claimants over time as they experienced changes in their welfare entitlement. Participants were interviewed three times between 2011 and 2013, enabling a dynamic picture to emerge of their responses to the changing welfare landscape. Welfare reforms experienced by the participants included the migration of Incapacity Benefit claimants onto Employment and Support Allowance, single parent's migration from Income Support onto Jobseeker's Allowance and the tightening of the conditionality and sanctions regime for young jobseekers. The findings from this research demonstrate a significant disjuncture between policy rhetoric and lived realities.

The hard 'work' of 'getting by'

Importantly, while David Cameron characterises out-of-work claimants passively 'sitting on their sofas waiting for their benefits to arrive' (Cameron, 2010), this research highlighted the very hard 'work' which 'getting by' (Lister, 2004) on benefits during times of welfare reform demands. Participants spoke of shopping daily to take advantage of the reduced shelves in supermarkets, and going to several shops in an area in an effort to get the cheapest deals. There was also evidence of creative efforts to secure a little additional income, with a disabled woman in her late 50s collecting scrap in the nearby streets, and many participants describing pawning and selling items during particularly straightened times. Managing on very low incomes often entailed having to make hard choices such as to heat or eat (Dugan, 2014) with frequent examples of individuals simply going without. Chloe, a single parent, explained:

> 'I go without my meals sometimes. I have to save meals for me kids. So I'll have a slice of toast and they'll have a full meal'.

Although not in paid employment, many of the participants were involved in other forms of socially valuable contribution in their work as volunteers, carers and parents. These important forms of contribution are too often neglected in Government accounts that equate paid work with dutiful, responsible citizenship behaviour. In the dominant narrative, 'hard working families' are praised as the 'beating heart of our nation' (Duncan Smith, 2010) with a notable silence on the contributions made by out-of-work claimants. The single parents in the study spoke of the hard work that bringing up a family alone involved, showing an awareness of how far this work went unvalued and unappreciated by Government and wider society. As Sophie put it:

> '[The Government] just think that we sit at home on our backsides all day. They don't realise the cooking, the cleaning, looking after the kids and that lot. That's a full time job in itself I think'.

Many of the participants were caring for family and friends, while there were also several examples of participants engaging in volunteering, which was often spoken about as being important for individuals' self-confidence and self-esteem. Those engaged in caring often described this work as demanding and time intensive. Jim, a disability benefit claimant, who cared for his partner and brother, both of whom had serious mental health issues explained:

> '[Caring is] all I do. I don't get any time apart from it'.

These lived experiences serve as a counter to the Government's rhetoric, challenging ideas of out-of-work benefit claimants as passive and inactive.

From 'welfare' to 'work'?

Perhaps even more significant, given the Government's reform agenda, were attitudes and orientations towards paid employment, attitudes which again showed a lack of fit with the dominant narrative. Research has repeatedly shown how out-of-work claimants typically demonstrate a strong work ethic (Shildrick et al., 2010), and describe clear aspirations to enter paid employment, where this is a realistic objective. Furthermore, while the Government characterises some out-of-work claimants as needing help to acquire the 'habit' of work, sometimes describing a 'culture of worklessness', research evidence suggests that most of those out-of-work have previous working experiences, something which this research also found.

Given that this research tracked people over time, it was possible to follow their intersecting and dynamic welfare and employment 'journeys', with several of the participants moving into and out of work during the research time frame, experiences characteristic of the 'low-pay, no-pay' cycle (Shildrick, 2012). Some of the employment which indivduals secured was low-paid, and arguably exploitative, with one young jobseeker, Josh, working 35 hours a week in a local shop for just £80 (£136.65 less than he was entitled to under the 2012 National Minimum Wage rate of £6.19 an hour).

Those who did not manage to secure employment during the time frame described and displayed enduring aspirations to enter the formal labour market, aspirations which were sustained despite the experience of repeated setbacks and rejections. Explaining why she wanted to find work, young jobseeker Sam described herself as a 'scrounger' demonstrating how the dominant, negative characterisations of claimants are being internalised in ways which can only be damaging to individuals' self-esteem. 'I need a job because I'm sick of scrounging. That's how I think of it anyway.'

Is welfare reform helping?

The Government's welfare reform policy approach is premised on the notion that its reforms, and in particular, its supposedly innovative 'Work Programme' will help people to make the transition from out-of-work benefits into paid employment. Indeed, the whole reform agenda is couched in a rhetoric that suggests that tough conditions and the threat of sanctions are necessary to help deliver the transformative rewards of paid employment to ever more of the population. While the strong aspirations to enter employment of most of the people in this research casts doubt on the need for tough conditions, there was also little evidence of welfare-to-work interventions being experienced as beneficial or helpful. Instead, participants spoke of courses that were formulaic and irrelevant, while encounters with advisers were described as brief, unhelpful and constantly framed by a relationship that was perceived as primarily supervisory and disciplinarian.

More generally, there was substantial evidence of the harm that welfare reforms were causing individuals, with participants speaking of their worry, anxiety and fear about current and future welfare reforms. Where individuals were sanctioned, they experienced significant material and emotional hardship, with young jobseeker Adrian describing how desperate his situation became following a lengthy sanction:

> 'I've lost a lot of weight because of it. That's really put me down ... I'm having like one, one and a half meals a day'.

Ironically, Adrian explained that his sanction made it harder for him to secure employment, as his gaunt appearance led potential employers to dismiss him as someone with substance misuse issues. Allied to this, the uncertanty associated with changing entitlement, as well as the increased work of trying to cover all the essentials with a small income, seemed to make it harder for people to actively plan for the future, occupied instead with coping day to day. This preoccupation with managing in the short term again makes successful and sustainable transitions into paid employment less rather than more likely, given the forward planning that such transitions demand.

Conclusion

Listening to what those experiencing welfare reforms have to say is essential if we are to better understand how changes to the benefits system are affecting individual lives. In doing so, what becomes apparent is the extent of the mismatch between the dominant Government narrative and lived realities, a mismatch with implications for the likely success of the welfare reform agenda. In particular, the logic for a strong emphasis on welfare conditionality is undermined by the evidence here presented, while the welfare reforms adopted may ironically be moving people further away rather than closer to the formal labour market (Roberts et al., 2014). The participants in this study dismissed the idea of their choosing benefits as a lifestyle choice, pointing to their difficult lives and asking 'who would choose this?'. As young jobseeker, James, put it:

'[Benefits is] enough for you to live on but you haven't got one bit of luxury left in your life. You're not living, you're existing. And that's how it feels.'

References

Cameron, D. (2010) *Together in the National Interest, Speech to Conservative Party Conference*, 6th October [Online]. London: The Conservatives. Available: http://www.conservatives.com/News/Speeches/2010/10/David_Cameron_Together_in_the_National_Interest.aspx (Accessed 7/10/10)

Dugan, E. (2014) *Benefit changes mean a choice of 'eat or heat' for an increasing number of families* [Online]. London: The Independent. Available: http://www.independent.co.uk/life-style/health-and-families/health-news/benefit-changes-mean-a-choice-of-eat-or-heat-for-an-increasing-number-of-families-9877801.html (Accessed 13/03/15)

Duncan Smith, I. (2010) *Our contract with the country for 21st Century Welfare, Speech to Conservative Party Conference*, 5th October [Online]. London: The Conservatives. Available: http://www.conservatives.com/News/Speeches/2010/10/Iain_Duncan_Smith_Our_contract_with_the_country_for_21st_Century_Welfare.aspx (Accessed 7/10/10)

Duncan Smith, I. (2011) *Reforming our pensions and welfare system, Speech to Conservative Spring Conference*, 6th March [Online]. London: The Conservatives. Available: http://www.conservatives.com/News/Speeches/2011/03/Iain_Duncan_Smith_Reforming_our_pensions_and_welfare_system.aspx (Accessed 7/3/11)

Osborne, G. (2012) *Speech to Conservative Party Conference*, 8th October [Online]. London: New Statesman. Available: http://www.newstatesman.com/blogs/politics/2012/10/george-osbornes-speech-conservative-conference-full-text (Accessed 10/10/12)

Hall, S., Leary, K. and Greevy, H. (2014) *Public attitudes to poverty*, York: Joseph Rowntree Foundation.

Lister, R. (2004) *Poverty*. Cambridge: Polity Press.

Roberts, E., Price, L. and Crosby, L. (2014) *Just about surviving: A qualitative study on the cumulative impact of Welfare reform in the London Borough of Newham. Wave 2 Report*, London: Community Links.

Shildrick, T. (2012) Low pay, no pay churning: the hidden story of work and worklessness, *Poverty* 142: Summer 6-9.

Shildrick, T., Macdonald, R., Webster, C. and Garthwaite, K. (2010) *The low-pay, no-pay cycle: Understanding recurrent poverty*, York: Joseph Rowntree Foundation.

Turning lives around? The Troubled Families Programme

Harriet Churchill, University of Sheffield
h.churchill@sheffield.ac.uk
@HarrieChurchill

Introduction

Announced in the aftermath of the 2011 August riots, the Troubled Families Programme (TFP) sought to 'turnaround the lives of 120,000 of the most troubled families in England' (Cameron, 2011). This article critically reviews the programme's aims and approach.

The Troubled Families Programme

In his post-riots speech, PM David Cameron announced 'urgent action on what some people call problem and others call troubled families' (Cameron, 2011). This led to the cross-departmental Troubled Families Programme (TFP), headed by the Department of Community and Local Government (DCLG), supported by £448 million of central government funding. The primary target group was highly specific – families with co-occurring problems of household welfare reliance; school exclusion, truancy and persistence school absence problems; and youth convictions or youth and/or adult anti-social behaviour problems (DCLG, 2012a). Local authorities (LAs) could also refer families that 'placed a high cost on local services'; experienced two out of the three problems listed above; and/or had 'high health needs' which included substance misuse problems, domestic violence and teenage pregnancy (Ibid).

The DCLG provided LAs in England with a target number of families to 'turn around' by May 2015 (DCLG, 2014a). LAs received funding for engaging families and for 'turning their lives around' measured in terms of:

- fewer school exclusions and improved school attendance over three school terms;
- 60% less anti-social behaviour interventions and 33% less offending;

social alarm about a growing social underclass. Cameron described the parents of young people involved in the riots as 'often welfare reliant single mothers', and the young people themselves as 'repeatedly failing in schools', often living 'without fathers' and 'without discipline' and as 'never wanting to work' (Cameron, 2011). This rhetoric strongly links social deviance, welfare reliance and lone motherhood – understating the diversity of the backgrounds of those involved, the role of peer and social media influences, and the complex socio-economic, local-specific and individual factors that were significant.

The social and economic threats posed by the social underclass were emphasised:

> '120,000 families are a big problem for this country. If you live near one you know very well who they are. And local services like police, health and schools also know who they are, because they spend a disproportionate amount of time and money dealing with them. These families are both troubled and causing trouble' (Pickles, 2011).

The target figure of 120,000 troubled families derived from the *Families at Risk Review* (Social Exclusion Task Force, 2007) which stated there were around 140,000 family households in the UK (117,000 in England), 2% of family households overall, affected by five or more of the following: household welfare reliance; poor/overcrowded housing; adults have no qualifications; mother has mental health problems; an adult has long-term health problems and/or disabilities; low income household; and family cannot afford food and clothing items. This was a dynamic figure, with an estimated 40,000 families moving in and out of this category each year (Ibid). These findings were based on data collected in 2004 by the former Family and Children's Survey (FACS), a representative longitudinal survey

- participation in the Department of Work and Pensions (DWP) welfare to work schemes and/or the end of a period welfare benefit receipt and the take up of paid work for six months (the latter secured the highest results payment overall);
- and/or, reductions in the cost of statutory measures associated with family problems (DCLG, 2012a).

The DCLG provided up to £4,000 total funding per family, an estimated 40% of the total average cost of intensive family interventions.

LAs had much discretion about local service approach. However, they were required to refer welfare recipients to the DWP's welfare to work programmes. Further, DCLG guidance promoted the former Family Intervention Projects, (FIPs) approach to time-limited, goal-orientated, assertive family support and family key worker/ lead professional roles (DCLG, 2012b).

By October 2014, 117,689 families had been referred to local TFPs, of which 85,303 had been 'turned around' (DCLG, 2014a). The majority had achieved the educational and crime reduction/ prevention targets (77,270 families) while 7,347 included individuals engaged with DWP Work Programmes and 8,033 included individuals, previously in receipt of welfare benefits, who had ended claims and taken up employment for six months (Ibid). Deemed a success, the Government announced the 'Extended Troubled Families Programme' (ETFP), pledging additional central government funding for its delivery starting in 2015/6 and broadening the programme's target group (DCLG, 2014b).

The TFP and social underclass politics

While a more in-depth review of local reforms, service user experiences and programme cost-effectiveness needs to await the findings of national and local evaluations, this section critiques the social underclass perspectives that inform the TFP aims and approach. Somewhat akin to the opportunism of some involved in the August riots, the Coalition acted opportunistically in the post-riots period to increase of 7,000 UK families. The figure, however, did not include data about 'troublesome families'. It would be better described as reflecting family households with multiple socio-economic, health and disability problems and adversities. Not reflected in this estimate was the FACS data about youth convictions and police warnings among families in the year prior to survey completion. Its findings suggested around 0.4% of UK families, around 28,000 families in 2004, were affected by this issue – a much smaller number. Nevertheless, researchers have warned that these figures are rough estimates due to issues such as the original sample size. The data is also out of date. Likewise, the DCLG (2013) claimed troubled families cost £9 billion a year, £75,000 per family in welfare and public service intervention costs. However, this estimate has been criticised as crude, given limitations in local comparable data.

Politically, social underclass perspectives sought to discredit alternative explanations for the August riots while at the same time mobilise support within and beyond the Coalition parties (divided over approaches to state intervention in families, especially among Conservatives) to take forward Coalition agreements to reform services for 'families with multiple problems' (HM Government, 2010: 19). However, they provide an insufficient basis for understanding and intervening in the lives of children and families with multiple, compounding socio-economic and psycho-social problems and adversities.

Turning lives around?

The DCLG programme data, reported above, claimed 73% of the target number of families were 'turned around' by October 2014 – the large majority of which (90%) achieved educational and crime prevention related targets while 17% achieved welfare to work and employment related targets. However, the educational and crime prevention targets sought to reduce problems sufficiently to reduce the need for statutory interventions such as school exclusions or Police interventions. Youth and family problems could remain relatively severe. The employment related targets sought to refer those in receipt of out of welfare benefits to DWP welfare to work schemes, reduce household welfare reliance and increase employment rates. But they were not accompanied by assessments of individual and household income or the impact of these changes for children, young people, parents and family households. With 63% of children living in relative household poverty in 2012/13 having at least one parent in paid work (DWP, 2014); employment earnings and prospects differentiated by gender, ethnicity and disability as well as other sources of social difference and inequality; young people at high risk of low wages and insecure employment; and families with children navigating rising childcare and living costs – there is a substantial need to evaluate and promote the degree to which employment secures higher incomes for young people, mothers and families.

A further programme aim was to reduce the demand for, and costs of, statutory measures and interventions among families, including those associated with child protection referrals, assessments and interventions. However, this places a premise on short-term reductions in service demand and costs, when for child-centred reasons, it is vitally important TFP practitioners are vigilant, and respond adequately to concerns about children's welfare and that they are able to facilitate individual and family access to welfare benefit entitlements, specialist health service provision, special educational needs assessments or social housing applications to address pressing social needs. The emphasis on short-term limited support is potentially harmful to child and family welfare, a concern which is exasperated by reduced welfare and family benefits for families (due to the Coalition's welfare reforms) and cutbacks elsewhere in children's services. The latter can restrict the capacity of other services to respond to problems and concerns in children's and parents' lives, particularly at an earlier stage before problems become severe and at which support could be more cost-effective.

This 'short, sharp, shock' approach to intensive family intervention orientated primarily towards reduced demands and costs on the welfare system and children's services also neglects the need for reforms in specialist children's and family services to: address gaps in specialist child and adult services, better support professional training, development and supervision; recognise challenges for inter-agency working between services; and ensure support is adequately tailored to family needs and circumstances based on anti-discrimination principles and comprehensive needs and risk assessments. Indeed the aims of the Extended TFP appears to include taking over the family support roles of professionals that have well established expertise in this area – such as social workers – with little national guidance or regulation around professional training, qualifications or workforce development.

Further, the TFP approach to programme evaluation makes it difficult to assess these concerns. The DCLG only requested LAs report total aggregate data about families identified and families 'turned around'. This means that unless LAs have maintained records linking family details, family data and aggregate data; it is not possible to evaluate the longer term nature of family circumstances. This is seriously problematic given the issues around repeat referrals and short-term service responses the TFP claims to address.

Conclusion

In conclusion, the TFP provides a limited conception of, and framework for, improving the lives of young people and families with multiple, compounding socio-economic and psycho-social problems and adversities. This is due to the significance of social underclass perspectives, committed to residual social policies. Alternative starting points for reform require more multi-dimensional individual-social-structural explanations for child and family problems which recognise the compounding nature of socio-economic, health and behavioural problems and adversities. Policy responses could better build on the growing expertise among specialist practitioners and services in this field, but require more investment and considered reform. They should include early intervention and prevention initiatives. Wide-ranging socio-economic policies and reforms are also needed to address high rates of material disadvantage and wide social inequalities. Given the scale of these problems in the UK context and the increasing recognition of the importance of a 'good childhood', there is a pressing need for greater political commitment to, and social investment in, harnessing the transformative scope of the welfare state to improve children's lives and prospects, and better support parents and families.

References

Cameron, D. (2011) *PM's speech on the fightback after the riots*, https://www.gov.uk/government/speeches/pms-speech-on-the-fightback-after-the-riots, [accessed 10.12.14].

DCLG (2012a) *The Troubled Families Programme: Financial framework for the Troubled Families Programme's payment by results scheme for local authorities*, London: DCLG.

DCLG (2012b) *Working with Troubled Families: a guide to the evidence and good practice*, London: DCLG.

DCLG (2013) *The Cost of Troubled Families*, London: DCLG.

DCLG (2014a) *Troubled Families: progress information at end of September 2014 and families turned around at end of October 2014*, https://www.gov.uk/government/publications/troubled-families-progress-information-at-september-2014-and-families-turned-around-at-october-2014. [accessed 26.12.14].

DCLG (2014b) *Estimating the numbers of families eligible for the Expanded Families Programme*, London: DCLG.

HM Government (2010) *The Coalition: our programme of government*, London: Cabinet Office.

Pickles, E. (2011) *DCLG Announcement: Tackling troubled families*, 15th December 2011, available at: https://www.gov.uk/government/news/tackling-troubled-families, [accessed 10th May 2013].

Social Exclusion Task Force (2007) *Families at risk: Background on families with multiple disadvantages*, Cabinet Office: London.

IMPACT OF WELFARE REFORMS

High-cost credit and welfare reform

Jodi Gardner, University of Oxford, and Karen Rowlingson, University of Birmingham
jodi.gardner@law.ox.ac.uk

Introduction

High-cost credit, in particular payday lending, has recently received unprecedented levels of academic and media interest. In the last five years from 2009 to 2014, the market for these products has grown significantly – from around £800 million to £2.8-£3.5 billion, depending on the definition used. This growth has occurred for a variety of reasons, many of which are intrinsically linked with welfare reform. Whilst the current government is spending a considerable amount of time and effort addressing the regulatory aspects associated with the supply of high-cost credit, it is doing little to tackle the underlying reasons why increasing numbers of people are turning to such expensive, and potentially harmful, financial products. Until these issues are addressed, we will only be dealing with the symptoms and not the root causes behind these issues. This article analyses the impact that recent welfare reform has had, and could have, on high-cost credit. There are three parts. Part I briefly analyses political and economic reasons behind the rise of high-cost credit in the UK. Part II highlights how the government has dealt with the problems created by this explosion, including the increased regulatory requirements on credit providers. Finally, Part III suggests a range of reforms which will help to provide a safer credit market for low-income borrowers in the UK.

Part I: The rise of high-cost credit

During the recent period of international financial turbulence, growing numbers of UK borrowers accessed short-term finance to close the increasing gap between their income and the cost of living. Due to a range of economic and political factors, there has been a consequent upsurge in the use of high-cost credit to 'make ends meet' – a form of credit which, as outlined above, has increased approximately fourfold in the last five years. The UK recently experienced the longest economic depression in over 100 years and a double-dip recession, wages stagnated or lowered, unemployment rose dramatically and the cost of living skyrocketed (Packman, 2014). Whilst the economy is beginning to show signs of improvement, these are being felt largely by the most well-off in our society, with little evidence of a 'trickle down' to those who need it the most.

Politically, a Conservative-led Coalition Government has enacted reforms that, when combined with the economic conditions discussed above, have resulted in an unprecedented increase in need for short-term credit. These include decreased access to welfare, the creation a universal benefits cap, dismantling the Social Fund (which was widely considered the 'lender of last resort' for vulnerable consumers in desperate need of funds) and the reduction in funding to a range of organisations designed to assist people who have fallen on hard times. The government also instigated a number of reforms which increased income insecurity, especially for low-income families, further contributing to people's need to rely on credit for many day-to-day expenses. It is therefore no surprise that in 2013 over two million people turned to payday lenders and other high-cost credit providers for short-term injections of much-needed cash.

Part II: The Government's response to high-cost credit

The increased attention paid to high-cost credit eventually led the government to review the legal regulation that previously existed in this field. For example, the government referred the industry to the Competition and Markets Authority for review (CMA) to determine what, if any, issues exist that may impact the competitiveness of the market. A new regulator for consumer credit, the Financial Conduct Authority (FCA), has also been created and replaces the Office of Fair Trading. The FCA has received increased funding and enforcement powers, and the impact of this is already evident with a number of firms having their licences revoked and actions taken against Wonga (UK's leading payday lender) for both unfair debt collection practices and irresponsible lending.

In conjunction with the transfer to the new regulator, the legislative and regulatory regime associated with high-cost credit has undergone significant reform, including:

- Enhanced affordability assessments, including a consideration of the borrowers' other financial commitments;
- Borrowers can 'rollover' (i.e. renew the loan for a further term without making any repayments) a maximum of two times;
- A maximum of two unsuccessful attempts at continuous payment authorities (CPAs) to pay off the loan in full allowed;
- Prohibition on the use of CPAs for part payments of outstanding loans;[1]
- Provision of a financial warning to be included in payday advertisements; and
- Provision of an information sheet, including how to access free debt advice, for borrowers who rollover a loan.

Whilst these go a considerable way to addressing some of the harm caused by high-cost credit, many in the consumer lobby, such as Stella Creasy MP and Unite, saw this as 'too little, too late'. One of the biggest concerns voiced by a number of consumer advocates and politicians was the lack of any cap on the cost of credit, which meant that payday loans of 3,000% APR were commonplace and loans of up to 16,000% APR were available on the market. These organisations believed that, despite the increased regulation, a cap was still necessary and in November 2013, an amendment to the Banking Reform Bill was passed which required the FCA to implement a cap on the total cost of credit by 2 January 2015. This cap involves:

1. The initial cost of credit limited to 0.8% per day, with an annualised percentage rate of 1,270%;
2. Default fees limited to £15 and default interest must not exceed 0.8% per day; and
3. A 100% repayment cap, meaning that the borrowers will never have to repay more than double the amount they borrowed (see FCA, 2014).

Whilst both the enhanced lending requirements and the newly established cap will help address some of the most heinous lender activities, they do not address the underlying causes of the high-cost credit crisis – the fact that large numbers of people in the UK do not have access to affordable and appropriate financial products in times of need (French et al., 2012; Rowlingson and McKay, 2014).

Part III: Looking beyond regulation – what more can be done?

The third and final part of this paper will consider, in light of the issues discussed above, what future reforms are needed to combat the problems associated with high-cost credit. The CMA has outlined that approximately 70% of all payday loans are obtained for 'everyday expenses', including groceries, bills and costs associated with car ownership (CMA, 2014: 68). This is in sharp contrast to how high-cost credit is often marketed, as a once-off loan for unexpected expenses or luxury items, such as a holiday. Unfortunately, using expensive, short-term credit for everyday expenses can easily result in the creation of credit dependency and a debt spiral, often with harmful consequences. It is therefore important to address the underlying needs behind the demand for high-cost credit in an attempt to decrease the number of people using this financial product in an inappropriate manner.

Lending to people on low incomes for short-term credit needs will always be relatively expensive, given the high cost of making such loans and the high risk of default. One way of making it more affordable is to subsidise it by assisting the non-profit sector. Demand for short-term credit will never cease completely and it is important that people, especially those on a low income, have access to appropriate and affordable credit. The government can assist this endeavour by increasing funding for Credit Unions and Community Development Finance Institutions (CDFIs), both of which provide affordable credit products. The banking sector also needs reform. The current vague and complicated fee structure of banks, including the high costs associated with unauthorised overdrafts, is one of the key reasons why many people turn to high-cost credit facilities. Pressure should therefore be put on mainstream banks to deliver increased short-term and affordable credit options to all customers. Unfortunately, for some of the poorest in our society, even low-cost loans from mainstream or not-for-profit institutions will have a detrimental impact on their financial position. Because of this, it is critical that the Social Fund is reinstated nation-wide, as this will ensure that people who are financially struggling do not exacerbate their situation by burdening themselves with problem debt.

It is an unhappy reality that many people turn to high-cost credit because their incomes are insufficient to cover their day-to-day expenses. Obviously further welfare reform is required to address this issue and ensure that all people have access to sufficient resources for a basic standard of living without having to resort to expensive and often harmful credit, including the promotion of a 'living wage' (see Davis et al., 2014). A wide range of further initiatives should also be implemented, including increased financial grants to low income families during times of need and enhanced funding for support organisations, such as money advice charities and, potentially, food banks. These reforms will, especially when complemented with the increased regulation discussed in Part II, address the underlying causes fuelling the explosion in demand for high-cost credit, as opposed to just managing the symptoms.

Conclusion – High-cost credit in the UK, more than just a regulatory issue

It is clear that we cannot deal with high-cost credit, in particular payday lending, without recognising the intimate and interconnected relationship it has with the welfare system. On one hand, the Coalition's agenda has allowed demand for expensive, short-term credit to flourish, thereby creating the high-cost credit crisis currently being experienced by many, largely low-income, people in our society. On the other hand, the underlying issues behind high-cost credit will not be adequately resolved without addressing fundamental problems of low and insecure income, whether sourced from the labour market or from social security benefits. Whilst the government has made great inroads into the regulation of high-cost credit products, it has largely ignored the broader issues – why and how we have created a society where so many people need to access expensive and often harmful credit just to 'get by'. Until this is addressed, the currently regulatory endeavours are unlikely to do anything more than merely push these problems onto a new area.

Notes

1 An automatic payment of outstanding debts through a debit or credit card, linked either to a bank account or credit card. Once a borrower agrees to a CPA, the lender will be able to obtain payment without any further action from the individual.

2 We would like to thank the AHRC for supporting the work on which this paper is based, through the FINCRIS project: Responsibilities, Ethics and the Financial Crisis.

References

Competition and Markets Authority (2014) *Research into the Payday Lending Market*, London: CMA.

Davis, A., Hirsch, D. and Padley, M. (2014) *A minimum income standard for the UK in 2014*, York: Joseph Rowntree Foundation.

Financial Conduct Authority (2014) *Proposals for a price cap on high-cost short-term credit: Consultation Paper*, July 2014.

French, S., Leyshon, A. and Meek, S. (2012) *The changing geography of British Bank and Building Society Branch Networks, 2003-2012*, Nottingham: University of Nottingham.

Packman, C. (2014) *Payday lending: global growth of the high-cost credit market*, Basingstoke: Palgrave Macmillan.

Rowlingson, K. and McKay, S. (2014) *Financial Inclusion Annual Monitoring Report*, Birmingham: University of Birmingham.

Financial inclusion

Lindsey Appleyard, University of Birmingham, Karen Rowlingson, University of Birmingham, and Stephen McKay, University of Lincoln
k.rowlingson@bham.ac.uk

Introduction – What is financial inclusion?

The OECD define financial inclusion as:

> 'the process of promoting affordable, timely and adequate access to a wide range of regulated financial products and services and broadening their use by all segments of society through the implementation of tailored existing and innovative approaches, including financial awareness and education with a view to promote financial well-being as well as economic and social inclusion' (OECD, 2014: 26).

In the UK, Kempson and Collard (2012) have suggested that people who are financially included have the ability to: manage day-to-day financial transactions via a transactional (bank) account; save to meet one-off expenses; manage a loss of earned income; invest in a pension; access insurance; and avoid/reduce problem debt.

Financial inclusion first emerged on the UK social policy agenda in response to bank branch closures in the early 1990s. From then on, this issue was championed by New Labour who set up the Financial Inclusion Taskforce in 2005 to help improve access to appropriate and affordable financial products and services. The Financial Inclusion Taskforce made some progress but since the global financial crisis, household incomes have become increasingly squeezed, making it difficult for people to achieve financial inclusion, as defined above. This paper explores current levels of financial inclusion and briefly reviews recent government policy before considering the future of financial inclusion.

Current levels of financial inclusion

There is no single measure of financial inclusion but one of its most fundamental elements is to have a sufficient and secure level of income with which to meet basic needs. Since the economic crash of 2007, however, unemployment has gone up and incomes have been squeezed still further. With wages stagnating and benefit cuts biting, it has become increasingly difficult for people to manage financially. In fact, survey findings suggest that in order to make ends meet, the majority of the population (57%) were cutting back on their spending in 2014. Much of this economising was on non-essentials such as eating out and luxury food but one in ten manual workers had cut back on basic food items (Rowlingson and McKay, 2014).

One of the key components of financial inclusion is to have sufficient savings to meet one-off expenses and/or shortfalls in income. Whilst many people recognise the significance of saving, only 41% of people said they were actively saving in 2010-11 (Rowlingson and McKay, 2014). It is unsurprising that those with the highest income were more likely to save than those on the lowest incomes and that those with the highest incomes were also able to save significantly more (half of the top 10% were saving a mean average of £526 whereas half of those at the bottom half of the income distribution were saving £50 per month) (Rowlingson and McKay, 2014). In 2010-11, 45% of households had less than £1,500 in savings, 28% had between £1,500 and £20,000, and 20% had over £20,000 (Rowlingson and McKay, 2014).

It is therefore not surprising that people have very little capacity to meet unexpected expenses, even relatively small ones. When asked whether or not they could find £200 at short notice, 16% of the population in 2014 said they would have to borrow money – either through a formal loan (credit card, overdraft, loan etc.) or through an informal loan from family/friends. A further 16% said they would not be able to meet this expense or preferred not to answer the question (Rowlingson and McKay, 2014).

An early focus of the financial inclusion agenda was to increase the number of people in the mainstream financial system through opening a bank account. Whilst increasing numbers of households now have a bank account, around 1.87 million adults remain unbanked in 2011-12 (Rowlingson and McKay, 2014). The majority of those without a transactional bank account are between the ages of 18-29 (15%) (Rowlingson and McKay, 2014). Not having a bank account (or a credit history) also has implications for accessing other financial products and services such as affordable credit, and to meet other needs such as private rented accommodation. However, it is not known how many people have a bank account but do not use it and the reasons for doing so (perhaps for fear of becoming overdrawn and the cost associated with it). Further research would be welcomed in this area.

Given the lack of savings, it is also no surprise that the number of households with unsecured credit or a form of credit commitment is high (64% and 75% respectively) (Rowlingson and McKay, 2014). This further suggests that household incomes are not meeting the needs of households and that these finances are under increasing pressure.

Some types of borrowing can be helpful to smooth the peaks and troughs of income and consumption but if people cannot afford their repayments they may get into 'problem debt'. 'Problem debt' also occurs when people fall behind with bill payments. Whilst it is difficult to access reliable data on 'problem debt', the evidence suggests that increasing numbers of households are experiencing difficulties in repaying unsecured credit and consider it to be a 'heavy burden' (18% in 2008-10) (Rowlingson and McKay, 2014). Furthermore, there were 34,000 mortgage repossessions in 2012, a fall from the peak in 2009 of 50,000 but still signalling major difficulties for people in repaying mortgages (Rowlingson and McKay, 2014). While mortgage repossessions have fallen in the last few years, evictions from rented accommodation have been increasing since 2010 (Rowlingson and McKay, 2014). Early evidence suggests that the impact of welfare reform and the so-called bedroom tax is exacerbating this trend. The government clearly has a responsibility to ensure that people have access to appropriate housing and greater forbearance is required particularly during financial hardship.

Coalition policy on financial inclusion

The Coalition has rarely used the term 'financial inclusion'. It has certainly not had a 'financial inclusion strategy' and it went ahead with the disbandment of the Financial Inclusion Taskforce in 2011. It had always been the intention for the Taskforce to be temporary but, given the economic situation, a government committed to financial inclusion might have considered extending its life for a few more years.

One of the first acts of the Coalition was to stop the introduction of the Saving Gateway. This was a financial inclusion policy designed to encourage low-income savers to save through matched saving. When piloted, the scheme was well regarded by its users. Instead, the government increased the amount an individual can save in a tax free ISA which caters for middle and higher income earners, people who already have access to appropriate financial services.

The Coalition also withdrew support from the Child Trust Fund, a universal savings scheme for all babies and was therefore fully inclusive.

Some elements of Coalition government policy have been more positive in relation to financial inclusion. For example, in 2013 the government have provided £38 million worth of financial support to Credit Unions to modernise under the 'Credit Union Expansion Project' and expand their operations for low income households, but this alone will not enable them to meet the potential market demand and many Credit Unions are unwilling to do so.

The government has also introduced various reforms of 'high cost, short term' credit including an interest rate cap on payday lending to reduce the cost and risk of this form of high-cost credit to individuals. From January 2015, the interest rate cap will be set at 0.8% per day, or 1,270% APR. More significant perhaps is that there is a 100% borrowing limitation, meaning that consumers will never have to pay back more than double the cost of their initial loan if they are experiencing difficulties with repayment.

Finally, the government's pension reforms around auto enrolment into workplace pensions looks set to include many more people than before into pension schemes.

Conclusions and recommendations

With the loss of the Financial Inclusion Taskforce in 2011 and in lieu of a clear financial inclusion strategy, recent financial inclusion policies have been fragmented and tokenistic. These policies alone do not go far enough to ensure that people are financially included, particularly around supporting those on the lowest incomes. And broader Coalition policies around welfare reform are causing levels of financial exclusion to rise still further in relation to low levels of income, problem debt and lack of savings.

UK household finances are under significant pressure. Many may have weathered the storm so far yet remain in an extremely precarious position. There is evidence of blue sky amongst the grey clouds in the UK economic outlook yet the Coalition plan to continue the drive for austerity and Welfare Reform. This suggests that the majority of households (particularly at the lower end of the income distribution) will experience financial challenges both in the short and longer term. It is fundamental that the work of the Financial Inclusion Taskforce is not diminished. The evidence presented here suggests that the reduction (in real terms) in household incomes is having the greatest impact on financial exclusion. This is also where government financial inclusion strategy could have the greatest impact. This could be achieved through instituting a minimum income standard via the minimum wage and through means tested benefit increases, progressive taxation and a reduction in VAT (as poorer households pay a disproportionate amount of VAT compared to wealthier households). Alongside this, savings schemes designed to support and reward low income savers that match regular small sums such as the Saving Gateway could offer a starting point for an effective financial inclusion agenda to be relaunched.

References

Kempson, E. and Collard, S. (2012) Developing a vision for financial inclusion, London: Friends Provident Foundation. http://tinyurl.com/p37ra77 [accessed 16.12.14].

Organization for Economic Co-operation and Development (2014) *PISA 2012 Results: students and money financial literacy skills for the 21st Century*, Volume VI. OECD Publishing. http://www.oecd.org/pisa/keyfindings/PISA-2012-results-volume-vi.pdf [accessed 16.12.14].

Rowlingson, K. and McKay, S. (2014) Financial Inclusion: Annual Monitoring Report 2014. Birmingham: University of Birmingham. http://www.birmingham.ac.uk/Documents/college-social-sciences/social-policy/CHASM/annual-reports/chasm-annual-monitoring-report-2014.pdf [accessed 10.12.14].

The value of local government for welfare

Annette Hastings, University of Glasgow, Nick Bailey, University of Glasgow, Glen Bramley, Heriot Watt University, and Maria Gannon, University of Glasgow
annette.hastings@glasgow.ac.uk

Introduction – The challenge facing local government

Local government has long played a central role in the British welfare system, particularly as the key provider of education and a range of social services. Historically, it was also the major provider of social housing although that role has become more of an enabling role in relation to planning and affordability since the 1980s. Local government has been supported through extensive financial grants from Central Government which have, broadly speaking, sought to equalise levels of provision across the country.

In recent years, local authorities in England have been at the forefront of efforts by the Coalition Government to manage the fiscal deficit by reducing public spending. That this is part of a longer-term agenda to reduce the size and scope of the state has been noted by commentators for some time, and is now being publically stated by the junior partner in the Coalition, the Liberal Democrats.

The scale of the cuts to local government budgets is of a scale not experienced previously and will radically reshape what they can do. There has also been (in England at least) a significant move away from the principle of equalisation. This is the evidence of a major research project for the Joseph Rowntree Foundation ongoing since 2011 which has charted the nature and pattern of cuts to local government budgets and the response of councils to these (see Hastings et al., 2015 for full details). Our own calculation of the scale of the cuts – borne out by evidence from bodies such as the National Audit Office – is of a real terms cut of 28% to English local government in the period 2010/11-15/16 (Hastings et al., 2015). Moreover, it is clear that authorities with the greatest concentrations of deprived people have been subjected to the biggest cuts in government grant.

It seems clear that, whichever party forms the next government, substantial further cuts in funding for local government can be expected. However, new research suggests that the capacity of English councils to continue to absorb further budget reductions without losing essential statutory services is close to being exhausted, and that the poorest and most vulnerable are likely to suffer the most significant impacts as this happens (Hastings et al., 2015).

So what has the Coalition been trying to achieve?

The Coalition Government's agenda for local government is not just about reducing spend, but also about bringing about fundamental change to the nature and scope of the sector. 'Localism' is clearly instrumental in achieving this – 'freeing up' local government from central control as well as 'dependency' on government grants, while passing over greater levels of responsibility for income generation and managing demand for services. The success of localism also depends on citizens and civic society organisations stepping forward to take over roles previously done by councils – such as managing the local leisure centre or library – and taking more responsibility for elderly relatives, neighbourhood cleanliness and so on.

The 'public service reform' agenda also aims to transform services so that budget contraction can take place without creating undue damage. 'Transformation' is conceived of encouraging services not only to work more efficiently but – as the recent report of the government-funded Transformation Panel indicated – more collaboratively and holistically: integrating different providers, data and technologies as part of a 'person-centred' focus.

Whether these agendas can indeed be delivered alongside fiscal austerity is a key question. Moreover, the effects of other elements of the Coalition's programme – not least welfare reform and the growing evidence of the disproportionate impacts of this on areas of concentrated deprivation as well as on the intensity of need – should also be considered.

How has local government responded?

The evidence from national data and local cases studies is that, while the response varies between authorities, it can be summarised as having two main elements:

1 Local authorities have sought to ***protect front-line services*** by trying to deliver the majority of savings needed through efficiency measures and cuts in 'back office' functions or overheads such as premises. However, it is clear that scope for these kinds of savings is rapidly diminishing, and indeed that later phases of efficiency savings have begun to undermine the capacity of staff working in front-line roles to deliver effective services. The evidence of our research is that the public *have* noticed a deterioration in service standards across a range of services particularly but not exclusively with respect to those focused on children and young people and on the environmental quality in residential neighbourhoods. The fact that front-line services are destined to bear the brunt of the burden of cuts in the years to come is concerning therefore.

2 Most authorities have sought to ***protect the services on which poorer groups are more reliant*** by targeting other services for a greater rate of cuts. Nationally, councils are striving to shelter services such social work and social care, as well as those focused on financial advice or homelessness by giving them a degree of relative protection. Our case study evidence suggests the substantial challenges which this can entail, not least because these 'pro-poor' services make up around 60% of the total expenditure of the case study councils. Whilst they may well have been subjected to a lower proportionate share, many have been subject to high absolute levels of cuts. Moreover, there is evidence that as austerity progresses, savings in 'pro-poor' services are making up a growing share of the overall burden of savings.

And what are the consequences?

First, ***front-line services are under increasing strain***. As cuts to council services interact with the impacts of the recession and reductions in welfare expenditure, some services – particularly those used most by poorer groups – are in danger of being overwhelmed by a rise in the level and intensity of needs:

> 'These people are coming to us at the end of their tethers and we're trying to help them. I don't think we've ever had people quite as bad as we have at the moment ... this last year in particular has been really, really hard on people, we are inundated with people coming in now' (Advice Services Provider).

> 'Social work are so stretched that I think they will not, unless it's an absolute must, go out to deal with something' (Housing Services Provider).

Second, the cuts are ***fuelling the rise in inequality between poorer people and places and their better off counterparts***. Even when authorities attempt to shelter poorer households from the worst effects of cuts, it is clear that these do fall most heavily on disadvantaged groups. Indeed, what can seem like quite small changes to services – the relocation of some services offered by a children's centre, reduced hours at the local swimming pool or increased charges for the uplift of refuse or public transport – can present an absolute barrier to some people's capacity to use a service.

Inequality is amplified by the fact that while poorer households may have few or no alternatives to council services, better off groups often do (the bookshop in place of the closed library, for example). Some councils have attempted to avoid withdrawing services altogether by centralising a range of services into 'hubs' operating from fewer locations but the costs of travel (money and time) may be prohibitive for low income groups.

Third, some of the cuts are ***storing up problems for the future*** because many council services play a preventative role. In the longer-term, these cuts may well result in higher levels of need and hence demand for services. Good quality care for older people maintains health and well-being and supports independent living. Children's Centres can help children get a successful start at school and reduce the need for more expensive social work interventions:

> 'And one important thing I'd say is like when it comes to social services this centre provides de-escalation from it. If a family is having problems and we come here with it first they help us deal with it. It can actually stop a lot of referrals to social services' (Children's Centre Service user, disadvantaged neighbourhood).

There is a real danger that the level of cut to local government budgets will lead to a loss of the preventative and transformative potential of council services.

Conclusions

The pace and depth of cuts to local government budgets is bringing about a fundamental shift in both the scale and the nature of local government. It is clear that the Coalition Government has a vision of the future which is radically different from the past: where local government provides fewer services, many to a smaller range of people; where it works in partnership with a wider range of public and voluntary organisations to meet needs; and where citizens play a greater role in provision and outcomes.

But it is not clear that the Coalition has put a coherent strategy in place for moving to this new landscape. Indeed, it seems that the pace as well as the scale of cuts is undermining the capacity of councils to invest in or develop new forms of partnership. Moreover, there is a glaring lack of resourcing focused on building capacity for citizen action to replace the activities of the local state.

References

Hastings, A., Bailey, G., Bramley, G. and Gannon, M. (2015) *'The costs of the cuts: their impact on local government and poorer communities'*, York: Joseph Rowntree Foundation (http://www.jrf.org.uk/publications/cost-cuts-impact-local-government-and-poorer-communities) Accessed date early March.

Housing and welfare reform

Ian Cole and Ryan Powell, Sheffield Hallam University
r.s.powell@shu.ac.uk

Introduction – The focus on housing in welfare reform

Housing has been described as the 'wobbly pillar' of the welfare state, a policy area which has been particularly susceptible to attacks on the post-war welfare settlement in the past thirty years, through reductions in public expenditure, a shrinking role for state provision and insistent rhetorical and material support for private market alternatives. This assault has continued unabated in recent years, despite the collapse of the mortgage debt market precipitating the global financial crisis of 2008. Given this legacy, it is therefore not surprising that housing has been at the centre of the Coalition Government's programme of welfare reform. A series of changes have been introduced to reduce the level of Housing Benefit (HB) received by working age tenants in both the social and private rented sectors. This focus is hardly surprising either, as HB is the largest single item of expenditure, apart from the state pension, in the Department for Work and Pensions (DWP) budget (£23.5 billion in 2012/13) (OBR, 2014: 55).

These measures have been justified as part of the wider deficit reduction plan, coupled with the familiar discourses of scapegoating the poor, while enhancing 'responsibility' and promoting 'fairness' for those renowned 'hard-working families' not receiving benefits who are struggling to afford their rents and mortgages. These measures have, however, failed to achieve significant reductions in overall expenditure as intended, and the overall HB bill has continued to rise. Any explanation of this trend has to acknowledge the critical importance of stagnant wage levels for the vast majority of people, set against a housing market dominated by escalating housing costs, acute pressures in the social housing sector, rising rents, tight constraints on mortgage borrowing and historically low levels of new building.

Despite this, a lot of distress and disruption has already been caused by these measures, with still more punitive policies in the pipeline, especially if the Conservatives win the 2015 election. This paper examines what the key measures have been, where the government has failed to achieve its objectives, and the impact so far on tenants.

The bedroom tax

The removal of the spare room subsidy, or 'bedroom tax', was introduced between April and November 2013, and has two stated objectives – to reduce HB expenditure and to reduce 'under-occupation' in the social rented sector. To achieve these objectives the policy makes a percentage reduction from the rent eligible for HB – by 14% for those households with one additional bedroom and by 25% for those with two additional bedrooms.

As with all elements of the Government's social policy it is important to set the stated aims against some empirical realities. First, if the target of the reforms really is under-occupation in the housing market, then it is hardy focused on the right housing tenure: only 4% of all spare bedrooms in the UK are in the homes of working age social tenants targeted by the bedroom tax. By contrast, 8% of owner-occupied households would fail the 'under-occupancy test'. Second, the estimated savings from the changes are not that large in proportionate terms: the estimate of £500 million savings (for 2014/15) is only just over 2% of the overall welfare budget cuts of £19 billion. Furthermore, an independent analysis by Professor Steve Wilcox suggested that this figure was in itself an overstatement – he estimated the net savings in the first year of operation at around £330 million (Wilcox, 2014). However, it is reasonable to suppose that the symbolic impact of these measures was always as important as its material impact. It attracted attention towards those social housing tenants living it up in their spare bedrooms and away from the critical state of the housing market that has caused more and more people to have to supplement their income with HB payments.

The bedroom tax also showed a woeful ignorance of the housing stock profile in the sector – in many areas there were simply not enough smaller properties to move to anyway. Even where tenants could move, and thereby release larger properties to be allocated, the consequences could create problems: in some lower demand housing markets there is a risk that these properties will now stay empty longer before being re-let. By targeting the social rented sector, it is inevitable that the costs of the bedroom tax will fall more heavily on the vulnerable. The DWP's own equality impact assessment estimated that more than three-fifths of those households would contain one or more registered disabled persons. And it was the consequences for disabled people that caused the Liberal Democrats to try and force an amendment to the policy, and for the Labour party to pledge to repeal it.

The bedroom tax prompted more concerted opposition and criticism than just about any other part of the Government's welfare reform programme. As a result of issues such as not making automatic provision for an additional room for a household where a member had a disability, or applying the size criteria penalties before a household has even been made an offer of suitable alternative accommodation, the Government was hoist on its own petard – a policy founded on a notion of 'fairness' was widely seen as palpably unfair. The political lesson that the Conservatives might take from the strong public reaction against the tax is that it is more difficult to withdraw benefit from those who already receive it than it is to deny access to the benefit in the first place.

Changes to housing benefit in the private rented sector

The range of measures introduced from April 2011 onwards to reform HB in the private rented sector (PRS), where the eligible rate is determined by a system of Local Housing Allowances (LHAs), are complex. They include changing the method for setting weekly LHA rates so that they are based on the 30th percentile rather than the median of local market rents; capping by property size the total amount that can be paid in HB (which has affected tenants in some parts of central London); limiting the property size for HB payment to four bedrooms; reducing the uprating of HB rates so that they are now set at 1% (or average local rent increases, if lower) for 2014/15 and 2015/16. It also raised the age at which the Shared Accommodation Rate applied from 24 to 34. This led to a sharp reduction in HB (on average over £13 a week) for those people in this age group without dependent children who had previously been living in self-contained accommodation.

While the bedroom tax proposals attracted more media interest, and were the focus of a sustained campaign of opposition, the changes to HB in the PRS are more important in terms of the amount of money to be saved. The measures have targeted nearly three times the annual amount of expenditure savings: £1,645m compared to £660m (Beatty and Fothergill, 2013). The relatively muted response to the impact of the measures, certainly outside London, reflects the disparate nature of the PRS, with no focal point for resistance and opposition. The changes involved are far more complex than the brutal simplicity of the bedroom tax ('reversing the reduction in LHA rates from the median to the 30th percentile of local Housing Market Rental Area rents' is hardly a strong basis for a populist rallying call). Some of the impacts have been blunted, or at least delayed, by the use of Discretionary Housing Payments, which began as a temporary stop-gap measure and have since become an essential, if extremely restricted, form of support for households most affected by the changes.

Most tenants who were affected by the bedroom tax or the LHA changes have responded in a similar way – attempting to find ways of staying put and paying up at first to avoid having to move, sometimes much further afield – only 6% of those affected moved in the first six months. The evaluation of the LHA reforms showed that nearly half the claimants tried to adapt to the shortfall in their HB by cutting down on essential items, and nearly a third had been forced to borrow from family or friends due to the changes. Only 9% had responded by spending their savings, which says more about their budgets than their lack of inventiveness in trying to make ends meet (DWP, 2014). These are all stopgap measures rather than a sustainable means of meeting the increase in their housing costs, and many claimants will be forced to move somewhere cheaper in the end – if, of course, there is any such accommodation available.

One reason for the more muted response to the HB cutbacks in the PRS than in social housing is that the effects of the changes vary widely from one locality to the next, so there is no single narrative about the scale of the impact or the response to them. For example, the reduction in LHA rates for a 2 bedroomed property in April 2011 ranged from £260 a week (reduced from £550 to £290) in Westminster to £6 a week (down from £75 to £69) in Rhondda. The changes also differ from other reforms in that they need to draw selectively on the repertoire of epithets used for those 'on benefit'. It is difficult, for example, to push the 'shirker/striver' distinction too strongly when one-in-four of all HB recipients, and around one in three in London, have a member of their household in employment. The increase in the number of people claiming HB over the past five years is not due to a sudden outgrowth of 'dependency' – it is the inevitable consequence of higher housing costs and stagnant wages.

But the dependency discourse has taken an unusual turn in terms of defining what it is to be young – now, it seems, anyone below 35 years old. Age is being used increasingly as a mode of rationing benefit support while keeping the pensioner standard of living (and the pensioner vote) free from such pain. The default mode for people under 35 without primary child care responsibilities is that they must share. This is a prelude to a much more aggressive attack on age-related support that would follow after the election. The rationale for changes to the SAR in effect inverts the usual 'cycle of dependency' scenario. In this Alice in Wonderland world, the problem is not that young people have failed to rouse themselves from their sofas and stand on their own two feet by living independently – the problem is that too many have done just that, and now must be forced out of self-contained accommodation, sell their sofas, and share, often in very unsatisfactory arrangements.

It is difficult to play the card of 'keeping separated parents actively involved in their children's lives', when those with weekend access arrangements for their children are in effect forced to move from their self-contained flat to share with other adult strangers instead. It can create specific problems for groups such as pregnant women, people with drug and alcohol dependencies, LGBT people, and those with mental health difficulties. And it is difficult for ministers to press a convincing case for people on benefits to move to areas 'where there are jobs', when the shortfall between the HB they receive and the rent charged is generally much higher in buoyant local labour markets. Such are the paradoxes of the policy discourse on welfare reform.

There are, as ever, two possible responses to these reforms: to tinker, for example by reversing the means for determining HB rates in the PRS, redefining exemptions from the bedroom tax or changing the rules on uprating; or adopting a longer term and more fundamental strategy. The two responses are not mutually exclusive.

Implications for future policies

The problem with focusing exclusively on HB to achieve housing outcomes such as lower rents or reduced under-occupancy is that such measures are trying to treat the patient through dosing them up with the disease they already have. The fundamental problem with public expenditure on housing is the complete mismatch between the high level of 'demand subsidies' such as HB, and the very low level of investment in supply, especially on building more genuinely affordable housing, not the parody of 'affordable housing' (with rents at 80% of the market rate) that we have at present. This has prompted a call from groups such as Social Housing Under Threat (SHOUT) to move from 'benefits to bricks'. The difficulty is that it will take an awfully long time before the stimulus to supply is reflected in lower rent levels or property prices. And the recent Lyons review of housing supply for the Labour Party offered a rather timid prospectus, hidebound by its fear of seeking to increase borrowing 'irresponsibly'. But marginal increase in housing output, or policy distractions such as Help to Buy, will not be enough. The appetite of developers for building and renewing homes across *all* localities, including areas of acute housing and social need, is always weak, especially when there is somewhere else more comfortable to be.

What is needed above all is more social housing, pure and simple. Thus was also the conclusion reached in a report on the housing crisis back in 2012 called *Building the Road to Recovery*. The authors of the report? A left-wing think tank? An independent charity like the Joseph Rowntree Foundation? No, Tullet Prebon, hedge fund managers *par excellence*. Yet for once the Coalition Government did not heed the siren voices of the City. It will be left to the next government to seize that opportunity if we are to go beyond the current malaise, going round in ever decreasing circles on cutting the funding for, and limiting access to, an increasingly divisive housing benefit system propping up an increasingly dysfunctional housing market.

References

Beatty, C. and Fothergill, S. (2103) *Hitting the poorest places hardest: the local and regional impact of welfare reform,* Sheffield: Centre for Regional Economic and Social Research, Sheffield Hallam University.

Department for Work and Pensions (2014) *The impact of recent reforms to local housing allowances: summary of key findings,* Research Report No. 874 London: DWP, https://www.gov.uk/government/uploads/system/uploads/attachment_data/file/329902/rr874-lha-impact-of-recent-reforms-summary.pdf [accessed 10.12.14].

Office for Budget Responsibility (2014) *Welfare Trends,* London: OBR http://budgetresponsibility.org.uk/welfare-trends-report-october-2014/ [accessed 10.12.14].

Wilcox, S. (2014) *Housing Benefit Size Criteria: impacts for social sector tenants and options for reform,* York: Joseph Rowntree Foundation.

'I'm thinking, god, what am I going to do, I've got no money, I need to pay this and I need to pay that, and then I'm going back to the tools that I'm getting from stress management ...'

Victoria Armstrong, Durham University
v.e.potts@durham.ac.uk
@stigmaresearch

Introduction

There is an emerging and significant body of evidence, of which this series is part, suggesting contemporary welfare reform operates to the detriment of individual recipients of welfare benefits and can often be harmful to the mental health of its claimants. Current mental health strategy and policy, specifically *No Health without Mental Health* (DoH, 2011) and *Closing the Gap* (DoH, 2014), acknowledge financial difficulties and poverty as contributory factors to mental distress yet this recognition seemingly fails to permeate wider welfare reform. Using empirical examples this article expounds the negative effect of recent welfare reform on many benefit claimants and suggests that the effect seems self-defeating when considered in light of mental health policy. The evidence suggests that the current system of claiming welfare benefits often causes stress and distress, frequently having the effect of undermining claimants and causing many to question their self-worth. Such sentiments appear to fuel a sense of hopelessness often 'coped with' or managed by attempts at employing individual techniques learned from talking therapies.

Method

The title quote is taken from an interview conducted as part of a doctoral research project exploring experiences of stigma and discrimination in environments providing support for people who have experienced or experience mental distress. The fieldwork involved a six month-long ethnography at two charitable organisations supporting people with 'mental health problems', 30 semi-structured interviews with 30 staff and members/service users of the organisations and six focus groups. All of the members/service users I spoke to directly (many are quoted below using first name pseudonyms) were in receipt of at least one welfare benefit.

Findings

At each organisation there was often a sense that the members regarded the government with suspicion. During a members' meeting discussing the possibility of particular activities receiving accreditation from an external body, a number of members expressed concern that their taking part might be 'used against us' by the government as an indicator of being fit for work. Their reluctance was described by one member as wanting to 'avoid falling into that trap'. On another occasion a group of members who were making a video for service users about Shared Decision Making explained to me how they were acutely aware that IAPT (Improving Access to Psychological Therapies) were 'targeting' thousands of people who experience depression and anxiety to 'move them off benefits'. An unsettling atmosphere of caution and mistrust was evident from the outset which became a line of inquiry during the interviews.

I spoke directly with many participants about the process of claiming benefits, including experiences at the Job Centre and Department for Work and Pensions (DWP) medicals. Under a third of participants in the research reported they had experienced no problems claiming benefits or any problems in terms of their interactions with the DWP. Thomas described being 'one of the lucky ones' and that 'the woman I saw, she was very sympathetic and she knows the government is wrong trying to force everybody to work'. However, there was consensus amongst the remaining two thirds of participants who described feeling scared and/or overly anxious when attending appointments at the Job Centre. Stewart explained a feeling of 'someone who is looking down on you and can easily take your money away from you … just fear'. Another member, Gary, reported receiving a letter from the DWP a week before Christmas. Gary approached the CAB for advice but they were unable to deal with his case until after the holidays. He called the DWP for advice and explained he was unable to read or write very well, the advisor's response was to 'fill in the form or your money will stop'. Gary describes feeling 'threatened' and 'alone and scared about what would happen'. Susan recalled attending a job centre appointment where the advisor proceeded to loudly discuss details of her psychiatric history in an open plan office and could only offer Susan, who is a qualified teacher, a basic literacy course. Susan reports her experiences as 'traumatic and humiliating' and that the experience impacted negatively on her self-esteem.

Members who had undergone a DWP/ATOS medical described similarly upsetting experiences. Amanda said she had been called in for medicals and interviews regularly, and was repeatedly requested to complete the same form over and over again. In the end she said it became too stressful for her, 'I got really annoyed and I just, I wrote down, you know, why are you making us write this down, you know I've been sexually abused, you know how it affects us, it's still affecting us in the same way and now I've got to think about this paedophile for the rest of the day …' Many members described feeling guilty about claiming benefits which they attributed to both the media and DWP representatives.

Guilty sentiments were often coupled with a sense of feeling compelled to rebut the implication that they were lying. Jon said he felt that during the medical the ATOS doctor 'was biased towards sort of nailing down any suggestions that I could be saying something that's not true … she was trying to pick up on possible deviations from the truth'. Jon went on to explain that that he understood the process was target driven but he describes feeling extremely 'guilty', harboured a sense of 'shame' as a result of the experience and felt that he was regarded with 'suspicion'. Similarly, Kathy told me about her experience of a DWP medical, 'you see a doctor and you're interviewed for between twenty and sixty minutes and they decide, they make their decision, so you see a doctor who has never seen you before, who has no medical notes whatsoever and he's supposed to make a decision of your life … but these people are not there to make a medical decision, they're there to get you off the benefits'. Kathy said it was a 'terrible' experience and in the months running up to the date of her medical she experienced more panic attacks than usual. Other members such as Jane said that as a result of the media portrayal of benefit claimants, she felt bad about herself and was initially fearful of claiming benefits but did so, as most people do, out of financial necessity. Stevie explained how she didn't feel 'up to measure as a person' because she claimed benefits and felt that this was a result of government and media attacks on welfare claimants.

The experiences and emotions recounted to me by the participants in the research, typified by the examples above, illustrate the impact on many benefit claimants who experience or have experienced mental distress. Erosion of self-esteem, feelings of guilt, increased stress and anxiety levels, perceiving that their claims are considered with suspicion, and regarding the government with suspicion appears to propel people into a cycle of stress and negativity. These effects seem diametrically opposed to mental health policy specifications about what support is supposed to achieve. However, there is evidence to suggest that talking therapy in the form of IAPT services is what many members turn to in order to cope or manage with stress of claiming benefits. As Maria explains, 'She says we're stopping your money in April, so, and I just didn't feel like I could go through another appeal … it's added a bit more stress because we're short of money and things like that and I'm thinking god what am I going to do, I've got no money, I need to pay this and I need to pay that, and then I'm going back to the tools that I'm getting, getting from stress management, anger management …' Maria and others use techniques they find useful in therapy to deal with financial worries which, on the face of it could be considered a success of IAPT. However, given the stress and anxiety caused to claimants by the process of claiming benefits, using therapeutic techniques in this manner could also be considered an insidious way of individualising inequality and encouraging people to accept and 'deal with' structural inequality.

Conclusion

Many people who are in receipt of or who attempt to claim welfare benefits because they experience mental distress or mental health problems find the process of claiming, receiving, and continually proving entitlement to welfare benefits extremely stressful. The administrative processes involved often exacerbate existing anxiety, depression and distress. With this in mind I suggest vociferous policing and curtailing of benefits by the DWP, scare tactics, and scapegoating by both the media and government is not the way to support people who have already experienced mental distress, or indeed any disabled person. Even those who don't have negative experiences of the benefits system don't feel particularly supported; they regard their situation as 'lucky' and breathe a sigh of relief. Existing mechanisms and processes relating to welfare benefits rarely feel supportive to those on the receiving end – at worst they perpetuate and aggravate inequality, and cause distress to individuals.

References

Department of Health (2011) *No health without mental health: a cross-government mental health outcomes strategy for people of all ages*. Available at: http://www.dh.gov.uk/prod_consum_dh/groups/dh_digitalassets/documents/digitalasset/dh_124058.pdf [accessed: 30 December 2014].

Department of Health (2014) *Closing the gap*. Available at: https://www.gov.uk/government/uploads/system/uploads/attachment_data/file/273649/Closing_the_gap.pdf [accessed 30 December 2014].

'Getting tough' on the family-migration route: A blurring of the 'them' and 'us' in anti-immigration rhetoric

Majella Kilkey, University of Sheffield
m.kilkey@sheffield.ac.uk
@mkilkey

Introduction – Migration policy under the Coalition Government: towards 'tens of thousands' of 'the brightest and the best'

David Cameron made a pledge in 2010 on behalf of the Conservatives to get net migration down to the 'tens of thousands' per annum by the May 2015 General Election. Writing just a few months ahead of that target date, it is clear that he will have failed, and dramatically so. Net migration (the difference between the number of people moving into the UK and the number of people moving out of the UK) in the year ending June 2014 was 298,000. This is 93,000 higher than in 2011 (ONS, 2014), and some 198,000 above the 99,999 upper threshold of Cameron's target. As is outlined below, the failure, however, is not for the want of trying.

While a firm commitment to reduce the level of net migration set the Conservative-led Coalition Government apart from the previous Labour administrations, their second key migration-policy mantra signals that there was continuity with Labour too: echoing the then Labour Immigration Minister's statement in 2000 that the UK was 'in competition for the brightest and the best', Conservative Home Secretary, Theresa May, stated in 2011 that 'we want the brightest and the best' (cited in Anderson, 2013: 58).

The dual aspiration of 'tens of thousands' of 'the brightest and the best', has collectively driven developments in the UK's migration regime under the Coalition Government. Thus, entry and settlement for all migrants, whether workers, students or family members, originating outside the European Economic Area (EEA), have been subjected to ever greater restrictions and conditionality, and while within the framework of European Freedom of Movement, the Government has not been able to restrict the entry of EU nationals, it has introduced tighter rules on their access to social welfare provisions in order to lessen what politicians perceive to be a 'magnet' for some EU migrants to come to the UK. This toughening of migration policies needs to be seen within the wider rhetoric of 'them' and 'us' that has been deployed by the Coalition government to justify the tightening of welfare entitlements in the context of austerity. Behind the apparent simplicity of binaries such as 'migrant' and 'non-migrant' / 'citizen' and 'non-citizen' / 'EU migrant' and 'British national', however, lies a much more complex and nuanced picture. Moreover, it is a picture that has been complicated by some of the very policies that rest on, and perpetuate, such distinctions. This is no more so than in the case of recent changes to the family-migration route, which the remainder of this article focuses on.

Changes to the family-migration route

The family-migration route provides the potential for entry to and settlement in the UK for non-EEA nationals wishing to join a partner (spouse, fiancé(e) or civil / unmarried partner) or family member (a parent or a child) who is living in the UK permanently – British citizens, settled persons or those who have asylum or humanitarian protection in the UK. This route makes up a smaller proportion of non-EEA migration to the UK than the work and study routes (ONS, 2014). In the context of the 'tens of thousands' target, however, all routes have been seen as contributing to overall numbers, and so legitimate for tighter control. Moreover, family migration takes on significance beyond its level at entry because it has a greater likelihood than either work- or study-related migration to lead to permanent settlement in the UK, and so contributes less than the other routes to *emigration* flows – the other side of the net migration coin. Additionally, as a result of human rights obligations and the establishment of a right to family reunification in the EU, the UK government cannot control family-related migration in the same way as work and study migration, and so it sits outside the 'points based' migration system, which since it was introduced by Labour in 2008 has served as the main tool for selecting the 'brightest and the best'. In this context, Kraler (2010: 8) argues that in many European countries 'family related migration is increasingly perceived to undermine migration control and to be in contradiction with selective migration policies ... [It therefore] appears as a form of unsolicited and by implication, unwanted migration'. In this vein, albeit facing constraints on their autonomy in this field, European states in recent years have sought to develop policies that allow for a more selective approach to admission through the family route.

It is in this context that Damien Green – then Minister for Immigration – in July 2011 launched a consultation on family migration (UK Border Agency, 2011). In parallel, the Migration Advisory Committee – established under New Labour in 2007 and composed mainly of economists to provide advice to government on labour market aspects of migration – was asked to review the minimum income requirement for sponsorship under the family-migration route (MAC, 2011). Despite an overwhelmingly critical response to the consultation (Home Office, 2012), Government pressed ahead with most of the proposals it had set out, and in July 2012, a series of changes took effect for non-EEA nationals applying for admission under the family route. The changes included:

- introduction of a new minimum income threshold of £18,600 gross per annum for those sponsoring admission, with a higher threshold for any children also sponsored; £22,400 for one child and an additional £2,400 for each further child;

- extension of the minimum probationary period for settlement of spouses and partners from two years to five years; during that five-year probationary, (as was the case previously) spouses and partners are subject to a 'no recourse to public funds' restriction, meaning that they cannot access most benefits, tax credits or housing assistance;

- abolition of immediate settlement for the migrant spouses and partner where a couple has been living together overseas for at least 4 years, and requiring them to complete a 5 year probationary period;

- restriction of adult and elderly dependants' settlement in the UK to cases where they can demonstrate that, as a result of age, illness or disability, they require a level of long-term personal care that can only be provided by a relative in the UK, and requiring them to apply from overseas rather than switch in the UK from another category, for example as a visitor; and

- restriction of family visit visa appeals, initially by narrowing the current definitions of family and sponsor for appeal purposes, and then, by removing the full right of appeal against refusal of a family visit visa.

Impacts of the changes

Sharpest criticism of the changes has been directed towards the raising of the financial bar for sponsorship. Under the previous rules sponsors were required to demonstrate their ability to maintain and accommodate themselves, their partner and any dependants without recourse to public funds. Since 2006 this maintenance requirement had been set at the level of Income Support. This required that the net income of the sponsor and non-EEA applicant, following deduction of housing costs, was not less than the equivalent amount that the family would receive in Income Support. In 2011, this equated to a post-tax income of £5,500 per year, excluding housing costs, for a couple with no child dependants; a figure that was well under a third of what was introduced in 2012. It is not only that the maintenance requirement has been increased so significantly; what is permissible as eligible income has also become more restrictive. Pre-July 2012, the couple could provide evidence of sufficient independent means, employment income of either or both parties could count, as could their employment prospects, and where a couple could not meet the maintenance requirement, they could provide evidenced undertaking of support from other family members. Under the new rules, the non-EEA partner's prior or prospective earnings are excluded, as is third party support, and the counting of self-employed is tightly restricted.

The exclusionary potential of the new £18,600 minimum income requirement was recognised from the proposal stage, with the Migration Advisory Committee estimating that 45% of the non-EEA partner applications made in 2009 would have failed under the proposed increase (MAC, 2011). Subsequent analysis has highlighted how because of disparities in average earnings, impacts are likely to be highly uneven geographically and by socio-economic group. Estimates suggest, for example, that 51% of British citizens in employment in Wales, 48% in Scotland and 46% in England would not meet the requirement on the basis of gross annual earnings (APPG on Migration, 2013). The All-Party Parliamentary Group on Migration's inquiry into the impact of the changes found evidence of a decline in the number of partner visas issued under the family-migration route, an increase in the number of refusals and an increase in processing times since the new rules came into force (APPG on Migration, 2013: 19-20). It also gathered evidence from those affected by the changes, and concluded that '... in today's internationally connected world, British citizens who are seeking to build a family with a non-EEA national – including from the USA and from Commonwealth countries such as Australia, Pakistan and India – are being prevented indefinitely from living together in their own country ... [Those impacted include] British citizens and permanent residents with considerable means, or access to means. In many of the cases children, including very young children, had been separated from a parent, with potentially severe effects on their future development' (APPG, 2013: 3).

Conclusion: a blurring of the 'them' and 'us'

The emphasis in the above of the impact of changes to the family-migration route on *British citizens*, as opposed to *migrants*, is an important one. In 2009, 59% of sponsors of partner visas were *UK-born British citizens*. In applying to British citizens, regardless of ancestry, in exactly the same way as they apply to recent and long-established migrant groups, the Coalition Government's changes have clearly blurred the boundary between 'them' and 'us'. In effect, in its efforts to 'get tough' on migration, the right to a 'family of choice' in the UK under the Coalition Government has become deeply contingent on socio-economic positioning *regardless of migration status*.

References

Anderson, B. (2013) *Us and Them?: The dangerous politics of immigration control*, Oxford: Oxford University Press.

APPG on Migration (The All-Party Parliamentary Group on Migration) (2013) *Report of the Inquiry into New Family Migration Rules*, http://www.appgmigration.org.uk/sites/default/files/APPG_family_migration_inquiry_report-Jun-2013.pdf [accessed 01.07.2013].

Home Office (2012) *Family migration: responses to consultation*, https://www.gov.uk/government/uploads/system/uploads/attachment_data/file/275300/cons-fam-mig.pdf [accessed 10.10.2012].

Kraler, A. (2010) *Civic stratification, gender and family migration policies in Europe*, Vienna: International Centre for Migration Policy Development.

MAC (Migration Advisory Committee) (2011) *Review of the minimum income requirement for sponsorship under the family migration route*, https://www.gov.uk/government/uploads/system/uploads/attachment_data/file/257244/family-migration-route.pdf [accessed 12.12.2011].

ONS (Office for National Statistics) (2014) *Migration Statistics Quarterly, February 2015*, http://www.ons.gov.uk/ons/rel/migration1/migration-statistics-quarterly-report/february-2015/sty-net-migration.html [accessed 11.03.2015].

UK Border Agency (2011) *Family migration: a consultation*, July 2011, https://www.gov.uk/government/uploads/system/uploads/attachment_data/file/269011/family-consultation.pdf [accessed 01.09.2011].

The coming of age of progressive neo-liberal conservative 'welfarism' under the Coalition government of 2010-15

Robert M Page, University of Birmingham
r.m.page@bham.ac.uk

Introduction

The election of David Cameron as the new Conservative leader in 2005 signalled the emergence of the 'progressive' neo-liberal Conservative approach to the welfare state (Clark and Hunt, 2007; Osborne, 2009; Cameron, 2010). Labour's success in rebranding itself as New Labour convinced Cameron and his associates that the Conservatives could gain electoral traction from a similar make over. This repositioning was not deemed to require any modifications to the party's neo-liberal approach to economic policy not least because of New Labour's conversion to the merits of this doctrine. In contrast, the construction of a progressive social narrative was deemed necessary to 'detoxify' the Conservative 'brand' and to highlight how the party's agenda in this sphere differed from the overly statist strategy of New Labour. Cameron wanted to develop a bolder, more enterprising doctrine that involved the recalibration, rather than the rejection, of neo-liberal conservatism. Although Conservatives have traditionally been sceptical about the notion of progress because of its association with the abstract, improving doctrines of socialism and liberalism as opposed to pragmatic forms of organic change favoured by party traditionalists, Cameron was keen to embrace this concept so that he could challenge Labour's claim to be the exclusive promoters of a forward looking agenda.

Mapping out the 'progressive' neo-liberal conservative agenda

It was in the broad area of social policy that Cameron sought to mark out the progressive elements of his neo-liberal Conservative doctrine. This involved, firstly, the adoption of a more sympathetic and less judgmental approach towards those who opted for alternative lifestyles of a 'non-harmful' kind. While the party remained resolute in its support for marriage and the 'two-parent' family, this was to be combined with a more inclusive approach to alternative family arrangements such as lone parenthood, provided that such parents 'played by the rules' and strove for economic independence. In addition, the condemnatory attitudes towards gay people that had come to the surface in Conservative circles as a result of the introduction of Section 28 of the Local Government Act of 1988 were rejected. Henceforth the party would adopt more positive forms of support for civil partnerships and gay marriage (McManus, 2010).

Secondly, the party's approach to state welfare, social justice and poverty was to be refashioned (see Hickson, 2008; Page, 2015, forthcoming). In the case of state intervention, Cameron wanted to lead a party which was not ideologically anti-collectivist but, rather, as was the case with Disraeli and Baldwin, supportive of those forms of interventionism were deemed conducive to the common good. For Cameron, the task of the Conservative progressive was not to oppose all forms of state intervention but rather to identify and support those measures that would enhance well-being and jettison those deemed harmful. Significantly, however, Cameron was keen to distinguish his progressive approach to state intervention from what he saw as the ineffective, outmoded, ideologically motivated, egalitarian statist strategy that New Labour had been pursuing in government. Cameron also sought to distinguish his progressive form of neo-liberal Conservatism from the 'reactionary' variant that had come to prominence during the Thatcher era by embracing a form of social justice that was not based on egalitarianism. Rejecting the earlier critiques of Hayek and Powell, Cameron believed that the pursuit of social justice was an appropriate goal for the right not least because of the painful social consequences that had resulted from the 'regenerative' neo-liberal economic reforms of the Thatcher era. Accordingly, a future Conservative government would seek to break down opportunity barriers and promote social mobility. In terms of poverty, it was now accepted that the concept should be regarded as a relative not absolute concept and that New Labour's allegedly narrow, mechanistic approach to poverty, which had focussed on halving the number of children living in households below 60% of median incomes, needed to be replaced by a broader, more holistic anti-poverty strategy based on non-financial as well as financial factors.

The promotion of a 'Big Society' was the third component of what can be described as Cameron's Progressive Neo-Liberal Conservative (PNLC) social agenda (see Ishkanian and Szreter, 2012). This emphasis on society was intended to distinguish Cameron's vision of Conservatism from the highly individualistic form of neo-liberalism that had characterised the Thatcher years in which active forms of civil engagement were treated with suspicion on the grounds that they were too often underpinned by a desire to move society in a social democratic direction. The emphasis on society rather than the state was intended to signify that it was possible to move in a progressive direction without resorting to the 'unwieldy' and 'inflexible' state initiatives favoured by New Labour. By invoking the notion of a Big Society, the PNLCs hoped that citizens would be inspired to take greater responsibility for tackling pressing issues in their local community rather than always looking to the state for support. Government would assist such activity by liberalising planning laws and providing practical support so that local communities could, for example, take control of facilities such as parks, libraries and other services.

Progressive neo-liberal conservatism in practice

The prospects for the PNLC cause did not seem particularly bright following the economic downturn of 2007 (Dorey, 2009) and the subsequent failure of the party to secure an outright majority in the 2010 General Election. However Conservative 'success' in linking the economic crisis to New Labour's failure to provide effective regulation of the banking industry and to its supposedly profligate approach to public spending coupled with the formation of a Coalition Government favourably disposed to PNLC ideas, enabled an 'austere' version of this doctrine to take root. Indeed, it is possible to argue that, despite criticisms from its opponents, PNLCs have set the pace in terms of the social policy agenda.

In the field of education, progressive neo-liberalism has been equated with creating a competitive school system which promotes rather than stifles 'excellence' and social mobility. During his tenure as Education Secretary, for example, Michael Gove ensured that that there will be no return to 'anti-aspirational' comprehensive schooling by expanding the number of 'autonomous' Academy schools and establishing Free schools. Gove also endeavoured to embed a more challenging education culture by encouraging pupils to study 'traditional' subjects and to undertake more testing forms of assessment. He also sought to introduce more rigorous forms of school inspections and introduced pupil premiums to encourage high performing schools to offer places to students from low income families as a way of enhancing social mobility.

In social security, neo-liberal progressivism has been equated with providing gateways out of poverty through paid work for those of working age and security for pensioners. In terms of the former, there has been a concerted attempt to 'rescue' working aged adults from the debilitating effects of poverty and 'benefit dependency' which it is contended that state-centric Labour governments have allowed to take hold in British society. Influenced by the work of Lawrence Mead (1986), Iain Duncan Smith has sought to reform the benefit system by introducing a Universal Credit scheme aimed at incentivizing unemployed people to find, and retain, paid work. This anti-poverty strategy has proved to be a testing one given that the social security budget was not protected from the government's deficit reduction plans. Working aged adults have had, to varying extents, to contend with the introduction of a benefit cap, a reduction in the value of their benefits and the imposition of a bedroom tax. Although the coalition recognizes that these measures have proved 'challenging' they are seen as being socially just measures in an age of austerity. It has also been deemed socially just to introduce a simplified single-tier retirement pension based on a 'triple lock' mechanism which ensures future payments are increased by no less than 2.5% per annum and to withdraw Child tax credits and Child Benefit from higher earners.

The Conservative-led Coalition government has found it more difficult to establish a 'progressive' narrative in relation to the NHS. The party's much vaunted pre-election commitments to defend the NHS were questioned after Andrew Lansley unleashed a major overhaul of the health system ostensibly designed to give professionals, patients and communities greater voice and choice in developing a modern NHS. Although Lansley's plans eventually found their way on to the statute book, the lengthy parliamentary process involved was indicative of deep rooted suspicions that the progressive Conservatives were intent on privatizing rather than modernizing the NHS. While Labour remains committed to stricter regulation of private sector involvement in the NHS if it returns to government the broader changes introduced by Lansley are unlikely to be reversed. As such, the progressive neo-liberal Conservative vision for the NHS is likely to be judged by the electorate not on the reforms *per se* but rather by the quality and availability of local health services.

Conclusion – The future for progressive neo-liberal conservatism

Emerging evidence suggesting that the poorest groups in society have been experiencing disproportionate forms of hardship in the Coalition era (Crawford et al., 2014; Hills, 2015) are likely to give ammunition to those who claim that the compassionate rhetoric of the PNLC serves to hide a desire to shrink the state along the lines set out by their older, non-progressive, neo-liberal conservative sister (Thatcher). However, there has been no sign as yet that the PNLC are willing to jettison their progressive motif. Given that the contemporary Labour party has been reluctant to provide a more compelling 'progressive' welfare vision, it seems that this strand of Conservatism will prove difficult to oppose despite the vociferous protestations of some of those experiencing the cold winds of 'reform'. While questions remain as to whether Progressive Neo-liberal Conservatism will survive in its current form after the forthcoming General Election, it may yet confound some of its critics and become the dominant welfare narrative of the contemporary era.

References

Cameron, D. (2010) 'Labour are now the reactionaries, we the radicals – as this promise shows', *The Guardian*, 9/4/2010.

Clark, G. and Hunt, J. (2007) *Who's progressive now?*, London: Conservative Party.

Crawford, R., Emmerson, C., Keynes, S., and Tetlow, G. (2014) *Fiscal aims and austerity: the parties plans compared*, IFS Briefing Note, 158. London: IFS.

Dorey, P. (2009) 'Sharing the proceeds of growth: Conservative economic policy under David Cameron', *The Political Quarterly*, 80, 2, 259-69.

Hickson, K. (2008) 'Thatcherism and the poor: Conservative party attitudes to poverty and inequality since the 1970s', *British Politics*, 4, 3, 341-62.

Hills, J. (2015) *Good times, bad times*, Bristol: Policy.

Ishkanian, A. and Szreter, S. (eds) (2012) *The Big Society debate*, Cheltenham: Edward Elgar.

McManus, M. (2010) *Tory pride and prejudice: the Conservative party and homosexual law reform*, London: Biteback.

Mead, L. (1986) *Beyond entitlement: the social obligations of citizenship*, New York: Free Press.

Osborne, G. (2009) 'I'm with the progressives', *The Guardian*, 7/5/2009.

Page, R.M. (2015) *Clear blue water? The Conservative party and the welfare state since 1940*, Bristol: Policy Press (forthcoming).

Austerity measures across Europe

Ludvig Norman and Katrin Uba, Uppsala Universitet, and Luke Temple, University of Sheffield
l.temple@sheffield.ac.uk
@LIVEWHATproject

Introduction: The austerity spectrum

With the exception of Switzerland, the nine countries in this following discussion[1] are members of the EU and therefore not fully independent in their reactions to the financial crisis of 2007-2008; evidence suggests that the role of the institutions of the EU and the European Central Bank (ECB) have been considerably strengthened in the wake of the crisis, particularly when the Eurozone crisis erupted in late 2009.

The initial response to the meltdown, prompted especially by the US Federal Reserve and the Bank of England, was to bailout collapsing financial institutions and stimulate the market through quantitative easing. However, the European focus since has predominantly been on implementing austerity policies to try and tackle government deficits.

Austerity measures have been pursued by governments of all colours, with measures that seek to reduce government spending by slashing department budgets, which inevitably leads to reducing welfare payments and cutting public sector jobs. For some, such as Prime Minister David Cameron in the UK, this has been taken further to a call for a permanently 'leaner' state.

There is a clear spectrum of severity when it comes to the austerity measures being implemented by governments across Europe. Austerity drives in Germany, Switzerland and Sweden have been moderate, and they generally mirror the weaker effects the 2007-2008 financial crisis had in these countries. This isn't to say there's been no acknowledgement of financial constraints; for instance, in Germany the narrative of *Sparpolitik* ('savings') and balancing the books is a prevalent one, but it isn't that new and it doesn't match the swingeing reforms being pursued in other countries. France didn't make it through the financial crisis unscathed but policy responses there haven't necessarily had a fundamental impact on labour market policy or the social security system.

However, the severity of austerity measures increases when we look at Poland and the UK. Here governments have introduced wide-ranging policies to cut public spending, with plenty more to come. And at the far end of the spectrum we find the most considerable austerity drives which, as expected, are those places hit hardest by the financial crisis: Italy, Spain and, most notably, Greece. In fact, the reforms in Greece have been 'all embracing', leaving practically no section of society unaffected.

Yet austerity-driven reforms of the welfare systems in these nine countries have been less comprehensive than might have been expected, especially in light of recent academic and public debates. There has arguably not been a revolution, but rather a constant gnawing erosion of the social security safety net. And what matters most is that this is happening alongside changing patterns of employment in the labour market which predate the financial crisis.

A precarious labour market

The labour market across Europe has clearly become more precarious since the financial crisis and job losses aren't the only indicator of this. For instance, according to the OECD, since 2008 the percentage of part-time workers who consider their work status to be involuntary has, with the exception of Germany, increased across all nine countries in the LIVEWHAT study. In 2013, it ranged from 6% of part-time workers in Switzerland to a staggering 66% in Spain, with almost half of part-time workers in Greece and Italy in this position, and a third in France (OECD Stat, 2014). Across all of the European Union this amounts to around 8.5 million people who might consider themselves lucky to have jobs, but are in need of more hours.

The most worrying labour market trends however are for the youth of Europe. In February 2014, unemployment rates for those aged 15-24 in the EU were double the overall unemployment rate. In the third-quarter of 2014 youth unemployment rates in Greece and Spain stood at over 50%, and at over 40% in Italy. In Sweden, Poland and France over a fifth are unemployed, a rate matched in the UK in 2012-2013 before it appeared to drop to around 17% in 2014. Much lower rates of 11% and 8% are recorded in Switzerland and Germany, respectively (OECD Stat, 2014).

Furthermore, of those who are employed in this age range, around 50% or more are in temporary contracts (the exception being Greece and the UK, where the numbers are much lower, at 27% and 16%, respectively). Worse still is the issue of entrenched youth unemployment, that is, those who have been without work for over a year: these account for over 50% of the unemployed youth in Greece and Italy, about 40% in Spain, and around a quarter in the UK, Poland, France and Germany (OECD Stat, 2014).

In the last two years these problems appear to be abating, but only slightly, and it isn't yet clear if this improvement is a definite trend. As it stands, a report from the House of Lords (2014) described the youth in Europe as being a potentially 'scarred generation'. Whilst the details vary from country to country, the report further acknowledges that the financial crisis rarely caused these problems, but accentuated existing and long-term structural issues that have been present in labour markets since the 1980s. Yet, when it comes to getting people into work during times of austerity, the overriding narrative of government responses across Europe has been focused not on structural issues but on the individual worker.

Austerity and flexicurity

In the UK the idea of worklessness being the fault of the individual, as opposed to the fault of the labour market, was most clearly articulated by the Freud Report, commissioned by New Labour and published in early 2007 – before anyone recognised the financial crisis was about to unfold.

This approach to the problem of unemployment chimes with the idea of 'flexicurity', an increasingly popular approach to labour policy. The idea is to create a job market in which workers are *flexible* and expected to accept the heightened loss of jobs if there is some *security* provided by unemployment benefits and other help such as further training (see Crouch, 2014).

The problem with an approach that emphasizes flexicurity is that during an austerity drive it is easier to do the first part (removing people from work), but harder to organise and fund the apparatus to achieve the second part (helping people get work).

For instance, let's say we want to dismiss a *middle-aged man who has been employed in the private sector for twenty years.* In Germany, he should be informed about the dismissal seven months in advance, while in Greece the period is four months (it was six months until 2010). In Poland, Switzerland, and the UK the period is only three months whilst in Spain he gets 15 days (it was a month until 2010). Collective agreements affect the notice period in France, Italy and Sweden.

If we dismiss *a young person with a short working history of six months*, then the notice period is significantly shorter – from one week in UK to four weeks in Germany, Greece, Sweden or Switzerland. In France and Italy, the notice period is still dependent on collective agreements.

Now let's say we're being dismissed, and we think our dismissal was unfair. If we wanted to argue such a case, we might find it a considerable struggle. Focusing just on the UK, as of April 2012, the length of required work at a company before an employee can claim for unfair dismissal was extended from one to two years. Consultation periods for large-scale redundancies were halved and compensation was capped. Workers making applications to employment tribunals must now pay charges of up to £1,200.

Yet even as dismissal times are reduced (or inadequate to begin with) and claims against unfair dismissals are made harder, not everyone is covered by them anyway: particularly workers with short-term contracts. Many younger workers in Greece, Italy, Poland and Spain are completely excluded from employment protection (see detailed analysis of this in McKay et al., 2012). And the next stage of worker dispute – taking strike action – has also been made more complicated. For instance, in the UK, stricter requirements on Trade Unions to keep their membership lists up-to-date or face fines were snuck through in the Transparency and Lobbying Bill of 2014.

So flexibility of the labour market has been on the increase – what about the security? It is quite clear that during the austerity drive, state support for the unemployed across Europe has not increased in scope to match. Most safety nets are not increasing at all. In fact, in many instances across Europe unemployment benefit has been frozen, reduced or capped, most dramatically in Greece, where the amount received for basic unemployment benefit was cut by 22% in 2012. Eligibility for receiving unemployment support has been made stricter in France, Spain, the UK, and in Poland, where budgets for services aimed at the unemployed were also cut by 50% in 2011. Finally, sanctions against those who do not follow the benefit conditions have generally increased; taking the UK again as an example, in the second half of 2010 there were 387,000 sanction decisions applied to people claiming Job Seeker's Allowance. By the second half of 2013 this stood at 473,000 (DWP, 2014).

So whilst it's clear that austerity measures which cut government spending will worsen the situation of public sector employees, we can expect negative long-term impacts on people in work or seeking work across all areas of employment. Because of imbalance in the flexicurity approach – weighted towards the creation of a flexible workforce – it doesn't even require large austerity drives or radical overhauls of the social security system for these problems to materialise for people out of or even in work. Italy serves as a clear example here as social insurance has remained more or less stable – even becoming more generous in specific areas – but it fails to cover an increasing proportion of the workforce: those who can only get temporary or freelance contracts.

Conclusion: Not revolution but erosion

This combination of austerity and flexicurity, then, has knock-on effects. For instance, standard maternity/paternity pay is linked to employment, as is saving up a pension. In some cases health insurance is an issue. Across these nine countries sick pay has escaped the worst of the cuts but it too has generally been made less generous (the UK sticks out here as the only country where the statutory sick pay is a flat-rate amount not linked to income: equal to only 17% of the median weekly wage). Whilst austerity has gripped Europe for half a decade, the long-term and cumulative effects are still yet to be felt.

Overall, reforms of the social security systems across Europe have been less comprehensive than might have been expected in light of recent media, public and academic debates. These systems still exist, even in Greece. There has not been a revolution in which the safety net has been completely withdrawn. However, governments everywhere are making the holes in these nets bigger, whilst simultaneously jobs become less secure and harder to get. In Europe the UK sits about halfway on the spectrum of severity when it comes to these issues, but this isn't a time to celebrate that we aren't at the bottom. What it shows is that the UK is not alone in travelling in a direction that points towards further insecurity and hardship for most workers. As this erosion continues, and if living costs continue to outstrip wage increases, another phenomena intensifies: working poverty. It reflects badly on governments if even those citizens in full-time work are struggling to get by; this does not happen under a 'leaner' state, it happens under a neglectful state.

Note

[1] Based on the analysis of policy documents and over 100 interviews with key informants in government and civil society the LIVEWHAT project (http://www.livewhat.unige.ch) has

compared welfare policy changes and austerity measures from 2005-2014 across nine European countries: France, Germany, Greece, Italy, Poland, Spain, Sweden, Switzerland and the UK. This project was funded by the European Commission under the 7th Framework Programme (grant agreement no. 613237).

References

Crouch, C. (2014) 'Introduction: labour markets and social policy after the crisis', *Transfer: European Review of Labour and Research*, 20, 1, 7-22.

DWP (2014) 'Jobseeker's Allowance and Employment and Support Allowance sanctions' London: DWP, https://www.gov.uk/government/collections/jobseekers-allowance-sanctions [accessed 05.01.2015].

House of Lords (2014) 'Youth unemployment in the EU: a scarred generation?', London: European Union Committee, http://www.publications.parliament.uk/pa/ld201314/ldselect/ldeucom/164/164.pdf [accessed 05.01.2015].

OECD Data (2014) United Kingdom, http://data.oecd.org/united-kingdom.htm [accessed 05.01.2014].

McKay, S., Jefferys, S., Paraksevopoulou, A. and Kees, J. (2012) *Study on precarious work and social rights*, Final report. VT/2010/084.

The impact of austerity on women

Fran Bennett, University of Oxford and member of Women's Budget Group
fran.bennett@spi.ox.ac.uk

Introduction

Initial analyses of the impact of the crisis in the UK, as elsewhere, tended to describe a 'man-cession'. It was said that it was largely men's jobs being lost, and that the number of female breadwinner households was increasing. The risk of poverty appeared to be converging, because of men's growing vulnerability; and the gender pay gap declined, because of men's pay falling more than women's (WBG, 2014). The benefits/ tax credits system acted to some extent as an automatic stabiliser in the immediate aftermath of the crisis, cushioning the blows of job loss and/or wage reductions for many lower-income households.

However, this was before the impact of the Coalition Government's austerity programme began to be felt (McKay et al., 2013). Although the government announced its plans to reduce the deficit primarily through spending cuts rather than tax increases in 2010, this took time to take effect. So it is only recently that the effects of austerity on women have become apparent.

Why focus on women? First, because they have more restricted incomes and opportunities. A higher proportion of women's incomes tends to be made up of benefits and tax credits – because they are more likely to be on lower incomes, and to receive benefits on behalf of others (especially children). They also more often act as intermediaries between families and public services, as well as being carers themselves (paid and unpaid); the Women's Budget Group (WBG) (2014) notes that over 300,000 care workers are employed on zero-hours contracts, including three-fifths of domiciliary care workers. For these reasons, women are likely to be affected more by reductions in benefits and/or services caused by austerity. Women also occupy a higher proportion of public sector jobs – more likely to provide decent pay, good quality conditions, and training for progression; a rebalancing of the economy from public to private sector jobs is therefore likely to disadvantage women.

So, as the Fawcett Society argued, cuts in benefits and services are a 'triple whammy' for women's lives and future life chances. The impact may also be exponential rather than merely additive, as one cut complicates other elements of women's multi-layered lives. The WBG, analysing the 2014 Autumn Statement, argues that the Chancellor failed to spot the real deficits – in care, affordable housing and high quality paid work – which affect women in particular.

The Fawcett Society filed for judicial review of the Coalition Government's Budget in 2010, arguing that it had not met all the requirements of the gender equality duty. The government conceded that it had not done so, and promised to do better in future. Nonetheless, the paucity of official gender impact assessments often means that others have to fill this gap instead.

What austerity measures?

There is not space here to give a detailed description of all the elements of the Coalition Government's austerity package. But one key characteristic is that reductions in social security are employed to avoid (more) cuts in other departmental budgets. Benefit expenditure is seen as a burden, with all major parties apparently aiming to reduce it – though in reality, benefits as well as services fulfil many positive social functions, including helping people to care and to cope. In addition, claimants are often identified as a group distinct from the taxpayers / 'hard-working families' who pay for benefits – whereas in practice, as Hills (2014) argued, these are often the same people at different points of the lifecycle.

The cuts 'saving' the largest sums are the changes in how benefits/tax credits for those under pension age are uprated (first by the Consumer rather than Retail Prices Index, and then largely by 1%, with some frozen). This contrasts with pensions, protected by the 'triple lock', and therefore increased annually by the highest of earnings/price increases or 2.5%. In addition, benefits have been reduced for families with children and disabled people in particular, affecting those in work and out, including through cuts to housing and council tax benefit. One key welfare reform whose aim was not principally to cut entitlements – Universal Credit – was delayed. The government capped annually managed social security expenditure, with only pensions and some cyclical benefits excluded, and a margin for forecasting errors.

Some public services budgets have been protected, including health and education (though the extent of this is contested). Local authorities have experienced significant funding cuts, especially those in more disadvantaged areas, with adult social care suffering in particular.

To give a rounded description of recent policy changes, reforms to taxation should also be included. The government implemented an immediate increase in VAT to 20% – though analyses of changes in households' disposable incomes exclude the effects of this increase. However, it has also implemented real increases in the personal tax allowance, with more to come. But, although lower-paid people benefit from such increases, once they are taken out of income tax they cannot benefit from further reductions. Such low-paid workers are more likely to be women. More of the benefit goes to men.

Moreover, De Agostini et al. (2014) concluded that, compared to price-linking, the revenue gained through reductions in benefits/tax credits between the 2010 election and 2014/15 has been spent on tax cuts, rather than contributing to deficit reduction. This means that there has been a transfer of resources from some groups in the population to others.

What has been the impact on women?

The analysis by De Agostini et al., (2014), as with most others, is based on households rather than individuals. This makes it harder to see the impact of changes on women as a group – although, as Browne (2011) shows, it is possible to show how single adult households of both sexes have fared. In 2013, Landman Economics for the WBG also analysed changes to spending on services and tax/benefits in England by family type, projected up to 2015/16, finding that lone parents lost the most in proportion to their income, followed by single pensioners. A majority of these groups are female anyway; but in addition, female lone parents and single elderly women lost a higher share of income than their male counterparts, losing nearly 16% and over 12% of income respectively.

It is more challenging to analyse impact in terms of individual rather than household incomes. But it is possible for benefits and tax changes. House of Commons library researchers assessed the impact of direct tax and benefit measures on individual incomes in 2014. The WBG (2014) reports that, taking into account the 2014 Autumn Statement, this shows £22 billion of the £26 billion 'savings' since June 2010 coming from women – 85% of the total. Analysis for the Equality and Human Rights Commission (Reed and Portes, 2014) has also found that, as a result of the direct tax and benefit changes carried out or planned between 2010 and 2015, women's average losses are twice as large as men's as a proportion of net individual incomes. Going back to gendered household analysis in order to include other public spending changes (on one method of calculating the value of services to households) in addition, they find that lone parents and single pensioners, as well as couples with children, experience the largest average fall in living standards; as noted above, the first two groups are dominated by women.

Some benefit cuts have a particular impact on women's access to *independent* income. Limiting the contributory element of employment and support allowance to twelve months for those in the work related activity group, for example, will leave many women with chronic health conditions with no income of their own (and will also affect many men). And although Universal Credit improves work incentives, this is not the case for many potential or actual 'second earners' in couples; the freezing of the work allowances will result in even fewer finding it worthwhile to earn an independent income, and/or to earn more.

In addition to the direct impact on women's incomes, in low-income families in particular it is often women who manage the day-to-day budgeting, and who bear the costs when this is not enough to meet the household's needs. Thus, they will be likely to be absorbing the impact of the cuts, whoever is directly affected; and the once-monthly lump sum payment of Universal Credit is likely to exacerbate these difficulties. Little is known about the support being given by extended families to those in hardship, but this is often likely to involve mothers and grandmothers helping out their adult children/grandchildren. The benefit cap and bedroom tax in particular may mean families with children having to move house, threatening to disrupt the informal support from relatives and friends relied on by many, especially lone parents. Cuts in social care may also involve women in particular making up the difference by increasing their unpaid care at home.

Conclusion

This contribution has focused largely on academic impact analyses and similar work by NGOs. It is also important, however, to highlight social media interventions by activists (see, for example, https://opendemocracy.net/5050/dawn-foster/whose-recovery-gendered-austerity-in-uk). Coventry Women's Voices, in co-operation with Warwick University's Centre for Human Rights in Practice, has developed a toolkit for assessing the impact on equalities (http://www2.warwick.ac.uk/fac/soc/law/research/centres/chrp/projects/spendingcuts/resources/database/resourceseia/), and their work was promoted by the Trades Union Congress. Looking to the future, the wider involvement of civil society will be crucial in forging a way out of the current situation. And in doing so, we should take as a guide the principle that 'the pursuit of gender equality needs to be considered part of the solution to the current endemic crisis and not treated as a luxury policy to be pursued only once growth has returned' (Karamessini and Rubery, 2014: 349).

Note

This section is written in a personal capacity and is not intended to represent the views of either Oxford University or the Women's Budget Group. The responsibility for any errors is mine.

References

Browne J. (2011) *The impact of tax and benefit reforms by sex: some simple analysis*, BN118, London: Institute for Fiscal Studies.

De Agostini, P., Hills, J. and Sutherland, H. (2014) *Were we really all in it together? The distributional effects of the UK coalition government's tax-benefit policy changes*, Working Paper 10, London: Centre for Analysis of Social Exclusion, London School of Economics.

Hills, J. (2014) *Good times bad times: the welfare myth of them and us*, Bristol: Policy Press.

Karamessini, M. and Rubery, J. (eds.) (2014) *Women and austerity: the economic crisis and the future for gender equality*, London and New York: Routledge.

McKay, A., Campbell, J., Thomson, E. and Ross, S. (2013) 'Economic recession and recovery in the UK: what's gender got to do with it?', *Feminist Economics* 19, 3, 108-23.

Reed, H. and Portes, J. (2014) *Cumulative impact assessment: a research report by Landman Economics and the National Institute of Economic and Social Research (NIESR) for the Equality and Human Rights Commission*, Research Report 94, London: EHRC.

Women's Budget Group (2013) *The impact on women of the coalition government's spending round 2013*, London: WBG. http://wbg.org.uk/wp-content/uploads/2013/10/WBG-Analysis-June-2013-Spending-Round.pdf. [accessed 4.1.15].

Women's Budget Group (2014) *Response to the Autumn Financial Statement 2014*, London: WBG, http://wbg.org.uk/wp-content/uploads/2015/01/WBG-AFS-final.pdf [accessed 4.1.15].

Child poverty and child well-being

Jonathan Bradshaw, Social Policy Research Unit, University of York
jonathan.bradshaw@york.ac.uk

Introduction – Children have been the victims of austerity

Children had been the focus of considerable investment by the Labour Government after 1999 in improved cash benefits and tax credits and in spending on child care, education and health. There was also an institutional transformation in favour of children culminating in the Child Poverty Act 2010. As a result child poverty fell and, on most indicators, child well-being improved (Bradshaw, 2011). Even after the start of the recession in 2008 the relative and absolute child poverty rate continued to fall thanks to the Brown government maintaining the value of transfers.

But after the Coalition came to power in 2010 the picture changed. The deficit reduction strategy they adopted tried to achieve the bulk of saving in cuts in expenditure rather than tax increases. The cuts included the freezing of child benefit, cuts in the real value of working age benefits and tax credits, limits to housing benefits in the private sector and the bedroom tax in the public sector, and the localisation of council tax benefits and the Social Fund. Useful benefits such as Educational Maintenance Allowances and the Health in Pregnancy Grant were abolished. Unemployment rose, real earnings fell for six successive years. The prices of essentials – food, fuel and private rents increased more rapidly than general inflation. The Child Poverty Action Group (2014) recently estimated that the failure to uprate child benefit by inflation since 2010/11 has meant it has lost over 15% of its value over this parliament compared to its worth had it been uprated using RPI. In practical terms, this means a family with one child has lost £543 of support over the five years, and a two-child family has sustained losses of £900. The failure to uprate the child element of tax credits over the course of this parliament has resulted in reducing the real value by 8.5%. As a result, a family with one child will have lost £628 in the last five years, and a two-child family double this (£1,256).

Out of work benefit income as a proportion of the Minimum Income Standard has fallen to 57% (Davis et al., 2014). So low has JSA become (currently £72.40) that it appears that an increasing proportions of the population have just stopped bothering to claim. Thus there has been a growing gap between the unemployment rate and the claiming rate – only about 47.5% of those registered unemployed are now claiming JSA (ONS, 2014). Some of these non-claimers will be ineligible for income tested JSA. Others will have been caught by the recent extension of waiting days before claims can be made. Others will have been caught by the increasingly harsh sanctions regime associated with the Work Programme. There is evidence that some unemployed people have drifted into part-time self-employed work supported by working tax credit in order to avoid oppressive sanctions.

The coalition had promised fairness in its deficit reduction strategy. But we now know that it was particularly unfair to low income families with children. The Equality and Human Rights Commission (Reed and Portes, 2014) shows that lone parents and couples with children have had the largest reductions in income. In contrast pensioners have been protected by the triple lock. Also the biggest cuts per capita in grants to local government have been in the areas with the highest child poverty rates (Beatty and Fothergill, 2013). Universal Credit, the big reform of social security, that might have mitigated some of this increase in poverty, if it had been implemented in 2013 as planned, is still mired in delay and has anyway been undermined by cuts. It may still never emerge.

The consequences of this are that although the relative child poverty rate has not increased yet (because the 60% median income threshold has fallen) the 'absolute' child poverty rate has increased both before and after housing costs. More than two-thirds of children in poverty have a working parent. A report by the Social Mobility and Child Poverty Commission (2014) concluded that the Child Poverty Act targets cannot be met, that it will be at least 2018 before falling average earnings are back to pre-recession level, and that by 2021 there will be 900,000 extra children in relative poverty. The Commission said that the next Government:

'... will have to adopt radical new approaches ... if Britain is to avoid becoming a permanently divided society. Even a world beating performance on employment levels, hours and wages would not enable the child poverty targets to be hit given current public spending plans and the current design of the tax benefit system .... We have come to the reluctant conclusion that without radical changes to the tax and benefit system to boost the incomes of poor families, there is no realistic hope of the statutory child poverty targets being met in 2020. None of the main political parties have been willing to embrace such a change, nor to speak this uncomfortable truth. They are all guilty in our view of being less than frank with the public. They all seem content to will the ends without identifying the means. It is vital that the next government comes clean.'

Child well-being

The impact of all this on child well-being will take time to emerge. However there is already evidence that child homelessness has increased sharply after a long period of decline, at a time when house building is at the lowest level since records began. The youth suicide rates are up, also after a period of decline. There is some evidence that the subjective well-being of children has stopped improving (The Children's Society, 2014). The number of nutritionally related admissions to hospital has risen. With so many health outcomes related to poverty we can expect deteriorating health indicators.

Conclusion

All this is such a waste, so short sighted – so costly. Hirsch (2013) has estimated that the costs of child poverty are over £35 billion in today's terms, equivalent to about 3% of GDP.

More is to come. We are less than halfway through reducing the deficit. Both Conservative and Labour have identified working age benefits for further cuts. Meanwhile the Trussell Trust, the largest food bank organiser, says that 913,000 people got at least 3 days' emergency food last year – an increase of 163% on the previous year (Stevenson, 2014) – the best possible evidence of the collapse of the safety net.

References

Beatty, C. and Fothergill, S. (2013) *Hitting the poorest places hardest: the local and regional impact of welfare reform,* Sheffield: Centre for Regional Economic and Social Research, Sheffield Hallam University. Retrieved from: http://www.shu.ac.uk/research/cresr/sites/shu.ac.uk/files/hitting-poorest-places-hardest_0.pdf.

Bradshaw, J. (ed) (2011) *The well-being of children in the United Kingdom*, Third Edition, Bristol: Policy Press.

Child Poverty Action Group (2014) *Policy note 2: uprating and the value of children's benefits*, December 20 http://www.cpag.org.uk/sites/default/files/CPAG-Uprating-childrens-benefits-policy-note-Dec-14.pdf.

Davis, A., Hirsch, D., and Padley, M. (2014) *A minimum income standard for the UK 2014* http://www.jrf.org.uk/sites/files/jrf/Minimum-income-standards-2014-FULL.pdf.

Hirsch, D. (2013) *An estimate of the cost of child poverty in 2013* http://www.cpag.org.uk/sites/default/files/Cost%20of%20child%20poverty%20research%20update%20(2013).pdf.

ONS (2014) *The UK Labour Market Statistical Bulletin* November http://www.ons.gov.uk/ons/dcp171778_381416.pdf.

Reed, H. and Portes, J. (2014) *Cumulative Impact Assessment. A research report by Landman Economics and the National Institute of Economic and Social Research for the Equality and Human Rights Commission*. Research report 94, http://www.equalityhumanrights.com/sites/default/files/publication_pdf/Cumulative%20Impact%20Assessment%20full%20report%2030-07-14.pdf.

Social Mobility and Child Poverty Commission (2014) *The State of the Nation 2014*, 20 October 2014 https://www.gov.uk/government/publications/state-of-the-nation-2014-report.

Stevenson, A. (2014) *UK Household Food Security: A Review of Existing Research*. CHASM Briefing Paper: http://www.birmingham.ac.uk/research/activity/social-policy/chasm/publications/briefing-papers.aspx [Accessed 5th January 2015]

The Children's Society (2014) *The Good Childhood Report 2014*, London: The Children's Society, http://www.childrenssociety.org.uk/what-we-do/research/well-being-1/good-childhood-report-2014.

Idle paupers, scroungers and shirkers: past and new social stereotypes of the undeserving welfare claimant in the UK

Serena Romano, University of London
serena.romano@unina.it
@SerenaRomanoSoc

Introduction

Negative public representations of the poor have always been used by governments to legitimise their actions, from the punishment/confinement option of the early English Poor Laws to current retrenchment trajectories of 'mature' welfare states dealing with an economic downturn. The introduction of austerity measures in advanced economies and their constant legitimisation by means of a 'moral argument' has recently been accompanied by the re-emergence of negative public representations of the poor, shedding new light on the relationships between economic crisis, austerity and the criminalisation of poverty in our society.

The idle poor

The history of the welfare state is one of stereotypes and public representations of deservedness. Past and present social representations (or stereotypes) of the poor have largely resorted to a number of common elements, primarily the criminalisation of the undeserving poor. Most of those stereotypes, arguably, emerged in the public debate precisely at times of economic, financial or social crisis. One of the most discussed stereotyped representations of the welfare claimant is the one found in pre-modern Britain with the visible explosion of the *social question*: the *idle pauper* who would intentionally sponge on community charity. Such a representation was part and parcel of the widespread belief at the time that poverty was a condition essentially derived from individual negligence. Eighteenth century British literature contributed significantly to the development of a certain negative public imagery of poverty and the poor. Daniel Defoe's famous pamphlet (*Giving Alms no Charity, and Employing the Poor a Grievance to the Nation*), for example, described poverty as being predominantly a result of 'casualty or crime'. The existence of pervasive stereotypes of idle paupers and their alleged moral characteristics, however, also had remarkable implications in terms of the effective social treatment of the poor. The predominant stereotype was gradually translated into a formal distinction between two alleged categories of welfare claimants: the deserving and the non-deserving poor. Not only did this separation go hand in hand with a strong *moral* judgements on the poor (destitute able-bodied individuals should blame their own behaviour for their conditions) but the 'idle poor' stereotype also encouraged the criminalisation of the 'undeserving' welfare claimant rather than stimulating efforts to eliminate indigence as a social problem. This process culminated in the formalization of the moral argument against the undeserving poor, brought about by the substitution of the Speenhamland system of poverty alleviation with a punitive approach towards those who failed to demonstrate their willingness to work. The repressive solutions of the new 'police' (Dean, 1991: 55) regime introduced by the Amendment Act of 1834 perfectly matched the orientations predominant at that time. The widespread resort to *confinement* (the so-called 'indoor relief') of able-bodied male individuals in the workhouses and the enforcement of the *less-eligibility* principle (social assistance should always be less desirable than labour) exemplify the extent to which British society came to discipline the undeserving unemployed poor by means of 'the threat of hunger' (Polanyi, 1944: 145).

The 'scrounger'

For many decades, the undeserving poor had disappeared as a concept in Britain. The expansion of inclusive welfare institutions, deriving from a new post-war social contract, mitigated the very need to differentiate between diverse categories of welfare claimants. This trend was interrupted with the outbreak of the oil shocks, when a new 'anti-scrounger' campaign emerged as early as 1976. A feeling of *suspicion* towards welfare claimants was fuelled by sensational tabloid headlines devoting exceptional coverage to unemployment 'dole' fraud cases and the 'alarming proportion' of welfare abuses. The reporting of welfare fraud cases was so intensive that public concern assumed the aspect of a proper 'scroungerphobia' (Deacon, 1978: 122). Public anxiety about welfare abuses was soon personified into the mythological figure of Derek Peter Deevy, a social security fraudster 'with 41 names [...] a luxury life style', spending '£ 25 a week on cigars' and who had admitted to obtaining 'a total of £36,000 by fraud'.[1] As was the case in the nineteenth century, the new negative orientation towards the undeserving welfare claimant soon turned into an institutional concern about 'dole' abuse and into a discussion over a prospective reform of the British social security system. The need to separate the 'deserving cases' from cheaters became the subject of debate and consequently transposed into action, marking the revival of the past 'less eligibility' approach in labour market policy-making.[2] While it is true that the real turning point in British 'welfare retrenchment' only came in the early 1980s, it is unquestionable that the revival of the *scrounger debate* came in conjunction with the introduction of much stricter forms of control over welfare claimants. In fact, the whole scrounger 'hysteria' exploded precisely in 1976, in the midst of a deep financial crisis that urged Britain to opt for an International Monetary Fund loan, conditional upon the introduction of drastic public spending cuts. Not surprisingly, under the Callaghan government austerity measures were enforced in tandem with a massive increase in prosecutions for fraud (25,000 cases in 1977) and with the introduction of much stricter eligibility rules for welfare payments.

The new undeserving poor: the 'shirker'

The economic crisis of 2008 and the consequent increasing call for austerity played a major role in the emergence of a new public concern for welfare abuse, as well as on the political legitimisation of social policy reforms diminishing social entitlements. Increasing emphasis on workfare incentives in social policy and on a moral argument against *welfare dependency* were paralleled by the revival of anti-scrounger feelings in most European countries. This trend is epitomised in the recent reinvigoration of the old 'welfare scrounger myth' in the British collective psyche, amplified by the political narrative around the undeserving poor. An alleged opposition between worker and 'shirkers' became a common talking point as of 2011 not only on the part of conservative politicians but also, surprisingly enough, among members of the Labour Party. In his speech at the Labour Party Conference in 2011 MP Liam Byrne expressed his concern about the fact that 'many people on the doorstep at the last election felt that too often we were *for* shirkers not workers'.[3]

As was the case with the pre-modern *idle pauper* and *the scrounger* of the 1970s, stereotypes of the undeserving poor also began to be reinforced by the negative portrayals of people on benefits on the part of certain media. The recent representation and even spectacularisation of the welfare recipient population (such as in Channel 4's Benefits Street and similar programmes) has led to widespread disapproval of the stigmatising stereotype of people who need benefits in order to survive. However, the media coverage of the new welfare scrounger debate reflects, in a way, the new dominant public attitude towards the undeserving poor, if not a tacit legitimisation of the welfare cuts already enforced by the Coalition Government. The media amplification of the 'scrounger's life' only provided new material for the 'hard' workfare argument, which has been at the heart of the UK welfare debate for years. Headlines such as 'Shameful scrounger boasts she won't have to pay back a penny' echoing the attacks on the welfare scrounger of the 1970s have become increasingly more frequent in the UK press over the last five years and increasingly used by the government to prove the need to reform the UK welfare system, which is accused of being far too generous. The infamous reference of the Chancellor of the Exchequer George Osborne to the *anger* of 'the shift-worker, leaving home in the dark hours of the early morning' while his next-door neighbour is 'sleeping off a life on benefits' is proof of a revival of the argument against people undeservingly receiving social benefits.

Conclusions

The current intensification of negative public representations of undeserving welfare claimants corroborates, as in the past, the emergence of a moralising shift in welfare policy-making and a not-so-new attitude of conservative policy-makers who repeatedly refer to the social perception of the undeserving poor in an effort to emphasise the distinction between socially acceptable behaviour (of the working class) and deplorable misconduct (of the able-bodied poor). Undoubtedly, media play a major role in reproducing and reinforcing prejudices and beliefs embedded in a given society. Politicians may have used the negative latent sentiments of 'striving families' towards the welfare scrounger to exaggerate the opposition between two worlds of welfare claimants: the deserving working man depicted by George Osborne and the undeserving, sleeping lazy fraud who sponge off society. Interestingly enough, the resurgence of a moralising drift in the welfare state and the new social representation of those undeservingly living on welfare – the shirker – present all the elements of the past stereotypes of the undeserving poor: the *parasitic* dimension, best summarised by the image of the welfare scrounger 'sleeping off on welfare', the criminalisation of unemployed people receiving social benefits by committing welfare fraud or by wasting their benefit payments on drugs/alcohol, the alleged luxurious standard of living of the lazy unemployed on the dole. There is also the new 'ethnic' dimension, now especially, and worryingly so, associated with emerging negative attitudes and misconceptions towards the *ultimate outsider* and welfare abuser: the unemployed migrant, who allegedly moves to the UK to exploit the system and sponge off the community.

Notes

[1] The Glasgow Herald, 14 July 1976.

[2] The Glasgow Herald, 5 August 1976.

[3] The Telegraph, 26 September 2011 (emphasis added).

References

Deacon, A. (1978) 'The scrounging controversy: public attitudes towards the unemployed in contemporary Britain', *Social and Economic Administration*, 12, 2, 120-135.

Dean, M. (1991) *The constitution of poverty: toward a genealogy of liberal governance*, London: Routledge.

Polanyi, K. (1944) *The great transformation. The political and economic origins of our time*, Boston: Beacon Press.

Legal exclusion in a post-'LASPO' era

Lisa Wintersteiger, Law for Life, Foundation for Public Legal Education
lisa.wintersteiger@lawforlife.org.uk

Introduction

Legal aid reforms mark a watershed in the relationship between the state and its citizens. The reduction in civil legal aid has effectively removed from scope the provision of legal help for many of the common issues that welfare recipients need to secure their entitlements and seek redress through the courts. Yet the proliferation of law makes ever-increasing demands on its citizens to understand the complex legal rules that circumscribe everyday life. The following article asks how we might reconsider the provision of legal aid in the future beyond the confines of the welfare state, and what the re-emerging public legal education movement can offer.

Legal aid and welfarism

The Legal Aid, Sentencing and Punishment of Offenders Act 2012 introduced changes that were implemented in April 2013, cutting spending to civil legal aid by £300 million per year in the long term (NAO, 2014). The legislation both reduced the range of issues for which civil legal aid is available and changed the financial eligibility criteria for receiving legal aid. The cuts affect people in many areas of law that impact on the most vulnerable in society: help with debt, welfare benefits, housing and many family problems is no longer available.

They also have a disproportionate effect on the wider voluntary and charitable sector. It has been estimated that the UK voluntary and community sector will lose around £911 million per year in public funding due to the wider cuts in local authority grants on which many not for profit legal advice service providers rely (Morris and Barr, 2013). Vitally, of course, it is precisely the services upon which many of the poorest people in society also rely. In light of these changes it is worth reflecting on the relationship between the unmet need for legal help, its historic relationship with anti-poverty work and the dangers of treating legal aid as a form of welfare. Within this rubric the potential for public legal education to meet needs is significant, but not without risks.

The relationship between welfare and legal entitlements is not straightforward. Law is not a neutral bystander in the process of poverty alleviation or welfare distribution. Law and legal systems have been accused of systematically undermining the interests of the poor by failing to provide legal services that meet their needs and failing to address the capacity of individuals to use legal services effectively (Carlin et al., 1967; PLEAS Task Force, 2007).

Yet resort to legal rights and remedies is essential both to the fair distribution of welfare services and to the protection from unfair treatment by employers, police, landlords and the state itself. These are the minimum protections that the law promises all of its citizens, regardless of means, and it is the point at which law and justice coincide. In the words of Reginald Herber Smith in his book *Justice and the Poor* written in 1919, 'Without equal access to the law the system not only robs the poor of their only protection, but it places in the hands of their oppressors the most powerful and ruthless weapon ever invented' (p.134-135).

At the centre of the uneasy relationship between law and welfare sits legal aid: the provision of publicly funded legal help for those who would otherwise be unable to gain redress through the courts to vindicate their rights. Legal aid has been described as a pillar of the welfare state. The recent suggestion by the Lord Chancellor that it is analogous to a social welfare benefit (PLP v Secretary of State for Justice, 2014) follows the line of argument that legal aid as all other welfare entitlements must be rationed in an era of austerity. But the analogy fails to address the fact that the costs to individuals of seeking legal redress are directly attributable to the law-making function of the state: 'There is a vital distinction between Beveridge's giants and these costs ... The costs arise because the state demands that individuals resolve their problems by means of its legal machinery' (Wilmot-Smith, 2014: 16).

The war on poverty and the emergence of the neighbourhood law services

Taking a step back in time, the association of law with attempts to fight poverty at its roots can be traced to the 1940s wartime legacy in the UK, and the 1960s developments in the US leading to the Office of Economic Opportunity legal services programme. Encapsulated in Lyndon B Johnson's declaration of war on poverty, law is a weapon to be used in order to win that war: 'Our aim is not only to relieve the symptoms of poverty, but to cure it and, above all, to prevent it. No single piece of legislation, however, is going to suffice.' The 1960s development of legal services manifested in the growth of neighbourhood law centres in a host of jurisdictions. The driving force was recognition of the pivotal role of legal services in meeting everyday legal needs and tackling the causes of deprivation. Without them, the newly enshrined rights to welfare would fail those who needed them the most.

A combination of advice, information, education and social policy work changed the face of legal services throughout the 60s and 70s. Yet precisely during this period of growth in provision for and spending on legal services, the overwhelming need and pressure on services was brought into sharp focus. This raised questions about the sustainability of publicly funded services with competing demands on the wider public purse and the allocation of funds at a local level. Burdens on caseloads served to detract attention from legal education and legal campaigns by communities themselves.

Advice agencies' activities to address systemic problems flourished during the 1970's, they included seminars, films, DIY kits, news columns, television and radio shows. The premise was that the wider education work was integral to individuals' empowerment and to the effort of supporting and generating community groups ability to assert their interest. According to the law centres working group on education in 1978: 'we use posters, leaflets and bulletins which relate to the working of the law in connection with local matters known to be of interest that can have immediate impact' (Garth, 1980: 202).

The rise of legal aid and decline of holistic services

But this broader focus of neighbourhood law centre services soon declined; in the US concerns about the radicalised nature of activities served to bring political pressure to bear on the activities of community legal centres. In the UK the more narrowly focused services sought to meet the demand for individual casework for clients (Garth, 1980).

The re-emergence of PLE debates around the world today reflects a changing policy landscape both in the UK and elsewhere. There are three broad rationales driving the growing prominence of PLE. Firstly, policymakers have become more alert to the ubiquitous nature of legal needs, with large-scale studies undertaken in various jurisdictions in the 1990s (Pleasance, 2013). Secondly, awareness of need has in many contexts led to alarm about growing costs, exacerbated in the wake of the financial crisis. Thirdly, in the development context, the failings of 'top down' rule of law initiatives have encouraged civil society development in community focused legal awareness raising and participatory models (Golub, 2007).

These three rationales are closely interrelated. Underlying them is the proliferation of law and the juridification of entirely new spheres of social life (Galanter, 2006) that has resulted in an ever-widening gap between the public's knowledge of the law and the legal frameworks that bind them as legal subjects. Legal need is no longer simply a problem of poverty: it is a problem of a decline in the substance of the rule of law.

In the UK, to take one specific example in a case concerning customs and excise rules, the judge observed: 'To a worryingly large extent, statutory law is not practically accessible today, even to the courts whose constitutional duty it is to interpret and enforce it' (Toulson, 2008 in Chambers, 2008). In the context of the recent raft of welfare reforms this means the expectation on the least legally able groups to know about and navigate the most complex rules relating to welfare entitlements is overwhelming. Not only is the burden of knowledge placed on individuals, but also the failure to be cognisant is increasingly met with punitive sanction regimes that can leave individuals entirely without a safety net. The impression is not one of the rolling back of the state, but rather the growth of legal interventions under the auspices of security and management, against a backdrop of legal exclusion.

The role of public legal education

The conundrum of how to meet legal needs and tackle legal exclusion is now more pressing than ever in the wake of legal aid cuts. The rise in litigants in person threatens to swamp courts with cases in which neither party is represented (an increase of 30% in family cases). Needless to say, court procedures and technical legal language is ill-suited for untrained lawyers seeking to resolve their disputes. Improvements in well-written self-help material and information can doubtless offer benefits. Yet the danger that the present policy focus presents is twofold. On the one hand, PLE may become a panacea for the absence of urgently needed advice and representation in primary areas of law that affect people's ability to secure their rights and the basic services on which they rely. On the other, it risks falling into the narrative that if only people were more capable (legally speaking) they could resolve their own legal problems outside of the courts and pull themselves up by their own boot straps.

Regardless of where on the ideological spectrum one stands with regard to the reduction on welfare spending as a whole, the law-making privilege and function of any government carries with it the responsibility that it gives meaningful effect to the laws that it makes. From the perspective of one law centre the problem is not simply that successive governments have failed to provide enough resources for legal services, 'Rather it is the near total failure to plan for or provide the means to enforce much of the legislation which is, at the moment, merely declaratory of rights and obligations' (Garth 1980: 167).

PLE is not an either/or to legal aid, nor is it an optional extra of social welfare provision. Without basic knowledge of a legal system the scale and extent of legal needs simply cannot be met. Moreover, the mandate for wider legal reform becomes questionable when the public is largely ignorant of its justice system. For the most vulnerable this means access to justice is illusory, for the more able but 'squeezed middle' it involves an increasing frustration and alienation from a costly and complex legal system.

Conclusion

The scandal of poverty and the agitation for civil rights was the driving force for reforms in the legal sector during the 60s and 70s. Today, the language of austerity has largely eroded the mechanisms by which hard won rights and protections are given substance. The task of meeting legal needs, however, has always been a challenge. Public legal education is a part of the continuum of legal help, not simply as concern for the social welfare needs of the most vulnerable but also as a locus for the meaningful engagement of citizens with the state.

References

Carlin, J., Howard J., and Messinger, S. (1967) *Civil justice and the poor: issues for sociological research*. New York: Russell Sage Foundation.

Chambers, R. (2008) EWCA Crim 2467

Galanter, M. (2006) *'In the winter of our discontent: Law, anti-law and social science'*, Annual Review of Law and Social Science, 2, 1-16

Garth, B. (1980) *Neighbourhood law firms for the poor: A comparative study* , Alphen aan den Rijn, Netherlands: Sijthoff and Noordhoff

Golub, S. (2003) *Beyond rule of law orthodoxy: The legal empowerment alternative,* Rule of Law Series, Number 41, Democracy and Rule of Law Project, Carnegie Endowment for International Peace, Washington: Carnegie Endowment.

Morris, D. and Barr, W. (2013) 'The impact of cuts in legal aid funding on charities'. *Journal of Social Welfare and Family Law*. 35, 1, 79-94.

National Audit Office (2014) *Implementing reforms to Civil Legal Aid.*

Pleasance, P., Balmer, N. and Sandefur, R. (2013) *Paths to justice: Past present and future*. London: Nuffield Foundation.

Public Legal Education and Support Task Force (2007) *Developing capable citizens: The role of Public Legal Education.*

Smith, R. (1919) *Justice and the poor: A study of the present denial of justice to the poor and of the agencies making more equal their position before the law, with particular reference to legal aid work in the United States*. Carnegie Foundation for the Advancement of Teaching.

Wilmot- Smith, F. (2014) Necessity *or ideology?* London Review of Books.

WELFARE PROVISION – CORE SERVICES

Pensions and the Coalition: a new way forward?

Liam Foster, University of Sheffield, and Jay Ginn, King's College, London
l.foster@sheffield.ac.uk

Introduction

Since its conception Beveridge's blueprint for pensions has been built upon in piecemeal fashion by successive governments in the context of social and economic change. This has resulted in a complicated pension system with considerable uncertainty about what people will receive in retirement. The long-term decline in the value of the Basic State Pension (BSP), increasing reliance on means-tested benefits, changes to private pensions including tax relief (where there is a £1.25 million lifetime limit on pension saving that qualifies for tax relief), contracting-out mechanisms and further regulation have all featured. Ultimately these changes have failed to halt concerns about the future sustainability of pension systems, their ability to remove the risk of poverty in retirement and incentivise pension saving. The Coalition government faces the same major challenge as its predecessors: ensuring that state pension transfers within the NI scheme remains sustainable while reducing pensioner poverty. Since its election the Coalition government has announced a number of measures designed to transform the pension landscape and reduce its complexity. This has largely involved implementing proposals made by the Pensions Commission and started by the New Labour government, which obtained cross-party and stakeholder consensus.

A changing landscape

Changes have included accelerating the equalisation of the State Pension Age (SPA) between men and women. This will be achieved in 2018 and a rise to 66 years will occur in 2020. In order to halt the decline in the value of the BSP, reform to its indexation has taken place. A 'triple lock' measure has resulted in the BSP rising in line with CPI, earnings or 2.5%, whichever is the highest. The State Pension system will be substantially reformed, with the BSP and state second pension (S2P) replaced by a new Single-tier State Pension (STP) for those below the State Pension Age in 2016 (see DWP, 2013a). The new STP will be set at approximately £144 per week (in 2012/13 prices), with 35 years of National Insurance (NI) contributions required to qualify for a full entitlement (an increase of 5 years compared to the current BSP). A minimum of 10 years' contributions will be required for any entitlement and all derived benefits will be phased out. The STP will eventually be easier to operate than the two-tier structure and may reduce the need for means-tested Pension Credit (PC), which suffers from poor take-up rates.

The introduction of the STP is intended to complement the expansion of private pensions by providing the foundation for the successful introduction of auto-enrolment. The intention of auto-enrolment, phased in from 2012, is to offer an occupational pension to millions of people without access to good-quality workplace provision, while coexisting with the latter if they have benefits or contributions above the minimal National Employment Savings Trust (NEST) scheme. Employees who are eligible in terms of age and earnings are automatically opted into the scheme chosen by their employer but may withdraw. Minimum contributions are being gradually increased and will be set at 4% for the employee, 3% for the employer and 1% in tax relief by 2018. It is estimated that around 11 million people will be eligible, with six to nine million people newly saving or saving more (DWP, 2013b). The stated logic behind auto-enrolment is that while structured advice and information may improve understanding, behavioural barriers, including myopia, cynicism and inertia, all inhibit pension saving (Foster, 2012).

Further changes under the Coalition government (announced in the 2014 Budget and due to come into effect from April 2015) allow flexibility in the way a Defined Contribution (DC) pension fund can be used from age 55, removing the requirement to annuitise 75%. Public sector pensions are also changing, including a switch to Career Average Earnings for new joiners and increasing pensionable age to match SPA. These follow previous cuts, such as indexation to the lower Consumer Prices Index (CPI) instead of Retail Price Index (RPI).

What will the changes mean for state pensions?

The accelerated rise in State Pension Age (SPA) means approximately 4.4 million people will have to wait up to a year longer for their state pension. This is on top of the gradual equalisation of women's SPA. These rises will affect eligibility for the winter fuel allowance, concessionary travel and other age-related benefits. This may be particularly problematic for those who have already made work, saving and retirement decisions, and who may struggle to adjust to delay in payment of the state pension. While the 'triple lock' measure is positive, a more realistic RPI which reflects rising costs of essentials, such as food and energy, for pensioners would help the poorest pensioners.

In principle the introduction of the STP is a welcome development for many low earners and for the self-employed, although the amount is barely above the threshold for means testing. In the short term it may provide a stronger foundation than the current system for some individuals (although long-term prospects are less positive). Those with a 35 year NI record will have a full state pension in their own right in retirement. However, women will be less likely than men to receive the full amount given their breaks in employment, if these do not all qualify for NI credits. The STP alone is insufficient for a decent standard of living, replacing about 25% of national average wages. There are large numbers of men and women who are already retired or due to retire in the near future who are excluded from the STP and will continue to receive the state pension in its current form. The change to STP is expected to reduce pensioner poverty from 11% now to 10% by 2025; but if the STP were available to all, including existing pensioners, this would reduce pensioner poverty to 7% (Carrera et al., 2012). Approximately 430,000 women born between 6 April 1952 and 16 June 1953 will miss eligibility for STP by a few months and will also suffer a particularly long wait for their pension due to the rise in their SPA (Ginn, 2013). The ending of derived rights for married and widowed women will adversely impact those who have been unable to build an adequate state pension in their own right.

What will the changes mean? Private pensions

The recent decline in return on investments together with increasing longevity has jeopardised the viability of private pension schemes. These are switching from Defined Benefit (DB) to Defined Contribution (DC), particularly in the private sector, transferring financial risk to employees. Guidance around pensions will also become more necessary due to changes in the way DC pension pots can be used from 2015. However, only £20 million has been allocated for a free independent guidance service in future. While choice may enable some people to use their pension pot more effectively, individuals will have increasingly complex decisions to make, both among different types of annuities and providers and among numerous other options for their money. Advice will be particularly important for those with small pensions. In the public sector, changes to pension scheme design and increasing pensionable age could reduce the average value of the pension by more than a third (PPI, 2013).

The introduction of auto-enrolment may increase the numbers of lower earners saving into private pensions with the bribe of an employer contribution and tax relief. However the distribution of tax relief (currently at £45 billion per annum) will benefit higher rate taxpayers, mainly men, more than basic-rate taxpayers. All DC schemes, including the government-sponsored NEST, individualise risk and there are barriers to portability of auto-enrolled funds (NEST cannot currently be transferred and is locked in until retirement and charges apply elsewhere). Contributing to such schemes may be inadvisable due to potential interaction with means-testing in retirement. Deciding whether to contribute to NEST or other schemes chosen by employers – which could be poorly managed or fraudulent – are difficult and free advice will be only generic. Many low to middle earners will lose where employers reduce their pension contributions to minimum levels: about half the average made by employers who now operate a scheme. Employees earning below £10,000 pa are not auto-enrolled although those earning between £5,772 pa and £10,000 pa may choose to opt in. Those earning below £5,772 pa may opt into NESTs but they will not attract an employer's contribution (figures are reviewed annually). This may incentivise employers to keep wages low and restrict hours of work. As in other private pensions, no credits are provided for periods of family care for children or parents. Thus the abolition of the S2P removes the only carer-friendly second-tier pension scheme. Alternatively a fully portable voluntary pay-as-you-go scheme, including carer credits as in state pensions could be operated (with cross-subsidy or an Exchequer grant in lieu of tax relief), thus avoiding the penalty for caring years which is incurred in private pensions.

Conclusions

The impact of the Coalition's pension changes is mixed. In the short term many women, others with low lifetime earnings and the self-employed are 'winners' in relation to the new STP. But its level and inclusiveness need to be improved if low earners are to benefit fully, especially given their continuing disadvantage in accumulating private pensions. The STP is meagre by international standards. Setting it at a higher level would reduce pensioner inequality. In the longer-term there will be many 'losers', with the new system less generous than the current one for most men and women as a consequence of a lower accrual rate than the combined accrual rate of the BSP and S2P. The introduction of auto-enrolment and NEST will offer new possibilities for those who otherwise lacked access to an employer's contribution. However, caring commitments are not taken into account and the lowest earners are excluded. Time will tell if it pays to save in a DC pension and for whom. Promotion of individual retirement provision through private pensions is likely to result in greater income inequality between older women and men, and between those with intermittent or low-paid employment and those with an advantaged labour market history. Therefore, while the new pension regime may eventually reduce complexity and encourage retirement saving, it will not reduce the gap between the poorest and most affluent pensioners.

References

Carrera, L., Redwood, D. and Adams, J. (2012) '*An assessment of the government's options for state pension reform*', London: Pension Policy Institute.

DWP (2013a) '*The single-tier pension: a simple foundation for saving*', White Paper, London: The Stationery Office.

DWP (2013b) '*Supporting automatic enrolment. The government response to the call for evidence on the impact of the annual contribution limit and the transfer restrictions on NEST*', London: The Stationery Office.

Foster, L. (2012) '"I might not live that long!" A study of young women's pension planning in the United Kingdom', *Social Policy and Administration*, 46, 7, 705-26.

Ginn, J. (2013) 'Austerity and inequality. Exploring the impact of cuts in the UK by gender and age', *Research on Ageing and Social Policy*, 1, 1, 28-53.

PPI (2013) '*The implications of the coalition government's public service pension reforms*', London: Pension Policy Institute.

A childcare system fit for the future?

Jana Javornik and Jo Ingold, University of Leeds
j.javornik@leeds.ac.uk
@JanaSvenska

Introduction

In the OECD, the UK appears a generous spender on childcare and early education: in 2011, government expenditure represented 1.1% of GDP (including pre-school), which was above the OECD average of 0.8%, but behind Denmark (2%), Iceland and Sweden (both 1.6%; OECD, 2014). In terms of child poverty and mothers' employment the UK lags behind countries such as Sweden, Finland and Slovenia, which spend more on services to families than cash benefits; the UK does the opposite. We argue that the UK's current demand-priming approach is too complex, inefficient and unsustainable and provides a low baseline of provision compared to other countries. This results in a shortage of supply, prohibitively high costs for parents, wide regional variation and negative impacts on women's employment. We argue that the next government's priority should be to move towards funding and developing a supply-led system with capped fees based on a sliding-fee scale.

Childcare reforms under Labour and the Coalition

Labour's introduction of the universal Early Years Entitlement marked a historically significant shift in UK childcare policy. This provides universal childcare for 3- and 4-year olds (equating to 15 hours of care per week for 38 weeks a year), intended to be gradually extended to the most disadvantaged 2-year olds from 2008, together with 'wrap-around' care for school-age children through Extended Schools and tax relief on employer-provided childcare vouchers.

The Coalition has committed to implementing Labour's proposed changes to the latter to ensure that higher rate tax payers do not disproportionately benefit and in 2013 announced its intention to double to 40% the number of 2-year olds qualifying for the Early Years Entitlement. Following the 2010 Comprehensive Spending Review, however, the maximum limit for childcare costs under Working Tax Credit was reduced from 80% to 70%, and from 2011 funding provided under the Extended Schools Programme was brought within overall schools funding, meaning no specific amount is earmarked for extended services, with schools deciding locally on what should be offered.

In 2013 the Coalition announced plans for a new tax-free replacement for the existing employer-provided voucher system from 2015. Families will receive 20% of yearly childcare costs, up to £10,000 per child; to be eligible both parents need to be in work, each earning less than £150,000 per year and not receiving support for childcare costs from tax credits or Universal Credit (HM Treasury, 2014). From 2016 the childcare costs covered under Universal Credit are planned to increase to cover 85% of eligible childcare (HM Treasury, 2014), going some way to addressing criticisms made. However, tax-free childcare is subject to the cap on social spending, and it is not clear how this will be financed over time.

Some of the effects of these changes are as yet unknown, although the impact of the reduction in the payment of childcare costs through Working Tax Credit has been negative. Increased subsidies may raise already prohibitively costly childcare, with the cuts made to the Sure Start Centres (with more closures planned) significantly affecting disadvantaged children.

Parental share of childcare costs amongst the highest in the OECD, with supply shortages and wide regional variation

The Family and Childcare Trust's Annual Survey (2014) found that since 2009 average childcare costs have risen by 27%, while wages have remained static. Figure 1 shows that in a two-earner family earning 150% of the average wage after accounting for government support, net childcare costs represent 34% of average family incomes, compared to an OECD average of 13%. At 167% of average earnings the childcare fees paid by a dual earner household typically amount to approximately 43% of household income and 14% for low-income single parent households.

Unlike relatively standardised childcare arrangements in most EU countries, the UK combines part-time universal free places with demand-led funding through the tax and benefit systems for both pre-school and school-age children. Parents are reimbursed through the tax and benefit systems for childcare purchased in an open market, where fees are set by providers to maximise profitability. They can receive financial help directly; other subsidies go directly to childcare providers through the Free Entitlement. Retrospective reimbursement through the tax and benefits system is inefficient and a deterrent for many families and an array of actors operating across sectors and funding mechanisms add to high costs. Regional variations in childcare provision are significant, with London and the South East offering the most expensive under-5 childcare; additionally 30% of parents report insufficient childcare in their area (DfE, 2014a).

High costs negatively affect mothers' employment

Childcare costs operate in the same way as a reduction in female wages: the higher they are, the lower the probability of women working. High childcare costs, coupled with cuts in Working Tax Credits and Child Tax Credits, reduce income gain for many families; even well-paid professional women report that after paying childcare, tax and national insurance contributions, they see little of their after-tax earnings. Figure 2 compares employment rates for mothers by education (proxy for wage) and the pres-

Figure 1: Net childcare costs for a dual-earner family with full-time earnings of 150% of the average wage, 2012

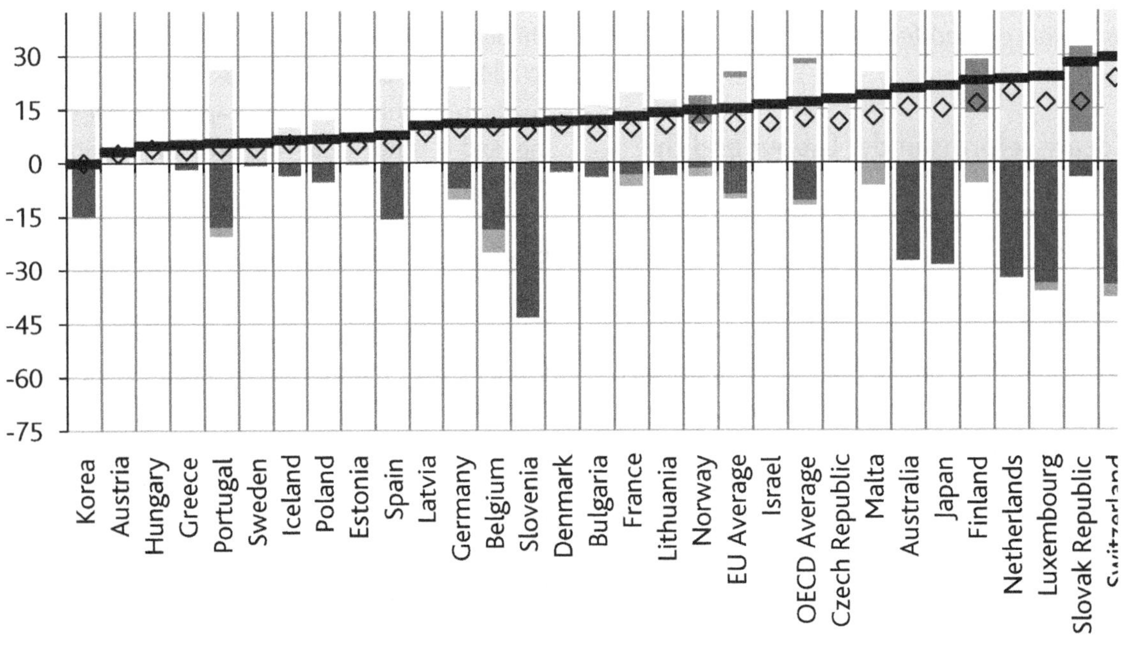

Note: The average wage reflects the earnings of an 'average worker' (see OECD, 2007: 186-7 for detail).

Source: OECD (2014), *OECD Family Database 2014*, OECD, Paris (www.oecd.org/social/family/database.htm).

Figure 2: Female employment rates (25-49 age cohort; FTE in %), by education and presence of children 0-5 years, UK, 2012

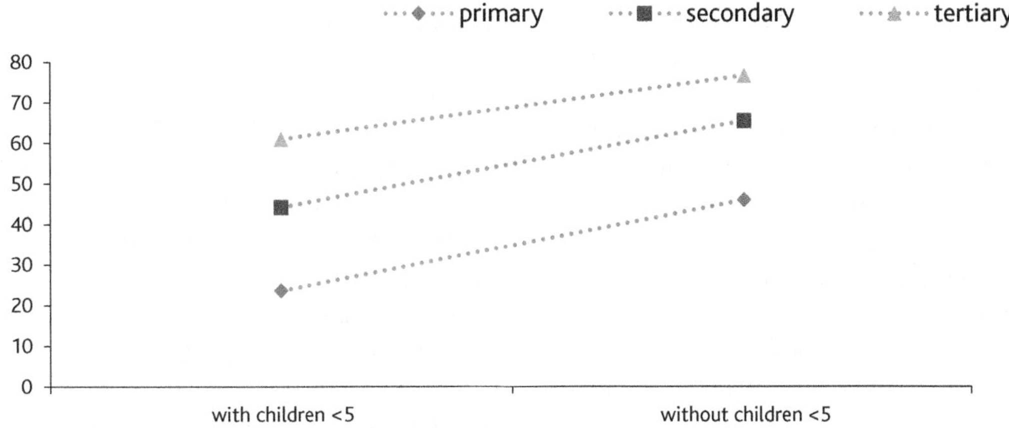

Data Source: Eurostat Labour Force Survey, 2012; own calculations.

ence of children aged 0-5 in the household in the UK.

A significant mismatch between service hours and working hours further creates tensions in a family's daily life and often leads to women reducing work hours, or leaving the labour force altogether. Once outside, women face difficulties getting back in; even a few years away has a significant impact on their lifetime earnings and pension rights.

The universal entitlement provides a low baseline compared to other countries, with subsidies tied to being in work

The extent to which childcare facilitates maternal work is increasingly recognised as an important component of service quality. But provision under both Labour and the Coalition has been piecemeal; the complexity of subsidies combined with inadequate high quality provision results in patchwork arrangements which are not suited to families' needs.

A very high (97%) take-up of the Early Years Entitlement (DfE, 2014b) is a clear indicator of high demand for quality childcare services. That it is limited to 15 hours a week, however, conflicts with the reality of their working life, as well as with the tax and benefits system which only recognise employment of 16 or more hours. This disparity is likely to become more pronounced with in-work conditionality under Universal Credit, which will compel recipients to take on extra working hours. The increase in casualised and zero hours contract work during the recession means that it is now even more difficult for families to plan care arrangements, with time required to travel between childcare and places of work being another, often hidden, factor.

Another key problem with current funding for childcare is that, aside from the Early Years Entitlement, the majority of funding is tied to being in work. For parents in education, training or seeking a job, or starting a business, childcare is essential. Time and again research on welfare to work programmes highlights that childcare is a barrier to work when parents are unable to find quality childcare *before* they move into work. The IFS (2014) finding that free places for 3-year olds helped only a small number of women into work is no surprise: entitlement to 15 free hours largely offers a discount on services families already are paying for, rather than helping more women into work.

Conclusion: Childcare cannot be an afterthought

Childcare policy reflects societal sharing of care responsibilities and obligations; who can access affordable quality childcare is an outcome of government decisions. The failings of current policy limit families' choice and force parents to craft their own solutions, leaving many disadvantaged. The forthcoming General Election is an opportunity to set out a vision for the future and decide whether care for children – the bedrock of our society – is indeed a shared social responsibility. Labour has stated that should it win the Election a key policy would be to increase the universal entitlement through an increase in the bank levy.

Regardless of the outcome of the Election, we would like to see a future government committing to a sustainable childcare strategy that will deliver for parents, and, crucially, for children. Priority needs to shift away from demand-priming through cash transfers and a focus on subsidies for parents in work towards funding and developing a supply-led system with means-tested and capped fees based on a sliding-fee scale. Direct funding and provision of quality childcare is a proven tool for poverty reduction and more equitable take-up.

The restructuring of childcare could pay for itself through reduced administration costs, jobs created and improved tax revenues. Increasing affordable and quality childcare raises the probability of women working as their reservation wage decreases. For example, a 10% increase raises the probability of working from 53% to 67% for less educated women and from 79% to 86% for more educated ones (Del Boca et al., 2008). Businesses retain female staff, government benefits from higher tax contributions, and adequate public childcare cuts down the price in commercial markets.

High quality public childcare ensures that parents are comfortable using the service. Quality will improve with nationally set standards and objectives (e.g. well-trained staff and staff:child ratios), while capacity planning and public oversight will reduce regional disparities. Childcare and early education frame the possibilities for later life, and hence strategically investing in quality childcare will yield significant returns for future generations.

References

Del Boca, D., Pasqua, S. and Pronzato, C. (2008) 'Market Work and Motherhood Decisions in Contexts,' *IZA Discussion Paper No. 3303*, Bonn: IZA.

DfE (2014a) *Childcare and Early Years Survey of Parents 2012-13*, London: DfE.

DfE (2014b) *Statistical First Release (Provision for children under five years of age in England: January 2014)*, London: DfE.

Family and Childcare Trust (2014) *Childcare Costs Survey 2014*, London: Family and Childcare Trust.

HM Treasury (2014) *Budget 2014 (HC1104)*, London: HoC.

Institute for Fiscal Studies (2014) *The impact of free early education for 3-year olds in England*, London: IFS.

OECD (2014) *OECD Family Database*, OECD: Paris.

'Universal childcare' and maternal employment: the British and the Swedish story

Ingela K. Naumann, University of Edinburgh
ingela.naumann@ed.ac.uk

Introduction

Over the last 25 years Britain saw a huge public investment in childcare. From New Labour to the Coalition Government the declared goals of new childcare policy was to bring more mothers into work, thereby reducing child poverty, and to improve child outcomes particularly for disadvantaged children by supporting 'early learning'. Hence the unwieldy term 'early childhood education and care' (ECEC) that is commonly used to emphasise both purposes.

Expenditure on ECEC more than doubled between 1997 to 2010, from 0.5% to 1.1% of GDP, moving the UK from one of the lowest to one of the highest spenders in the OECD. The number of 3 and 4 year olds attending ECEC increased from around 65% to 93%, and for Under-3s from 25% to 42% (Stewart, 2013; OECD, 2014). A flagship policy of New Labour was the introduction of universal free part-time early education for 3 and 4 year olds in England, which was extended to some 2-year olds by the Coalition Government. Similar policies operate in the other UK nations. Further, various forms of tax credits and childcare vouchers are aimed at reducing childcare costs for working parents.

Recently however, frustration is mounting: despite an investment of around £2bn a year in childcare, the increase in maternal employment has fallen short of expectations and childcare costs for working parents have soared. In particular universal ECEC has come under scrutiny: whereas a study by the IPPR predicted universal childcare to bring more than 250,000 parents into work (Cooke and Pearce, 2013), research by the IFS found that the expansion of free part-time childcare places, costing around £800m a year, had only helped a modest 12,000 more mothers into employment, thus being a very expensive employment policy (Brewer et al., 2014).

Along predictable ideological battle lines, some argue that the universal childcare policy does not go far enough; others see it as an expensive, even dangerous, policy failure (see e.g. www.day-nurseries.co.uk, 2014). This debate distracts from the fact that 'universalism' is but one aspect of the British childcare system – or rather, the UK nations' childcare systems (which nevertheless, share common traits), and possibly not the element that is in most need of reform. From countries with higher levels of maternal employment we can learn what kind of childcare, as regards policy design, policy integration and funding, supports working parents, and what obstacles there are in the UK. We shall in particular look at Sweden, one of the world's 'childcare champions' – not least due to our British fascination with the 'Swedish Model' and Nordic 'universalism'.

Universal childcare works: it supports early development of all children

To start with both Sweden and the UK nations share a very similar universal policy of 15 hours free early education per week for all children aged 3 to school-entry. There is international consensus on the positive effects of early childhood education for child outcomes. For England, this has been confirmed by the large-scale 'Effective Provision of Pre-school Education' Project (EPPE, 2004). Especially children from disadvantaged backgrounds profit from early childhood education, as long as it is of good quality. And here lies a crucial importance of public spending on ECEC: childcare markets are poor guarantors for quality in deprived neighbourhoods as they gravitate towards areas where purchasing power is high. At the same time universal policies have been shown to reach disadvantaged children more effectively than targeted approaches. There is thus a clear case to be made for public spending on universal early childhood policy. Most OECD countries now offer some form of early education entitlement assuming future social and economic benefits. Finally, with the UN Convention on the Rights of the Child emphasizing the importance of education for children of all ages, we are past the point of no return. Universal ECEC for pre-school children is here to stay.

The question is whether, or under what conditions, universal ECEC policy also supports maternal employment.

Why universal childcare does not really help mothers into work in the UK: lack of full-time places and high costs

On the face of it, a 15 hours/week childcare guarantee is ill-suited to help parents into work: there are very few jobs with working hours that could be squeezed into the time frame of a daily 3-5 hours early education session. And even where the entitlement can be taken more flexibly over two days, as is now the case in England, it would be difficult to find a job that precisely matches the free offer.

In the UK, most parents of 3 and 4 year olds who work need to purchase additional childcare, either from the same provider, or they need to find someone who can pick up their child from nursery school and look after them (often a childminder or relative) – a logistical feat; and the multiple childcare arrangements common in working households with small children speak a silent story of stress, contingency and making do. Parents who do not want to delay returning to work until their child is 3 are left to organise all their childcare themselves. Most of this childcare is provided by the market, and availability and quality differ considerably across regions, councils, cities and neighbourhoods.

Market-based childcare is expensive, in the UK extraordinarily so. A full-time dual earner couple with average earnings and a 2 year old spends around 34% of disposable family income on childcare, compared to an OECD average of 13% and 4.5% in Sweden respectively (OECD tax-benefit model, 2014). It should thus not come as a surprise that in the UK, universal part-time ECEC has not brought significantly more women into the labour market, but eases the costs for those who have already successfully solved their childcare conundrum.

Lack of adequate childcare and costs have internationally been identified as key obstacles to women's labour market integration. Where costs exceed 10% of disposable family income, the barrier for women to enter work, particularly for low-skilled women, increases. In the UK tax credits have helped cover up to 70% of childcare costs on a means-tested basis (there is a new system in place with Universal Credit). However, real costs in many parts of the UK exceed the set ceilings and childcare costs after subsidies remain too high for many low and middle income families. As a consequence, the 'motherhood penalty' is significant with the employment rate of mothers with children below 15 at 65%, almost 10% lower than the general female participation rate (24-54 age cohort) (OECD, 2014). The majority of employed mothers work part-time and rely strongly on informal care (Naumann et al., 2013).

... and why it does in Sweden: availability and affordability

It is here, with respect to availability and affordability, that the Swedish childcare system differs from the UK, not in the universal, free part-time element. In fact, when Swedes speak about their 'universal preschool' they don't primarily think of the free early education for 3-5 year olds, but refer to the entitlement of all children from age 1 to a full-day, all year round place in a daycare centre, if their parents are in employment – in essence a targeted policy. It is the extent of take up rates that gives this policy its 'universal' character: the vast majority of Swedish pre-school children attending ECEC do so on a full-time basis. The average usage amongst Under-5s is 33 hours per week, and maternal employment is at 80% almost as high as the general participation rate of Swedish women (OECD, 2014).

This childcare is not free of charge, but heavily subsidized. In Sweden parent fees cover on average 7% of the actual costs, they are capped and means-tested, and for some groups of parents the fee is waived altogether (Naumann et al., 2013). Childcare costs are not an issue for Swedish families, irrespective of household income. To reduce barriers to work further, there is an entitlement to 15 hours free childcare for children aged 1 whose parents are in education or looking for a job. In the knowledge that childcare is available to them, Swedish parents are more confident than their British counterparts to 'take the plunge' and return to work while their children are young, or continue education or professional training.

But how can Sweden, with similar spending levels than the UK, afford such a generous childcare system?

Funding a comprehensive childcare system

The main difference lies in the respective prioritization of funding streams: in the UK a big chunk of ECEC spending goes directly to parents helping them with their childcare costs via tax credits and childcare vouchers; the rest is channelled to providers to fund the free entitlement. Administering this complex system is costly and experiences in other countries such as Australia, Canada or the US have shown that demand-side funding does not necessarily reduce costs.

In Sweden, the emphasis since the 1970s has been on supply-side funding, thereby gradually building up a childcare infrastructure and workforce that made it possible for high quality daycare to be offered to all families across the country, which contributed to key characteristics of the 'Swedish Model': high employment, high tax revenue, low gender inequality and child poverty. The link between parental employment and childcare entitlement in the policy design ensures that public investment yields direct economic returns.

It is important to note however, that it is not the extensive childcare provision alone that boosts Swedish employment levels: a long paid parental leave policy of 16 months, and a seamless transition from parental leave to childcare entitlement; flexible working time that even includes an entitlement to leave when a child is sick; and generous family benefits all add up to a 'policy package' that helps parents reconcile family and work.

Conclusion

In conclusion, if the 'Swedish Model' serves as inspiration, ironically the question whether there should be more or less 'universal', that is free, childcare in the UK becomes less relevant vis-à-vis, the challenge to transform the currently fragmented and costly provision into an integrated system that offers reliable and affordable early education and care to all children and their families where they need it, when they need it. This will not be possible without further public investment – investment which spans election cycles – but restructuring childcare can offset the costs in the longer run by creating new jobs and increasing tax revenue.

One last caveat: whilst a well-designed childcare system can indeed bring more mothers into work, it cannot solve all problems. As long as new jobs in the labour market are primarily of a low-pay, part-time nature, economic returns for public spending on childcare will remain meagre.

References

Brewer, M., Cattan, S., Crawford, C. and Rabe, B. (2014) *The impact of free, universal pre-school education on maternal labour supply*, Institute for Fiscal Studies, London: IFS.

Cooke, G. and Pearce, N. (2013) *The Condition of Britain: Interim Report*, Institute for Public Policy Research, London: IPPR.

Daynurseries.co.uk: 'Should the Government Provide Free Universal Childcare? 06. March 2014, http:www.daynurseries.co.uk/news/article.cfm/id/41/should-the-government-provide-free-universal-childcare, [accessed 03.01.2015].

The Effective Provision of Pre-school Education (EPPE) Project (2004) *The Final Report*, Technical Paper 12, London: Institute of Education.

Naumann, I., McLean, C., Koslowski, A., Tisdall, K. and Lloyd, E. (2013) *Early childhood education and care provision: international review of policy, delivery and funding*, Scottish Government Social Research Paper, Edinburgh.

OECD (2014): OECD Family Database, OECD: Paris, www.oecd.org/els/family/database.htm, [accessed 03.01.2015].

Stewart, K. (2013): *Labour's Record on the Under Fives: Policy, Spending and Outcomes 1997 -2010*, CASE/LSE Working Paper 4, London.

Education: who runs our schools?

Stephen J Ball, University College London
s.ball@ioe.ac.uk

Introduction

The Coalition government announced in 2010 that it intended to achieve change in compulsory education by reducing and stripping out regulation, and giving schools and head teachers more autonomy. Supply-side measures were to be put in place to 'set education free' by introducing new providers and new choices, and wresting schools from local authorities by creating many more academies, cutting excessive red tape, scrapping unnecessary quangos, and creating a streamlined funding model where government funding follows the learner and is dispensed directly to schools from central government:

> 'We will change the laws – on planning, on funding, on staffing – to make it easier for new schools to be created in your neighbourhood, so you can demand the precise, personalised, education your children need . . . The money currently wasted on red tape and management consultants instead invested in books and teachers' (Gove, 2009).

In all of this, the relationship between educational quality and social deprivation was to be addressed by the proliferation of academies and free schools and plans for a 'Pupil Premium' (a LibDem policy commitment) first suggested by American pro-marketeers Chubb and Moe (1990) – that is extra money per head where pupils come from 'poorer homes', 'making schools work harder' for pupils in these circumstances.

Recent developments

The Academies Bill, laid before Parliament just 14 days into the Coalition government and passed in July 2010, enables secondary schools, primary and special schools classed as 'outstanding' to become academies without a requirement to consult local authorities. In November 2010, the possibility of schools applying for academy status was extended to those deemed 'satisfactory' by Ofsted, if partnered by an 'outstanding' school. Michael Gove, then Secretary of State for Education, said that he expected that academies would become the norm among English schools. The Academies Act also authorised the creation of Free Schools. A Free School is a type of Academy, a non-profit-making, independent, state-funded school, which is free to attend, but which is not controlled by a Local Authority. The Free School concept is based on similar schools found in Sweden, Chile, New Zealand, Canada, and the United States. In both the US and Canada they are known as charter schools. The first 24 Free Schools opened in autumn 2011 including five proposed by faith groups, two involving ARK Schools (an academy chain), and one each The Childcare Company, King's Science Academy, and Discovery New School. In December 2013 after a series of inspections the Discovery New School was closed. By Oct 2014,111 Free Schools were opened or approved; by December 4,344 academies were open or had been approved – in addition 42 Studio schools have opened or been approved (http://www.studioschoolstrust.org), and there are 30 University Technical Colleges (http://www.utcolleges.org).

The Academies programme is both imposed on 'failing' schools and is self-generating – ambitious chains and individual sponsors wanting to run more schools, and head teachers and governors looking for budget maximization – 'failing schools' are handed over to existing chains or 'brokered' by DfE consultants to new sponsors. 'Outstanding' schools are encouraged to form relationships with less well-graded schools and *superheads* are parachuted in to 'save' under-performing schools. At the same time, Local Authorities, Trades Unions and Universities are marginalized or their participation in educational work is fundamentally reworked – although some Universities act as Academy sponsors. The Conservative, New Labour and Coalition governments have all been keen to get new actors into service delivery in response to a continuing 'discourse of derision' that constructs public sector schooling as dysfunctional. As a result the distribution of responsibility for the solution of educational problems is changing and philanthropy and business are now essential parts of the policy process, redefining policy problems and constructing and enacting new 'market-based' solutions.

One further intention of these reform moves, both those of New Labour and the Coalition, is a whittling away of the national agreements on teachers' pay and conditions, the introduction of fixed term contracts and performance related pay and opening up new routes of entry into teaching – most recently for ex-service personnel. Increasingly schools themselves (Teaching Schools) and Teach First are taking over the responsibility for teacher training and entry into teaching and some University based preparation routes are being closed down. Teach First is a social enterprise registered as a charity. It coordinates an employment-based teaching training programme whereby participants achieve Qualified Teacher Status through the participation in a two year training programme that involves the completion of a PGCE along with wider leadership skills training. Its focus is on schools in areas of social disadvantage.

The new governing space of education in England is an incoherent, ad hoc, diverse, fragile and evolving network of complex relations. It contains possibilities, inconsistencies and contradictions – both business and religion, localism and corporatism, equity and privilege. It rests on new relations of regulation, competition, funding and performance management. The process of public sector 'modernization' or transformation involved here is both creative and destructive, a process of attrition and reinvention. Although the transformation process may sometimes appear to be disjointed it has an internal logic, a set of discernible, if not necessarily planned, facets.

The process of transformation is both recreating the difficulties and inconsistences it was meant to address and creating new ones. Both academies and free schools were created as responses to what was presented as the low standards of performance of some state schools, especially in areas of social disadvantage. These schools, it is argued by their sponsors (see for example http://www.arkschools.org/) will bring creativity and energy to bear upon entrenched social and educational inequalities. In fact, a number of Academies and Free Schools have been deemed by Inspection and performance outcomes as 'under-performing'; some chains of academies have been found to be unable to manage their schools effectively; some chains and academies and free schools appear to be indulging in dubious financial practices; the free schools were supposed to be targeted at areas of social disadvantage but recent research by Rob Higham (2014) indicates their distribution does not reflect this aim; and indeed DFE figures indicate that the majority of the 24 free schools that opened in 2011 have a lower proportion of children eligible for free school meals than the local average (Guardian, 2012); 18 Academy chains are now 'paused' – that is concerns related to their performance and management abilities mean they cannot take on further schools (the list includes AET, the largest academy chain with 77 schools, and E-ACT which runs 25); furthermore 68 academies have received pre-warning letters and 7 warning letters from the DfE about their poor performance.

The Ofsted assessment of E-Act academies reported 'overwhelming proportion of pupils ... not receiving a good education'. Inspectors visited 16 of E-Act's 34 academies over a two-week period – one was judged Outstanding, four were Good, six were judged as Requires Improvement and five, including Hartsbrook E-Act Free School, were Inadequate. Hartsbrook has now been closed twice and has its third sponsor. Key weakness in the 16 academies inspected included:

1 Poor quality teaching

2 Work not matched to pupils' abilities

3 Weak monitoring

4 Poor use of assessment data

5 Insufficiently challenging lessons for more able pupils.

Inspectors also discovered E-Act had deducted a proportion of pupil premium funding from each academy until 1 September 2013. Ofsted was unclear how the deducted funding was being used to help disadvantaged pupils.

Of the 41 that have had judgments published as of April 2014 four free schools have been rated 'inadequate' by the inspectorate – this is 9.7% compared with the national average for all schools of 3%. Overall, 79% of state schools are rated good or outstanding compared with only 68% of free schools (watchsted.com 2014).

In December 2014 the Chief Inspector of Schools, Sir Michael Wilshaw, a one-time academy super-head, stated in his annual report that struggling schools are 'no better off' under academy control and said there could be little difference in school improvement under an academy chain or a council. Imagining the position of a head teacher of a newly converted academy, he said: 'In fact, the neglect you suffered at the hands of your old local authority is indistinguishable from the neglect you endure from your new trust' (The Guardian, 10 December 2014).

Finally, a report for the House of Commons Select Committee on conflicts of interest in academy trusts (Greany and Scott, 2014) identified a number of dubious practices and inappropriate financial arrangements and concluded 'that the checks and balances on academy trusts in relation to conflicts of interest are still too weak. In the course of the research we came across a significant number of real or potential conflicts of interest that we found concerning' (p. 3). There have been a number of high profile examples of financial malpractice.

Conclusion

As noted already Academies and Free schools are specifically intended to break the local authority monopoly of school provision, indeed to residualise LAs. However, evidence indicates that many academy trusts are unable to manage their schools effectively, that many academies and free schools are underperforming compared with their LA counterparts, but that many recruit a more socially advantaged intake than their LA counterparts. In all of this there is a lack of oversight and transparency. The response to these problems by the previous Secretary of State, Michael Gove was to reinvent a geographic system of school 'authorities' – Regional Commissioners (all appointed by him) and Regional Boards, elected by school head teachers. The majority of those elected to the Boards are school head teachers. The new Schools Commissioners are now formally charged with both managing and growing the Academy sector. Local democratic oversight has been almost totally displaced. Our relationship to schools is being modelled on that of the privatised utilities – we are individual customers who can switch provider if we are unhappy, in theory, and complain to the national watchdog if we feel badly served – but with no direct, local participation or involvement.

Putting all of these policy moves together, we are moving back towards a pre-universal 19th century 'system' of education that is messy, patchy and diverse, involving a variety of providers – voluntary, philanthropic, faith, self-help (parents), trusts of various kinds and, on a small scale so far, private; although at this point in time, public sector providers remain as the main providers.

So what should the incoming government do?

- ✓ Establish a framework for an ethical audit of educational providers.
- ✓ Require much greater accountability and transparency from providers – including the Inspection of academy chains.
- ✓ Consider ways in which outsourced services might be brought back 'in-house' – as inspections are to be – and/or replace for-profit providers with mutuals.
- ✓ Commission and publish a systematic review of evidence on the relations between profit, performance and equity.

References

Chubb, J. and Moe, T. (1990) *Politics, markets and America's schools*. Washington, D.C.: The Brookings Institution.

Gove, M. (2009) Speech to The Conservative Party Conference: http://news.bbc.co.uk/nol/shared/bsp/hi/pdfs/07_10_09govespeech.pdf.

Greany, T. and Scott, J. (2014) *Conflicts of interest in academy sponsorship arrangements:* A report for the Education Select Committee, London Centre for Leadership in Learning, Institute of Education, University of London.

Guardian, (2012) http://www.theguardian.com/education/2012/apr/23/free-schools-deprived-pupils-average.

Guardian, (2014) http://www.theguardian.com/education/2014/dec/10/ofsted-sir-michael-wilshaw-struggling-schools-academy-neglect.

Higham, R. (2014) 'Free schools in the Big Society: the motivations, aims and demography of free school proposers', *Journal of Education Policy*, 29, 1, 122-39 .

Watchsted.com (2014) http://www.theguardian.com/education/2014/apr/29/free-schools-ofsted-failure-rate-higher-state.

The impact of the Coalition austerity drive on English statutory homeless service delivery

Sarah Alden, University of Sheffield
sop11sla@sheffield.ac.uk

Introduction

In legal terms a person(s) is entitled to present as homeless to an English local authority if they are threatened with homelessness within 28 days. For the authority to accept a full duty it must further be determined that the household had not made themselves intentionally homeless, have a local connection and reach the threshold of priority need. In respect of the latter a household would normally be assessed as vulnerable if it contained dependent children, a pregnant person, a person under 18, or a care leaver under 21; alongside these are categories that require more interpretation, such as vulnerability due to health issues, institutionalisation, violence, or older age. Over the last decade or so the main political parties in England have remained committed to reducing statutory homelessness levels and rooflessness through the adoption of preventative strategies. For example alongside accepting eligible households as statutorily homeless, with a legal duty to provide settled accommodation, local authority housing option services (LAHOS's hereafter) may provide financial assistance or support to ensure a household can remain in their home, or secure alternative private rented accommodation.

It has been argued that the main political motive for prevention schemes are to ease pressure on oversubscribed social housing, and avoid 'damaging' homeless statistics, rather than a genuine desire to assist those in housing difficulty, meaning 'non vulnerable' households may struggle to access these services (Lund, 2011). Further, it has been found that stringent targets and the need to ration scarce resources (alongside inadequate training around housing law) may lead to unlawful gatekeeping (Reeve and Batty, 2011), whereby households are denied their legal right to present as homeless.

Due to an assessed link between scarce resources and gatekeeping, it was predicted that LAHOS users may experience worse outcomes in the current politically austere climate. Since the Coalition Government came to power in 2010 its main policy objective of reducing public spending has meant cuts to both central and local budgets, and local authority departments and expenditure toward housing and welfare is at its lowest level since 1945 (Nevin and Leather, 2012). Alongside this, the Coalition has charged LAHOS's with identifying cost savings and in some cases front-line staff have been reduced through redundancy and redeployment (ONS, 2011). Further, recent research has shown that welfare cuts and related policy changes introduced by the Coalition have lessened the options available to low income households. For example whilst social housing has been perennially scarce, reforms relating to local housing allowance have meant that private rented accommodation is becoming increasingly unaffordable. For example Lister et al. (2011) estimated that as a result of the shortfall between LHA and due rent over 90% of private rented stock in just over a third of local authorities (excluding London) will be unaffordable by 2023, rising to 60% by 2030.

When these factors are taken in conjunction, it is perhaps unsurprising that statutory homelessness acceptances (Gov.UK, 2014), and households requiring help due to the threat of homelessness (Fitzpatrick et al., 2012) have followed an upward trend, with the former having risen by nearly a quarter following the economic downturn (DCLG, 2014). Alongside this the Localism Act has provided LAHOS's with new powers to discharge a homeless duty into private rented accommodation. If utilised this essentially weakens the position of a household in terms of the security of tenure they can expect if accepted as homeless. This is because private tenants are normally given an assured shorthold tenancy, whereby landlords are only required to provide a six month agreement, whereas local authority or housing association tenancies offer longer term security of tenure (Fitzpatrick et al., 2012).

Service delivery in an age of austerity

To explore in greater detail how the current political climate is impacting on statutory homelessness and housing advice services a national baseline survey and follow on interviews with a selection of line managers and staff were carried out by the author between December 2012 and July 2013. A total of 272 practitioners completed the survey, and 27 practitioners in 12 LAHOS departments participated in interviews.

The survey findings, in line with other research in this area, confirmed that statutory homelessness acceptances had increased, with three-fifths of LAHOS stating that they had risen in their area. Further, around 40% of practitioners surveyed felt the ability to undertake the role was adversely affected by the resulting heavy workload, and nearly half due to departmental budgetary decreases. In a similar vein nearly all interviewees reported a higher workload due to the impact of welfare cuts and many felt this growth would continue as austerity measures continued to take hold.

When survey respondents were asked to consider the current challenges faced the most common response was local housing allowance reform, cited by nine out of 10; this was closely followed by welfare reform/general effects of the downturn and lack of private rented accommodation, with each being cited by over four-fifths of respondents. All bar one survey respondent named at least one challenge to service delivery, and 99% cited two or more; just over 70% of respondents reported five or more challenges. An equally high number of challenges were reported in the minority of LAHOS where statutory acceptances had not increased. The follow up interviews suggested that this was likely to reflect a growth in households seeking help who were not necessarily owed a full housing duty. These findings provide a strong indication that LAHOS's are under considerable pressure in the current climate.

All practitioners who reported challenges to the service were asked in what ways these impacted upon their ability to effectively undertake the role. Over half of survey respondents felt unable to give appropriate advice and assistance to all who required it and a similar number reported that unacceptable alternatives may be offered to some service users. In support of this some interviewees reported that an increased requirement to ration services had meant further barriers had been put up. For instance one practitioner said that they had previously allowed service users directly into their offices, but this ceased due to an increase in footfall, another stated that in the near future service users would no longer be able to contact them directly by telephone, as a central department was to be set up which would field all calls.

The interviews were able to provide a richer understanding of the pressured environment in which front-line staff operated. For example many officers advised that whilst groups assessed as 'vulnerable' tended to be prioritised, resource shortages would result in authorities practicing unlawful gatekeeping. The pressures most reported by interviewees included a lack of temporary accommodation and concerns around increasing statutory homelessness numbers due to the rise in footfall over the last few years, which is supported by official figures highlighted in the introduction.

> 'I have got into a situation where I am turning around and saying to people, your priority need, you fit the criteria, go away, I have got nothing for you' (Manager, LAHOS B).

Sending people away due to a lack of local connection was also remarked to be as a result of inadequate staffing within any given authority, which a few practitioners advised had worsened in recent years.

As touched upon above, adequate (particularly legal) training is viewed as an important element to ensure effective delivery, yet less than a handful of LAHOS's interviewed felt training was sufficient in their department. Alongside workload issues resource scarcity was a central factor in understanding the lack of training and in some cases this was overtly connected to the choices departments were required to make in the current austere climate:

> 'Since the cuts last year we were basically told we had the choice between losing one member of staff or there would be no more training in the next few years. But they had to save money, it is really really horrifying how much money they have had to save' (Officer One, LAHOS J).

Finally, although administration difficulties due to lack of staffing resources and suitable landlords were commonly reported, some interviewees stated that their authority planned to embrace elements of the Localism Act. Of particular concern was the suggestion by a few interviewees that the Act could be used to prevent people making a homeless application in the first place, as households may be discouraged if led to believe social housing would not be awarded if they were accepted as statutorily homeless.

The impact of austerity on homelessness services

Whilst LAHOS are a perennially lean service the findings of this research indicate that greater challenges are faced in the current austere climate due to a lower level of available resources and greater workload levels as a result of an increase in service users. Related to this a few authorities were setting up enhanced 'screening' to make it harder for households at threat of homelessness to see a specialist adviser, which may increase incidences of preventable homelessness.

Of particular concern was that nearly all interviewees reported practices of gatekeeping to protect limited resources and reduce homeless acceptances. This may ultimately hide the true picture of homelessness, which may in turn impact upon the level of resources assessed as necessary to tackle it. Dependent on the focus of the authority we may develop very different insights into the extent to which there is a homelessness problem in a particular area, which will likely be formed on the basis of how it is recorded, rather than the actual reality. It is argued that if the number of households losing their home is shrouded in these ways, this may arguably give politicians less reason to address this important issue.

Conclusion

It is concluded that as the likelihood of practitioners practicing gatekeeping is chiefly linked to resource scarcity and the requirement to ration services, its incidence is likely to progressively worsen in the current political climate. It is also important to note that suitable quality training may also suffer due to funding shortages, which will have a negative impact on the provision of effective advice. Linked to this was a concern that implementation of the Localism Act may be influenced by the need to protect limited resources, rather than providing choice. For example some practitioners advised that execution of this part of the Act, even if viewed as unworkable due to shortages of private rented accommodation, may potentially be treated as a weapon that could be brandished to discourage households from presenting as homeless.

The problems identified ultimately call for an injection of resources, which runs counter to the main Government drive toward reducing public spending. However, as an essential service, it is argued that ensuring statutory homelessness departments are provided with suitably qualified staff and sufficient options to stem homelessness is necessary and the provision of funding to help achieve this should not be skimped. Furthermore, if politicians are genuinely motivated to reducing homelessness, this should relate to all forms, not just the most visible.

References

DCLG (2014) *Statutory Homelessness: April to June quarter 2014*, England, London, DCLG.

Fitzpatrick, S., Pawson, H., Bramley, G. and Wilcox, S. (2012) *The homelessness monitor: England 2012*, London: Crisis.

Gov.UK. (2014) '*Homelessness statistics*' https://www.gov.uk/government/collections/homelessness-statistics [accessed 10.06.2014].

Lister, S., Reynolds, L. and Webb, K. (2011) *Research report the impact of welfare reform bill measures on affordability for low income private renting families*, London: Shelter.

Lund, B. (2011) *Understanding housing policy, 2nd edition*, Bristol: Policy Press.

Nevin, B. and Leather, P. (2012) *Localism, welfare reform and housing market change: Identifying the issues and responding to the challenge a report for nash*, London: Nevin Leather Associates.

ONS (2011) '*Statistical bulletin labour market statistics*', http://www.ons.gov.uk/ons/dcp171778_232238.pdf [accessed 12.10.2011].

Reeve, K. and Batty, E. (2011) *The hidden truth about homelessness: experiences of single homelessness in England*, London: Crisis.

Combating modern slavery

Gary Craig, Durham University
gary.craig@durham.ac.uk

Introduction

What's not to like about a Bill aimed at combatting modern slavery? After years of lobbying by prominent NGOs such as AntiSlavery International, ECPAT, the Poppy Project, Kalayaan, Unseen, and many children's and church-based charities, the institution of a UK Anti-Slavery Day, the failure of Michael Connarty MP's Private Members Bill on slavery in supply chains (talked out by Tory Whips), a growing volume of detailed research on modern slavery, initiated by the Joseph Rowntree Foundation (see for example Craig et al. (2007) and the range of research studies funded by JRF on forced labour: www.jrf.org.uk/research/forced-labour), and the creation of an All Party Parliamentary Group on Trafficking (APPGT) in 2008, the seriousness of modern slavery within the UK was finally accepted by government when the Home Secretary announced in August 2013 she would be presenting a Bill to Parliament later that year.

Early criticisms

The draft Bill finally emerged in December 2013 and in the period before and after its publication, its provisions were subject to the most intense scrutiny, including a special inquiry chaired by Frank Field MP, an investigation into data on trafficking chaired by Fiona McTaggart MP, of the now-renamed APPGTrafficking and Modern Day Slavery (in recognition of the much wider range of slavery offences coming to light), intense lobbying by NGOs and researchers, and a joint Select Committee of Lords and Commons. The outcome of this scrutiny was a tacit acknowledgement by government that the draft Bill was deficient in many respects. As a result, a final version of the Bill was published in June 2014 and welcomed in principle across the political spectrum as it had its first and second readings.

Since then, however, as the Bill has begun to progress through Parliament, the fault lines have begun to emerge. A number of key issues have been highlighted which have underlined the difference between the current government's over-emphasis on criminal justice issues and on defining the precise nature of offences on the one hand, and a wider understanding of the nature, causes and scope of modern slavery on the other (see for example the report of the Joint Committee on Human Rights report on the JCHR (2014)) Some of these wider issues may be picked up as the Bill becomes an Act (by March 30 2015); however, it is likely that some remain to be dealt with by an incoming government.

Some plus points

First, the good news. The government has stressed that the Act will make it clear that victims of modern slavery (such as trafficked women – perhaps 5,000 or so in the UK now according to a variety of estimates[1] – and young men often smuggled under violent conditions into cannabis farms – of which there are thousands now in the UK) will not be criminalised for any acts they are forced to undertake. Secondly, government has also agreed at the time of writing – under pressure, unexpectedly, also from big businesses afraid of losing market share to less scrupulous employers making use of forced labour – that they will introduce a clause along the lines of Michael Connarty MP's original Bill requiring companies to report in their accounts what they are doing to scrutinise their supply chains – of, hopefully, both labour and products – for evidence of slavery practices. Thirdly, offences will result in very heavy punishment – including life sentences – for those found guilty of promoting them.

And now the bad news

However – and it is a big however – there is much yet to be done which is unlikely to be reflected in the final form of the Act as compromises are done to ensure it reaches the Queen for royal assent by the end of March. First, perhaps most worryingly, the Bill as a whole has a continuing emphasis on human (both child and adult) trafficking for sexual purposes as the major focus. Trafficking for labour exploitation (which numerically is beginning to overtake cases of sex trafficking), and particularly forced labour, have yet properly to be reflected within the Bill as separate and highly significant forms of modern slavery within the UK. It is still the case that labour exploitation is perceived by many as something which happens in poor 'underdeveloped' countries. (It is of course important to recognise that most such incidences of forced labour do happen outside the UK and that is why the issue of supply chains – which result in slave-produced goods such as Bangladeshi clothing and Thai prawns being sold within this country – is so significant.) And the system for identifying and dealing with victims of trafficking has been shown to be not fit for purpose with government undertaking a review of the National Referral Mechanism (NRM) which processes alleged victims. We do not know yet what this will show but there remains intense anxiety that the NRM is still far too closely linked to the needs of immigration policy – and we know what that does to serious and evidence-based debate! For example, the chances of a victim of trafficking having their claim accepted as such are about three times higher if they are white European than if they are Black African in origin.

We also know that most organisations tasked with identifying victims are hugely underprepared and ill-trained to do so. This is both reflected in the failure of many agencies to understand the nature of human trafficking and what precisely they are looking for in terms of victims – as many cases of child sexual abuse have also shown – and of the legislature in particular to understand the nature of forced labour. Cases have fallen or derisory punishments applied because judges, magistrates and prosecutors do not understand the circumstances under which a person may be said to be in forced labour; for example, freedom physically to move around or visit local shops does not imply freedom from psychological, financial or emotional pressure which effectively keeps a person in bondage. The Act needs to clarify the nature of the offences, identify all the slavery-like practices as separate and distinct, and require the Home Secretary to use effective guidance and instructions to all those organisations with a responsibility for addressing the issues.

Secondly, despite intense lobbying (which resulted in a tied vote in Committee with the Chair finally casting his vote for the government position) the government has refused to give ground on the issue of overseas domestic workers' (ODWs) visas. Until 2010, ODWs, often coming to work for a specific employer such as a diplomat or businessman, were able to change employers if they found they were being abused or exploited, as was often revealed to be the case in the work of Kalayaan (2014) the major NGO operating to support ODWs. The incoming government in 2010 changed this arrangement so that any ODW seeking to change employers would be deported, thus trapping the ODW in an exploitative situation. ODWs' families are dependent on their income for children and family either with them or back at home (in the Philippines for example) and are more or less forced to accept their exploitation or lose their status and thus their income. Lobbying continues around this issue with Labour attempting to find a compromise such as a visa which can be renewed annually under certain conditions.

More work to be done

Thirdly, the government committed early on to establishing the post of an Anti-Slavery Commissioner, effectively the National Rapporteur called for by UN, EU and Council of Europe conventions and protocols, a role which is being performed very effectively in several countries such as the Netherlands and Finland. However, whilst the government has agreed to include the term Independent in the title for this role, it is clear that the person would not be independent in any meaningful sense: the Commissioner reports to the Home Secretary (and not to Parliament), who has the power to redact reports. Clearly, the government also sees the role as a criminal justice role: it has profoundly annoyed many Parliamentarians who discovered late in the day that the post had been advertised and candidates interviewed before it had even been debated in parliament, and most of the candidates turned out to be senior serving police officers. The person appointed was a recently retired Metropolitan Police Officer. As it stands, the Commissioner's mandate is weak and narrow and it is unlikely to enjoy the confidence of campaigning organisations, victims or indeed of Parliament as a whole, as National Rapporteurs do in other countries where they exist.

Fourthly, there remains concern about the remit of the Gangmasters Licensing Authority (GLA) which is the major regulatory body with powers to combat forced labour (introduced after the Morecambe Bay tragedy in 2004 where 23 Chinese cocklepickers were left to drown by an illegal gangmaster). The GLA is acknowledged to be effective in what it does, given its limited remit (three industrial sectors) and resources (which were actually cut substantially in 2013). Government moved the departmental home for the GLA from the agriculturally based departmental home DEFRA to the Home Office, which again appears to emphasise the links between forced labour and immigration policy.[2] Many have argued that a more appropriate home would either be in BIS, with its interests in business development or even DWP, with a labour market-wide purview. Wherever the GLA finally ends up, although government appears to acknowledge that its remit needs to be extended to other industrial sectors such as construction, care and hospitality and leisure, this will be meaningless without a significant increase in its resources. At present, the number of prosecutions of criminal gangmasters through the GLA has fallen dramatically (from 19 in 2010 to 3 in 2014) (Guardian, 14 November, 2014) with the government cuts underpinned by a policy line suggesting that the GLA should only pursue likely high profile cases (and, presumably, leaving other criminals to flourish?)

Finally, there is a concern that, although the devolved administrations are all introducing some form of legislation to address various aspects of modern slavery, there appears to be little attempt to align these to ensure that comparable offences are recognised and dealt with in a comparable fashion. Without this alignment it would be possible, for example, for a criminal gangmaster in one territory to decide to move to another territory where the legal and regulatory regime was less unhelpful.

Conclusion

It is 182 years since Wilberforce's second anti-slavery legislation in the UK Parliament; it seems likely that a new government might need barely a year to identify the obvious weaknesses in the Modern Slavery Act 2015 and legislate again to address them.

Notes

1 The report of last full year of the UK Human Trafficking Centre (NCA 2014) indicated that there were at least 3,000 referrals of people alleged to have been trafficked but most commentators have suggested this is a substantial underestimate.

2 In fact most people found to be in forced labour in the UK are either UK nationals or EU migrant workers with a legal right to be working within the UK (Scott et al., 2012)

References

Craig, G., Wilkinson, M., Gaus, A., McQuade, A. and Skrivankova, K. (2007) *Contemporary slavery in the UK*, York: Joseph Rowntree Foundation.

JCHR (2014) *Report of Joint Committee on Human Rights on the Modern Slavery Bill*, London: TSO, HL62, HC 779.

Kalayaan (2014) see www.kalayaan.org.uk for accounts of their work and case studies.

NCA (2014) *The UK Human Trafficking Centre Annual Report 2013*, London: National Crime Agency.

Scott, S., Craig, G. and Geddes, A. (2012) *The experience of forced labour in the UK food industry*, York: Joseph Rowntree Foundation.

Adult social care

Jon Glasby, Robin Miller and Catherine Needham, University of Birmingham
c.needham.1@bham.ac.uk
@DrCNeedham

Introduction

Going into the 2015 election the policy direction of adult social care is the subject of a high degree of political consensus. All mainstream parties agree that, in contrast with NHS clinical services, individuals should contribute to the cost of their social care package unless they have low income or few assets, and that a mixed economy of provision with a substantial role for the private sector will continue. The Care Act 2014 affirmed that support must be preventative rather than crisis-led; once people need care it should be integrated with health services; and care and support should be personalised, so that people have choice and control. Whoever wins the election, this policy direction will continue to shape the experiences of older people, people with disabilities and people with mental health problems. In the sections that follow we consider the progress to date on prevention, integration and personalisation, what is proposed for the future and the likely barriers to success.

Prevention can be harder than cure

There is obvious appeal in preventing people from experiencing deterioration in their physical or mental well-being to the point at which informal social networks can no longer cope and they therefore rely on formal social care services. Not only could preventative services enable people to maintain their autonomy, independence and current quality of life but should make public funding stretch further. This thinking has underpinned recent social care policy as it has numerous whole sector and user-group specific social care policies of the past. These have resulted in a well-developed typology of prevention services that include those that: prevent people from becoming frail, disabled or unwell in the first place (primary); avoid a worsening in people's conditions or social situation or at least slow this process (secondary); and seek to enable people to recover from a crisis or minimise the social impacts of a disability or illness.

The Care Act reflects this typology, and emphasises that all adult social care services should be seeking to 'delay and prevent' care needs in 'every interaction' with individuals and their families, i.e. prevention is not just the responsibility of bespoke services (DH, 2014). Other services provided or overseen by the local authority and its partner agencies are also seen to have a role, with health, housing, leisure and transport sectors seen as important pieces of the prevention jigsaw. Furthermore many if not most mainstream and informal activities that individuals undertake (such as paid or voluntary work, keeping fit and active, maintaining friends and family) are recognised as potentially helping to maintain people's well-being. Local community resources, developed and delivered by the third sector, are often central to the establishment of supportive networks, offering advice on what is available and more innovative approaches.

This whole-system, asset-based, person-centred and locally permissive approach to national preventative policy, has much to commend it. Despite these positives, it is clear that if we see the main outcome of prevention as ensuring that limited public sector budgets will be sufficient for the future then prevention is an endeavour doomed to failure. Demography and advances in medical science dictate that increasing numbers of people will become older and frailer and therefore in need of support, even if this uptake is delayed or minimised for a period of time. Rather than abandon prevention, however, we need instead to be realistic in what can be achieved and celebrate improvements in quality of life and delay in resource usage for individuals and families. We need to be smarter in measuring relevant impacts and sharing learning, and have greater patience over when these can be achieved, to avoid quick fixes being favoured over those that may make more difference but work over longer timespans.

Stronger together but happier apart? The challenges of integration

Under New Labour, there was a stated commitment to 'joined-up solutions to joined-up problems' and to bringing down the 'Berlin Wall' between health and social care (Hansard, 1997, col. 802). Under the Coalition government from 2010, it seemed initially as if this would be different, with many people fearful that the government's health reforms (eventually embodied in the Health and Social Care Act, 2012) would lead to greater competition and fragmentation. In response, the NHS Future Forum (2011), which was established to review the proposed changes, placed significant emphasis on the need for 'integrated care' – ensuring that the support delivered is joined-up around the needs of the individual and is experienced in a seamless fashion by people using services.

This has since become a key part of the policy rhetoric, with a series of pronouncements and initiatives designed to promote more 'integrated care'. This includes the creation of new Health and Well-being Boards to oversee the integration of services at local level, the creation of a series of 'integrated care pioneer' pilots to test out new ways of working and the establishment of a Better Care Fund to encourage a greater pooling of health and social care resources. The difficulty with such initiatives is two-fold:

- While few would disagree that it makes sense to work together in situations where people have complex or multiple needs, the current health and social care system has not been designed with integrated care in mind. Each agency has different legal powers and responsibilities, accountability structures, budgets, geographical boundaries, cultures, IT systems, and so on – let alone the fact that one service is universal/free at the point of delivery and the other is heavily targeted/means-tested. A famous article on 'the five laws of integration' (Leutz, 1999: 93) argues that 'you can't integrate a square peg into a round hole' – and yet this is exactly what front-line services are being asked to do.
- The very fragmented nature of the health reforms and the intense financial pressures facing public services (especially local government) means that potential partners are having to navigate a much more complex, congested environment, and are having to try to make time and space to develop local relationships in incredibly stressful and difficult conditions. In one sense, it has never been more important to work together, and yet – ironically – it's never been more difficult.

Going forwards, it seems unlikely that current tinkering around the edges will be sufficient to generate more integrated care. While we have a system based on a rigid distinction between 'health' and 'social care' needs, we can ask local services to try their best to work across such fault lines – but expecting them to genuinely solve such embedded problems would be a triumph of hope over experience.

This time it's personal(isation)

The third impetus for change in adult social care comes from the aspiration to personalise support around the individual. This became a formal policy commitment following the signing of the Putting People First Concordat between the then New Labour Government and the social care sector in 2007 (HM Government, 2007) – although its genesis lies in much older campaigns to increase choice and independence for people with disabilities.

Enhancing choice and control has primarily been achieved through financial devolution, making those people who are eligible for state funding aware of how much money is available and then giving them as much control as possible over how that money is spent. Efforts have also been made to increase people's social capital and enhance their access to universal services and spaces, rather than relying only on bespoke social care services.

Over almost a decade of implementation, there are many powerful stories of people's lives being transformed through personalisation – of being able to employ their own staff, or to buy in services that enhance their well-being but don't come off a traditional menu of care services (a laptop, a family holiday to Centre Parcs, for example). The perceived success of personal budgets in social care has led to their extension into the NHS for people receiving Continuing Healthcare.

However, the extent to which personalisation has been a success in social care is highly contested. It does not appear to work well for older people (the largest group of adult social care users), where take up of personal budgets is lower than for people with learning disabilities (45% of older people compared to 59% of people with a learning disability (Age UK, 2013)). The difference is particularly stark for direct payments, which are associated with the most transformative outcomes for people: only 7% of older people are in receipt of a direct payment, compared to 25% of people with learning disabilities (Age UK, 2013). The per head care spend for older people tends to be so small that it is difficult to identify creative ways to cut it up differently. Social workers have expressed grave concerns about the problems of overlaying personalisation on top of austerity – with additional bureaucracy and time spent on brokerage or support planning limiting the scope to review and support people once they are in the system. People committed to using personalisation as a way to enhance citizenship rights have clashed with those who appear to see it as an effective lever to dislodge longstanding state responsibilities for welfare support (Needham and Glasby, 2014).

Despite palpable shortcomings in the current approach, it is hard to give up on the aspiration that care and support should be person-centred, and efforts to extend this will continue in the future. Tackling the underlying funding settlement for social care is key to securing a version of personalisation which supports citizenship, overcoming the 'deficit' model of social care in which people are viewed as a bundle of needs rather than of assets. Making it easier for people to access peer support, and meaningful advice and information is also vital.

Conclusion

All of the major parties going into the election are promising to make real progress on the three aspects of adult social care discussed here. There are differences of emphasis in the party proposals but not of broad intent. A casual glance at the 2010 manifestos would indicate that this was also the case. Making the policies happen will require a willingness to rethink the post-1945 welfare settlement more fundamentally so that structures and incentives allow a substantive commitment to preventative, integrated and personalised care. The pots of money that come with system redesigns cannot continue to paper over the cracks of a system which urgently requires adequate public funding. Forthcoming changes such as the introduction of the cap on care spending risk adding to the complexity of the system without bringing in sufficient new money to ensure adequate coverage.

References

Age UK (2013) *Making Managed Personal Budgets work for older people*, London: Age UK, http://tinyurl.com/cbblznv [accessed 23.1.2014].

Department of Health (2014) *Care and Support Statutory Guidance, issued under the Care Act 2014*, London: DH, https://www.gov.uk/government/uploads/system/uploads/attachment_data/file/315993/Care-Act-Guidance.pdf [accessed 24.12.2014].

Hansard (1997) House of Commons Debates, 9 December, http://www.publications.parliament.uk/pa/cm199798/cmhansrd/vo971209/debtext/71209-07.htm#71209-07_spnew1 [accessed 23.1.2015].

HM Government (2007) *Putting people first: a shared vision and commitment to the transformation of adult social care*, London: HM Government.

Leutz, W. (1999) 'Five laws for integrating medical and social services: lessons from the United States and the United Kingdom', *Milbank Memorial Fund Quarterly*, 77, 77-110.

Needham, C. and Glasby, J. (eds) (2014) *Debates in personalisation*, Bristol: Policy Press.
NHS Future Forum (2012) *Integration – a report from the NHS Future Forum*, London: NHS Future Forum.

Independent living and disabled people

Jenny Morris, Previously policy analyst and researcher on disability issues, now retired
jenny@jennymorris.net

Introduction

There was much political consensus on disability policy during the 20 years to 2010. Campaigning by disabled people's organisations had led to all-Party support for an additional costs benefit (Disability Living Allowance), anti-discrimination legislation, and measures to increase disabled people's employment rate and reduce the numbers living in poverty. In addition, Labour, Conservative and Liberal Democrat parties all came to support disabled people's wish to have choice and control over the support required to go about their daily lives. This piece will summarise the resulting commitments to independent living and review progress made since 2010.

In 2005, with all-Party support, the Labour government published *Improving the Life Chances of Disabled People* (Prime Minister's Strategy Unit, 2005), which stated that:

'By 2025, disabled people in Britain should have full opportunities and choices to improve their quality of life and will be respected and included as equal members of society' (p.7).

In 2008 the Independent Living Strategy (ILS) (HM Government, 2008) set out an aim that, by 2013:

- disabled people who need support to go about their daily lives will have greater choice and control over how support is provided
- disabled people will have greater access to housing, transport, health, employment, education and leisure opportunities and to participation in family and community life.

This five year strategy included outcomes against which progress was to measured and stated that, if sufficient progress was not made by 2013, further consideration would be given to the need for legislation to deliver an entitlement to independent living.

The Coalition Government's approach

On entering government, the Coalition parties restated their support for the Independent Living Strategy but then spent three years developing another strategy and action plan, *Fulfilling Potential* (Department for Work and Pensions, 2013a). The Independent Living Scrutiny Group, intended to report on progress, was disbanded and the government refused to carry out the promised five year review of progress in 2013.

Fulfilling Potential has some similar outcomes to the ILS, but many of the databases against which progress was to be measured were discontinued or affected by changes in the definition of 'disabled person' in the Equality Act 2010, resulting in breaks in the time series of a number of data sources. This means that the government's 2014 progress report on *Fulfilling Potential* is limited in what it measures – on most outcomes 2013 is taken as the baseline year. It is also difficult to fully measure progress on ILS commitments. Nevertheless, there is serious cause for concern when key outcomes of the ILS are measured against what data is available.

Choice and control

An increase in the proportion of disabled people saying they have choice and control over support needed to go about daily life is a key outcome for the ILS and *Fulfilling Potential*. However, there has been a significant fall in choice and control since 2008 (Department for Work and Pensions, 2014a: 20) despite the increase in 'self-directed support' in the form of personal budgets for social care. Most personal budgets take the form of council-managed services, only 17% are direct payments and there is evidence that inadequate funding and restrictions on how personal budgets can be used inhibit choice and control (see e.g. Needham and Glasby, 2014).

Participation in family and community life

Expenditure on social care fell by £4bn between 2010/11 and 2012/13, and is predicted to fall by a further £4bn by 2015 – a total reduction of 33% (Duffy, 2014). The consequences are significant for people who need support to live at home and to participate in 'family and community life'. For example, between 2010/11 and 2013/14, the numbers of older people receiving home care support fell by 31.7%, the numbers receiving equipment and home adaptations by 41.6% and those receiving by meals on wheels by 63.7% (Age UK, 2015). Home care providers are worried about risks to dignity and safety of service users, and many report that levels of service purchased by local authorities or via direct payments are not sufficient to cover the support required (Angel, 2012).

There has been a significant increase in the percentage of people with learning disabilities who receive no support, and increases in charges for those that do (Mencap, 2012). Closure of the Independent Living Fund to new applicants in 2010 and to current recipients in 2015 means people with high levels of support needs are at increasing risk of institutionalisation. The money to be transferred to local authorities is less than that currently spent on supporting ILF recipients, confirming evidence from the Association of Directors of Adult Social Services that they are unlikely to provide equivalent replacement funding. More local authorities are being open about their practice of limiting the amount of money they will spend to support someone at home to the cost of alternative residential provision (Disability Rights UK, 2013).

Employment and economic well-being

The ILS (and *Fulfilling Potential)* committed the government to narrowing the employment gap between disabled and non-disabled people. In 2010 this was 30%, having fallen by 10% since 2002. In 2014 – using the new definition of 'disabled person' – it had risen slightly to 33% (Department for Work and Pensions, 2014a: 10). There is no evidence that current policies to support disabled people into work are improving employment opportunities: only 5% of disabled people on the Work Programme have found a job (Department for Work and Pensions, 2014b). The reported success rate for the Work Choice programme is better but only 1% receive this form of support (Department for Work and Pensions, 2014c). There was a 16% decline in the numbers of disabled people receiving support from the Access to Work programme between 2009/10 and 2012/13, and although there was a slight increase during 2013/14, the number is projected to fall by a further 31% during 2014/15 (House of Commons Library, 2014: 5).

The proportion of disabled people and their families living in poverty has fallen over the last 10 years, although they are still more likely to be living in poverty than non-disabled households. This improvement is largely because of reductions in the numbers of pensioner households living in poverty (McInnes et al., 2014: 32-33). Large numbers of disabled people have experienced, or will experience, a reduction in their household income as a result of welfare reform. Demos calculated 3.7 million disabled people will experience some reduction of income, and, over the period to 2017 they would lose £28 billion as a group (Wood, 2013). For many, this will be compounded by the reductions in funding for social care and the increase in VAT, which has a disproportionate impact on poorer households.

There is mounting evidence of substantial negative impact on disabled people's quality of life. Research carried out by Ipsos Mori on behalf of the National Housing Federation found that amongst households affected by the bedroom tax (61% of whom include someone with a disability or long-term illness), 9 out of 10 are concerned about meeting their living costs, 32% have cut back on meals and 26% on heating (National Housing Federation, 2014).

Housing and transport

Disabled people are experiencing a reduction in housing opportunities. In 2001, 33% of households containing a disabled person were social housing tenants but by 2011 this had fallen to 13% (Department for Communities and Local Government, 2013: 72). The numbers of people accepted as homeless by local authorities reduced considerably between 2003 and 2010 but has increased since then, and this pattern also applies to people accepted as homeless because of old age, physical disability, or mental illness (Department for Communities and Local Government, 2014).

In 2011, 15% of households that included someone with a long term limiting illness or disability felt their current home was not suitable for their needs (Department for Communities and Local Government, 2013: 70). One in five people with learning disabilities are living in accommodation which 'needs improvement', 4 in 10 live with their families and of these 7 out of 10 want to change their housing situation (Mencap, 2012).

Funding for home adaptations rose each year from 1997-98 until 2011-12 but has since levelled off (House of Commons Library, 2013), although it has been estimated that the need for adaptations is more than ten times higher than the total amount of disabled facilities grant allocated (Department for Communities and Local Government, 2011: para 2.2).

Research on older people's housing opportunities concluded 'there is very limited choice for older person households moving home to accommodate their support needs (in terms of tenure, location, size, affordability and type of care/support)' (Pannell, et al., 2012: 7). Around 5% of older people live in specialist housing with support and there is evidence of a reduction in on-site support which has 'affected the quality of life for some residents, especially those aged 85+ and/or with high support needs' (Pannell and Blood, 2012: 1).

The Good Practice guide on Planning and Access for Disabled People has been cancelled following the publication of the National Planning Policy Framework; and Design and Access statements have been scrapped for the majority of planning applications. A survey of district councils in England, found 'most new-build homes are still not designed to meet the needs of disabled people, nor to be readily adaptable' (Astral Advisory, 2013: 1).

In terms of transport, there has been no improvement in the proportion of disabled people experiencing difficulties, which remains at about 1 in 4 (Department for Work and Pensions, 2014a: 24). Forty-two percent of disabled people claiming Job Seekers' Allowance and 36% of those in the Employment and Support Allowance Work-related Activity Group cite difficulties with transport as a barrier to employment (Department for Work and Pensions, 2013b:13). Since 2010 there have been significant reductions in expenditure on important programmes intended to increase transport opportunities.

Conclusion

For the first time in the history of modern social policy things are getting worse for disabled people. Independent living opportunities amongst the current generations of disabled people are diminishing, and will only worsen for future generations unless urgent action is taken to reverse current trends. Such action would need to address not only the support that many disabled people need in their daily lives but also their access to housing, transport, education and employment opportunities. Without such action, our society will never achieve the goal, set out in *Improving the Life Chances of Disabled People*, that disabled people in Britain 'will be respected and included as equal members of society'.

Note

This is a summary of evidence contained in Morris, J. (2014) Independent Living Strategy: A review of Progress, http://www.disabilityrightsuk.org/sites/default/files/pdf/IndependentLivingStrategy-A%20review%20of%20progress.pdf

References

Age UK (2015) 'Age UK's 'score card' – the devastating truth of the social care crisis', *Age UK Press Release,* 21st January. Accessed on 21/1/2015 at http://www.ageuk.org.uk/latest-press/social-care-funding-falls-by-billion/

Angel, C. (2012) *Care is not a commodity: UKHCA Commissioning Survey 2012*, United Kingdom Homecare Association, http://www.ukhca.co.uk/downloads.aspx?ID=356 [Accessed 10.12.14]

Astral Advisory, 2013. *Disabled Facilities Grants in England.* http://districtcouncils.info/files/2013/07/DFG-Report-Final-pdf.pdf [Accessed 12.12.14]

Department for Communities and Local Government, 2011. *Disabled Facilities Grant allocation methodology and means test,* DCLG. https://www.gov.uk/government/uploads/system/uploads/attachment_data/file/6335/1850571.pdf

Department for Communities and Local Government, 2013. *English Housing Survey: Households 2011-12.* https://www.gov.uk/government/uploads/system/uploads/attachment_data/file/212496/EHS_HOUSEHOLDS_REPORT_2011-12.pdf [Accessed 12.12.14]

Department for Communities and Local Government, 2014, Live Tables on Homelessness https://www.gov.uk/government/statistical-data-sets/live-tables-on-homelessness – Table 773: Statutory homelessness. Households accepted as owed a main homeless duty by local authorities, by priority need category, England. [Accessed 12.12.14]

Department for Work and Pensions (2013a). *Fulfilling Potential: Making it happen*, https://www.gov.uk/government/uploads/system/uploads/attachment_data/file/320745/making-it-happen.pdf [Accessed 10.12.14]

Department for Work and Pensions, 2013b. *A survey of working age benefit claimants,* DWP. https://www.gov.uk/government/uploads/system/uploads/attachment_data/file/224543/ihr_16_v2.pdf [Accessed 12.12.14]

Department for Work and Pensions (2014a). *Fulfilling Potential – Outcomes and Indicators Framework Progress Report,* https://www.gov.uk/government/uploads/system/uploads/attachment_data/file/348867/Fulfilling_Potential_Outcomes_and_Indicators_Framework_Progress_Report_2014.pdf [Accessed 10.12.14]

Department for Work and Pensions (2014b) *Work Programme statistical summary,* https://www.gov.uk/government/publications/work-programme-statistical-summary-march-2014 [Accessed 10.12.14]

Department for Work and Pensions (2014c) *Work Choice: Official Statistics.* https://www.gov.uk/government/uploads/system/uploads/attachment_data/file/309798/work-choice-statistics-may-2014.pdf [Accessed 10.12.14]

Disability Rights UK (2013). 'Court upholds policy limiting home care spending', http://www.disabilityrightsuk.org/news/2013/august/court-upholds-policy-limiting-home-care-spending [Accessed 10.12.14]

Duffy, S. (2014) *Counting the Cuts*, Centre for Welfare Reform, http://www.centreforwelfarereform.org/library/by-date/counting-the-cuts.html

HM Government (2008) *Independent Living Strategy,* http://webarchive.nationalarchives.gov.uk/20130703133823/http://odi.dwp.gov.uk/docs/wor/ind/ilr-executive-report.pdf [Accessed, 10.12.14]

House of Commons Library, 2013. *Disabled Facilities Grants (England) Standard Note SN/SP/3011,* House of Commons Library. http://www.parliament.uk/business/publications/research/briefing-papers/SN03011/disabled-facilities-grants-dfgs [Accessed 12.12.14]

House of Commons Library (2014) *Access to Work*, Standard Note SN/EP/06666. http://www.parliament.uk/business/publications/research/briefing-papers/SN06666/access-to-work [Accessed 10.12.14]

Ismail, S, Thorlby, R. and Holder, H. (2014) *Focus on: Social care for older people*. Nuffield Foundation, http://www.nuffieldtrust.org.uk/publications/focus-social-care-older-people [Accessed 10.12.14]

McInnes, T, Aldridge, H, Bushe, S, Tinson, A and Born. T.B. (2014) *Monitoring Poverty and Social Exclusion*, http://npi.org.uk/files/8214/1658/1400/Monitoring_Poverty_and_Social_Exclusion_2014.pdf [Accessed 23.1.15]

Mencap, 2012. *Housing for people with a learning disability*, Mencap

National Housing Federation (2014) *One Year On: The impact of welfare reforms on housing association tenants.* http://www.housing.org.uk/publications/browse/one-year-on-the-impact-of-welfare-reforms-on-housing-association-tenants-1/ [Accessed 10.12.14]

Needham, C. and Glasby, J. (2014) 'Taking stock of personalisation' in C. Needham and J. Glasby (eds) *Debates in Personalisation*, Bristol: Policy Press, 11-24.

Office for Disability Issues, 2014. https://www.gov.uk/government/uploads/system/uploads/attachment_data/file/348867/Fulfilling_Potential_Outcomes_and_Indicators_Framework_Progress_Report_2014.pdf

Pannell, J. and Blood, I. 2012. *Supported Housing for Older People in the UK: an evidence review*, Joseph Rowntree Foundation. http://www.jrf.org.uk/publications/supported-housing-older-people-evidence-review

Pannell, J, Aldridge, H. and Kenway, P. 2012. *Market Assessment of Housing Options for Older People*, New Policy Institute. http://npi.org.uk/files/5213/7485/1289/Market_Assessment_of_Housing_Options_for_Older_People.pdf [Accessed 23.1.15]

Prime Minister's Strategy Unit (2005) *Improving the Life Chances of Disabled People*, http://webarchive.nationalarchives.gov.uk/+/http:/www.cabinetoffice.gov.uk/media/cabinetoffice/strategy/assets/disability.pdf [Accessed 10.12.14]

Wood, C. (2013) 'Destination Unknown – April 2013' http://www.demos.co.uk/blog/destinationunknownapril2013 [Accessed 10.12.14]

How not to do big reorganisations in social policy: the NHS

Ian Greener, Durham University
ian.greener@durham.ac.uk
@ijgreener

'Tony Blair once explained his priority in three words: education, education, education. I can do it in three letters. N – H – S. 'David Cameron, Conservative Party Conference, 2006

'We will stop the top-down reorganisations of the NHS that have got in the way of patient care' – The Coalition: Our programme for government, May 2010

'Andrew Lansley (Greedy), Andrew Lansley (Tosser), The NHS is not for sale you grey-haired manky codger' – MC Nxtgen. March 2011

'We're f*cked' – David Cameron's reported response to the scale of criticism of the NHS reorganisation – February 2012

Introduction

Welfare reorganisations are expensive, and big reorganisations carry substantial risks. It is therefore imperative that we get them right – and rather sobering how infrequently healthcare reorganisations of any type have much success at all. The Coalition Government created a storm of protest against their NHS reorganisation, and Labour appear to be gearing up to make healthcare a big election issue in 2015. The Coalition Government's NHS reorganisation is confusing in that it is clearly a continuation and extension of Labour's approach in the previous five years especially, but at the same time led to them being accused of privatising and dismantling the NHS in ways their predecessors were not. This led to a situation where the former Labour Secretary of State, Alan Milburn, criticised the final version of the proposals as not being radical enough because of their dilution of competitive market structures, whereas Conservative supporters criticised the reorganisation for being too radical and so risking them losing the next election. What follows here is not a chronological account – Nicholas Timmins' excellent 'Never Again' can be downloaded from the King's Fund website for that (Timmins, 2012). This short piece attempts to draw lessons for big reorganisation from its events.

Lesson 1 – If you're going to big welfare reorganisation, get a mandate for it

During the 2010 election campaign, the NHS wasn't much discussed – there appeared to be a consensus that large-scale reorganisation was not on the table, and Labour found themselves outflanked by Conservative commitments to 'ring-fence' NHS spending. Upon election, the Coalition Government made a promise to end 'top-down' reorganisation, suggesting a period of relative calm.

Six weeks later, the government released its White Paper 'Equity and Excellence' (Secretary of State for Health 2010). Very few people were consulted about its contents. Little wonder that, once both the public and NHS staff became aware of what was going on, the former signed a petition in their thousands to demand a debate in Parliament on the proposals (ironically, aided by a measure introduced by the Coalition Government to allow greater public involvement in the Parliamentary process) and the latter began, especially through the Royal College of GPs, to campaign vigorously and actively against the proposals. Both the public and those working in the NHS felt that the government had no mandate for its reorganisation – with some justification.

Lesson 2 – If you're going to reorganise welfare services, give a reason why you are doing it

The new government's NHS reorganisation sought to increase the pace of marketization (and indeed privatisation). However, it seemed to have forgotten to explain what problem this was the solution to.

By early 2010, levels of reported public satisfaction with the NHS recorded in the British Social Attitudes Survey were at an all-time high. Increased funding was beginning to show results, with the UK catching up on success rates in a range of clinical indicators where it had been behind its peers. There was still a long way to go (the events at Stafford Hospital certainly showed that), but things seemed to be going in the right direction. In their rush to publish their plan for healthcare, the government forgot to explain to anyone what their reorganisation was for.

This led to two big problems. First, it left the government having to come up with a reason why the NHS needed such major change. There were two broad strategies. First, the government published data showing the NHS lagging behind comparative nations in key clinical indicators. This provoked a furious response from clinicians, who challenged the government's data, often via blogs or other web commentaries. These online responses showed that, in a connected era, the government's authority was open to vociferous, rapid and highly credible challenge. The government's second strategy was to try and show the reorganisation was necessary because of the future challenges facing healthcare. The problem was that their reorganisation did little to address arguably the most significant challenges facing the NHS – the boundary between health and social care, or its big public health challenges. So again, these claims were quickly challenged by highly-mobilised and informed on-line communities.

The second problem was that the lack of a credible reason for reorganisation left space for alternative theories to flourish. Claims about stealth privatisation and vested interests began to appear. Now, of course, it may be the case that these theories were right – that the reorganization was largely about privatising healthcare and generating profit for multinational healthcare organisations – but the government's lack of ability to provide an alternative narrative meant that the case for reorganisation was never made.

Lesson 3 – If you are to consult people about your welfare plans, be prepared to admit you got it wrong

The legislation outlining the NHS reorganisation was subject to a 'pause' because of the mounting criticisms against it. Whereas the political process had by then actually largely approved the Bill, the national mood had moved very much against it. In announcing their 'pause', then, the government appeared to be prepared to stop and listen.

However, what quickly became apparent was that the pause did not include the option to stop the reorganisation in its tracks and get the government to think again – it was about amending the Bill only. This was partly due to the reorganization having a timetable that meant it had already moved ahead of the legislative process (leading to accusations of it being unconstitutional as well as undemocratic), and partly due to the government not wanting to back down from their plans, even when they were faced by criticism from within their own ranks of the reorganisation potentially wrecking their chances at the next election. This made the pause appear to be less about listening and more about working out the bare minimum the government needed to change to force through its plans. This was to store up problems in implementation later.

Lesson 4 – Making policy is not the same thing as making things happen

What the aftermath of the two year debate over the Health and Social Care Bill makes clear is that it is one thing to make policy (or publish a White Paper), and another to implement it. This is the case in two key senses here. First, the transition from White Paper to Health and Social Care bill was fraught, chiefly for the reasons outlined above – the proposals were a surprise to the public and those working in health services, who were not consulted and so had no ownership or stake in agreeing with them. That the government could give no coherent reason for their reorganisation led to space for accusations about vested interests to be spread. Then the 'pause' tried to address concerns by making its structures more complicated and to the Bill being heavily amended. Lansley's original vision was so extensively modified during the process through which it was turned into law that it was almost unrecognisable by the end.

But these problems fade into the background compared to the problems that are involved in actually making the reorganisation happen. We don't know what the effects of the coalition's reorganisation are yet – it is too early to judge. But we do know that the funding crises of the past appear to be resurfacing (despite the 2010 claims that budgets would be 'ring-fenced') and as health leaders find themselves closing down organisations (such as PCTs and SHAs) only to end up often re-employing many of the same staff in similar roles in new organisational structures, while at the same time trying to get those new organisations to work.

Lesson 5 – Another reorganisation is probably not the answer

Health services, in common with other welfare services, are about relationships, not ideal types such as markets (or hierarchies or networks), and relationships are about people. It is perfectly possible to provide excellent healthcare in the most dreadful of circumstances, or to provide dreadful care even if surrounded by the best possible facilities. Looking for organisational solutions to complex service problems is probably to look in the wrong place. It is certainly the case that organising things well can help deliver good care, but it can't do the whole job – that requires hard work, professionalism, and commitment. What is remarkable is not only that policymakers appear to continue to overlook this basic fact, but that they continue to alienate and distract those who deliver welfare services by continually reorganising their workplaces, disrupting their lives and, quite often, making their jobs more difficult. We need to support those who deliver care in doing a better job, not reorganise them every few years and take their attention away from those they are doing their best to serve.

Conclusion

We don't know how much the NHS reorganisation of 2010-2012 cost. If we include not only its direct costs, but also the redundancy payments, the costs of setting up new organizations and the extra time and effort GPs have had to put in as a result of their bigger role in commissioning, often on top of their 'old' jobs, then the sum comes to billions and billions. A key question is whether any benefits at all have accrued, never mind ones sufficient to actually cover the costs of the reorganization. We need policymakers to face a more substantial burden of proof before they go ahead with large scale welfare reorganisations, as well as for them to learn that reorganizing, in itself, is seldom the answer. Welfare services are about people – about helping those who need them, and about supporting those who provide them. The role of government is surely to try and provide the resources and structures to these ends, not to continually disrupt them through unnecessary and expensive change.

References

Secretary of State for Health (2010) *Equity and excellence: liberating the NHS*. London: The Stationery Office Limited.

Timmins, N. (2012) *Never again?* London: King's Fund and the Institute for Government

Domestic violence

Rachel Robbins, Manchester Metropolitan University
r.robbins@mmu.ac.uk
@DorisDayRobbins

Introduction

There are long-rehearsed arguments about estimating the scale of domestic violence linked to its reporting and recording. Despite the problems associated with estimating the scale of the issue, all the evidence points to domestic violence as being widespread, with findings broadly consistent across studies. In the UK, for example:

- It is generally recognised that over 90% of domestic violence is experienced by women (Welsh, 2005)
- On average two women are killed each week in England and Wales by a partner or former partner, this constitutes nearly 40% of all female murder victims (Home Office, 2006)
- In 2012, 1.2 million women suffered domestic abuse (Home Office, 2013)
- Fewer than one in four people who suffer abuse at the hands of the partner report it to the police (Home Office, 2013)

However, domestic violence was not one of Beveridge's five giant evils and has therefore struggled to find an easy place in relation to welfare provision for its victims and survivors. This oversight, it could be argued, is because the welfare state was built on gender norms and assumptions that did not question the presence of violence in family life or see it as a cause for public concern. However, since the feminist refuge movement of the 1970s there has been a creeping recognition of the need to protect (predominantly, but not exclusively) women and children from abuse and violence in the home. Most noticeably, domestic violence has been acknowledged as a child protection issue with the new category of harm 'impairment from seeing or hearing the ill-treatment of another' being introduced in the Children and Adoption Act of 2002. This is not unproblematic, not least because in practice it places an emphasis on mothering behaviour rather than the abusive partner and also does not address violence where children are not present. However, it is an example of the mainstreaming of the issue. More recently Teresa May in 2010 addressed the National Women's Aid (May, 2010: online) conference and declared that:

'Violence against women is not an aside for me; it is not an afterthought or a secondary consideration. It was a priority for me in opposition and it is a priority for me now I am in government'.

So, it could be argued that concern for survivors and victims of domestic violence has moved from the fringes of feminist action to state interest. However, policy, provision and practice remain piecemeal and fragmented across a range of organisations from across the economy.

Progress in domestic violence

Whilst in opposition Theresa May launched a Conservative Party strategy document 'Ending Violence against Women' (2008), which stressed that domestic violence was a priority for the Conservative Party, with an emphasis on tackling inequality, prevention and multi-agency working. However, the financial crisis and 'austerity' policies have produced a shift in tone that highlights the lack of resources. So that in the Home Secretary's (May, 2010: online) address to Women's Aid, there was an emphasis on efficiency, reducing the deficit and not 'throwing money at a problem'.

This is not to say that domestic violence has been ignored. The government has introduced a new definition of domestic violence that was extended to include 16 and 17 year olds and placed greater emphasis on the patterns of coercive and controlling behaviour that characterise abusive relationships. Furthermore, in August 2014 the Home Office announced plans for writing a new domestic abuse offence into law. Within the domestic violence sector these moves were generally welcomed, but underline a criminal justice approach to domestic violence rather than acknowledging it as a wider welfare and social justice issue. In particular, these moves need to be seen alongside the impacts of the coalitions' spending review and continued cuts in welfare spending.

Cuts to domestic violence services

Given its complicated history, the terrain of domestic violence services remains difficult to navigate. Domestic Violence services are provided by a range of statutory and voluntary organisations. Statutory provision centres on child protection, safe-guarding, criminal justice, probation and some Independent Domestic Violence Advocate (IDVA) services. The voluntary sector provides a wide range of services from a national network of specialist refuges to locally provided self-help groups and confidential telephone helplines. Much of the expertise around prevention, support, crisis management and longer-term establishment of rights and resources for victims resides in the voluntary sector and much of it is provided locally from community-based groups.

Despite May's (2010) assertion that local authorities must not see this sector as an 'easy cut' when making difficult decisions, Towers and Walby (2012) found that there was a dramatic reduction in local services with a 31% cut to the funding for domestic and sexual abuse sector from local authorities in 2011 – 2012. Commissioning practices meant that the impact was greater on smaller organisations, with smaller providers of specialist services being bid out of the commissioning market by larger, general housing associations. There has also been a significant reduction in the numbers of IDVAs, with recent reports suggesting a 30% shortfall in the service as a result of local authority cuts (Community Care, 2012).

In terms of practice, the shift from feminist theorising about power and control has been replaced by a more managerial approach (Robbins et al., 2014). Central to this new approach is the concept of managing and reducing risk. This move, alongside the reduction in finances has led to the concentration of activity on those cases designated as high risk. Despite evidence that domestic violence is a common experience, services are limited to the few. This is unfortunate in its own right. However, research by Walby (2009) suggests that the cost of domestic violence to the public purse decreases with the amount invested in public services as injury and harm reduce, economic input can increase.

Cuts to related welfare services

However, the complex nature of domestic violence means that it is not just cuts to the sector itself that are problematic for provision. For example, the restrictions on legal aid, imposed by the Legal Aid, Sentencing and Punishment of Offenders Act (2012) have tightened regulations and access to legal aid, with strict evidential eligibility requirements. With the current emphasis on criminal justice remedies, this has serious implications for women who would require support to provide the evidence. There has also been an £819 million reduction in budgets and services from children's services impacting on the prevention and referral work in Youth Services, Early Years and Children's Centres (Higgs, 2011). The NSPCC has since disbanded many of its local intervention projects (Gadd, 2012).

The endemic levels of domestic violence prompt the conclusion that 'domestic violence is no respecter of class, creed or colour,' (Hague et al., 2003: 9) and there is an emphasis in the literature on the universal nature of domestic violence. Some commentators, however, contest this view, pointing to evidence that domestic violence is suffered disproportionately by certain groups, and that some women are particularly vulnerable to domestic violence, or less able to escape it, because of restricted access to resources and assistance. Increased poverty, therefore, could lead to worse outcomes for women living with violence. Increased taxation and benefit reductions associated with 'austerity' are predicted to impact more harshly on women (Women's Budget Group, 2010). This, alongside persistent gender inequality in income, will lead to more impoverished families. Therefore, it could be argued that if current trends persist, more abused women and their children will be forced to stay with their abusers as benefits, subsidised childcare and employment opportunities diminish (Gadd, 2012).

Conclusions and alternatives

This review has highlighted particular issues for those in need of welfare and support owing to the violence they are experiencing or have experienced in their homes within the current climate of 'austerity' and financial constraint. Key concerns include:

- Domestic violence, whilst a stated government priority, has not received additional funding and remains vulnerable to welfare cuts. However, government has made steps in securing domestic abuse as a criminal justice issue. If the law is going to be central to state approaches to domestic violence, attention needs to be paid to recent cuts and constraints on access to legal aid.

- Provision of welfare services within the domestic violence sector has relied heavily on voluntary sector expertise built up over a number of years by activists and professionals. However, there has been a significant shift in the balance of power between statutory and activist, front-line services, with commissioning practices placing an emphasis on outcomes, individualist approaches and unit costs. This has had severe ramifications for locally organised services and the national network of provision by the voluntary sector.

- Despite endemic levels of violence the cuts have forced a hierarchy of risk within statutory services, with resources being focussed on 'high risk' cases meaning that 'low-level' bullying and isolation are unlikely to meet thresholds for services. Not only will this impact on the quality of life for families living with violence, it means that expertise in prevention and support is being lost to crisis management and in the long term will become more costly.

- All of the above is exacerbated by the unequal burden of welfare cuts on women who will have less opportunity to disclose their circumstances to welfare professionals and fewer resources to secure living arrangements.

However, there are other ways of constructing domestic violence. Currently, the key area for progress by the government has been in securing domestic abuse within a legal framework. Whilst this is helpful, the criminal justice system is not necessarily the only or the best way to confront the issues that abusive relationships have for wider society. Given the scale of the problem and the small number of convictions, it could be argued that it would be better to divert funds back into locally based voluntary sector activity, where domestic violence is seen primarily as a social justice and welfare issue and where there is expertise and experience of supporting women and families to make a range of choices to secure their futures.

References

Community Care (2012) '30% shortfall in domestic violence advisers as council cuts bite' *Community Care,* 20 November 2012 (www.community care.co.uk)

Conservative Party (2008) *Ending violence against women: Conservative Strategy Paper* https://www.conservatives.com/~/media/Files/Downloadable%20Files/ending-violence-against-women.ashx?dl=true [accessed 27 December 2014].

Gadd, D. (2012) 'Domestic abuse prevention after Raoul Moat' *Critical Social Policy,* 32, 4, 495 – 516.

Hague, G., Mullender, A. and Aris, R. (2003) *'Is anyone listening?' Accountability and women survivors of domestic violence,* London: Routledge.

Higgs, L. (2011) 'Exclusive survey: youth services and children's centres worst hit as cuts average 13 per cent in one year', *Children and Young People Now*, 25 January http://www.cypnow.co.uk/cyp/news/1044853/exclusive-survey-youth-services-childrens-centres-worst-hit-cuts-average-cent [accessed 27 December 2014].
Home Office (2006) *Crime in England and Wales 2005/6 Home Office Statistical Bulletin*, London: Home Office.
Home Office (2013) *Policy: ending violence against women and girls in the UK* published 26 March 2013 https://www.gov.uk/government/policies/ending-violence-against-women-and-girls-in-the-uk [accessed 27 December 2014].
May, T. (2010) 'Address to the 36th Annual Women's Aid National Conference 2010', 16 July http://www.womensaid.org.uk/page.asp section=0001000100150008000400002 andsectionTitle=Theresa+May%27s+Speech [accessed 27 December 2014].
Robbins, R., McLaughlin, H., Banks, C., Bellamy, C. and Thackray, D. (2014) 'Domestic violence and multiagency risk assessment conferences (MARACs): a scoping review', *The Journal of Adult Protection*, 16, 6, 389-98.
Towers, J. and Walby, S. (2012) *Measuring the impact in cuts in public expenditure on the provision of services to prevent violence against women and girls*, Report for Northern Rock Foundation and Trust for London.
Walby, S. (2009) *The cost of domestic violence: update 2009*, Cardiff: CAADA.
Welsh, K. (2005) 'The Disassociation between Domestic Violence Service provision and multi-agency initiatives on domestic violence', *International Review of Victimology*, 12, 3, 213-34.
Women's Budget Group (WBG) (2010) *The impact on women of the Coalition Spending Review 2010*, http://wbg.org.uk/RRB_Reports_4_1653541019.pdf [accessed 27 December 2014].

The environment

Tony Fitzpatrick, Nottingham University
tony.fitzpatrick@nottingham.ac.uk

Introduction

In May 2010 David Cameron announced that he wanted the Coalition government to be the 'greenest government ever'. As he and Nick Clegg declared:

> '... we need to protect the environment for future generations, make our economy more environmentally sustainable, and improve our quality of life and well-being' (Cabinet Office, 2010: 17).

By the end of 2013 Cameron was reported as telling aides to 'get rid of all the green crap' in order to reduce energy bills (Daily Mail, 2013).

How did we get from there to here? Was the government ever committed to real change? What have its principal successes and failures been? Are we now closer to an alignment of social policies and environmental policies than we were 5 years ago?

The key to answering such questions lies in the extent to which policy has been preventative, strategic and forward-looking rather than reactive and makeshift. And that distinction turns on how the government perceives the relationship between the economy and nature.

Economy, society and nature

There are three possibilities:

1. The inherent value of the natural environment and the needs of future generations are regarded as essential to social well-being.
2. Ecological issues are seen primarily as a business opportunity.
3. Ecological issues are low priority ('we'll spend money on nature when we can afford to').

The more policies are framed by (2) or (3) the more likely decisions will resemble post hoc, 'crisis management' interventions. Of course, governments often invoke (1), but do their actions follow suit? George Osborne (2009) once said:

> The global market for green goods and technologies is worth trillions of dollars a year, but with less than a 5% share of that market Britain is failing to take advantage.... I want a Conservative Treasury to lead the development of the low carbon economy.

This and subsequent developments correspond more closely to (2).

Indeed, in 2011-12 (the most recent available statistics) the green economy was employing a million people, with low carbon goods and services worth £128bn, or 8% of GDP – representing one third of Britain's economic growth at that time (Carrington, 2014a). The sector was growing at 4.8% per annum (above the global average) and Britain ranked sixth in the world, in a sector worth £3.4 trillion worldwide (Carrington, 2014a).

Take wind power. The industry attracted £2.6bn of investment in 2013-14, of which £1.1bn stayed in the UK, and full-time jobs in the wind industry rose 8% in the 12 months to June 2014 (Carrington, 2014b). Ironically, these are genuine successes the Coalition has not been interested in publicising. One possible reason is that onshore wind turbines attract the ire of UKIP. With their right-flank vulnerable the Conservatives have felt the need to tack into that particular political storm. With local communities often excluded from the early stages of decision-making processes, failures in planning and consultation may have also stimulated opposition to wind farms.

So, Britain maintains its position close to the top of various environmental league tables. This is partly because of historical legacies, i.e. the shift from coal to gas and from manufacturing to services. But the government deserves some credit. It vowed to pursue the Labour government's targets for cutting carbon emissions by a third by 2020. More recently, progress has been made on 'Electricity Market Reform' and low-carbon power generation. And the deployment of offshore wind has been increased, as necessitated by the EU Renewable Energy Directive. It also donated almost £1bn to the Green Climate Fund to help developing countries adapt to global warming (Martin, 2014).

Missed opportunities

But the last five years have largely been ones of missed opportunities, as the country has shifted more towards (3).

- The government has stressed a market-based approach, yet not provided the long-term security that investors in renewables require.
- Labour's plans for more eco-towns were severely scaled back.
- Basing recycling schemes entirely upon incentives (replacing the planned 'pay as you throw' approach) has not been shown to work with the effectiveness and comprehensiveness that is needed.
- Labour's boiler scrappage scheme was discontinued; the Energy Company Obligation has a free boiler scheme but only for those who meet strict eligibility criteria.
- Air quality has been declining since 2010 and the UK faces action from the EU if improvements are not made.
- The progress in domestic solar power which was being made under Labour has halted.
- The Green Deal allows people to borrow money from a private provider to improve boilers and insulation. There has, however, been very little take-up and only the most ideological could regard it as a success.

What accounts for this? The Tories have always been resistant to environmentalism. Cameron's pre-2010 'hug a huskie' approach was an implicit acknowledgement of this as the Tories tried to detoxify and reposition themselves as compassionate conservatives. But austerity and an attempt to shrink the state quickly pushed that emphasis to one side. With the Liberal Democrats trumpeting their social conscience and green credentials, many conservatives have had even more of an excuse to regard the environment as liberal-leftie obsession that a business-minded government should not indulge. The following developments illustrate this.

The UK currently risks reasserting its addiction to fossil fuels (Bast et al., 2014: 60). Investment in them soared in 2014-15 to £15.2bn; while investment in low-carbon energy fell to £10bn (Carrington, 2014c). This is despite increasing recognition of the fact that a large proportion of remaining fossil fuels have to be left in the ground if global warming is to be limited to 2°C. A recent report suggested that 82% of remaining coal deposits, 49% of available gas and 33% of oil reserves should not be extracted and used (Bast et al., 2014; McGlade and Ekins, 2015).

The hostility to onshore wind power contrasts with the enthusiasm for hydraulic fracturing ('fracking'). The environmentalist objection is well known – that fracking pollutes water tables, releases methane, causes earth tremors and overloads social and natural infrastructures. Yet even the business case is lacking – in 2015 only 11 exploratory wells for shale gas are to be drilled (Vaughan, 2015) – unless you are persuaded by those corporations whose economic self-interests are at stake. The deposits to be released beneath villages, shires and towns (including those in the 'derelict North') may yet turn out to contain electoral poison for the Conservatives. Ironically, the fashion for fracking is a subtle, if unintended, acknowledgement that we are now in the latter stages of the fossil fuel era. A proper 'transition strategy' to clean energy is needed. Yet fracking has not been sold on that basis, not by a government salivating for revenue as the economy continues to stall.

Similarly, since nuclear power counts as low carbon energy support for it has revived. While some environmentalists welcome this commitment, many others worry about waste disposal and the eventual costs of decommissioning plants.

Like so many of its predecessors, the government also regards roads and airports as crucial for British competitiveness. Without a change of direction, this is what will dominate transport spending until 2020. Yet the Department for Transport (2014: 8) concluded that local sustainable transport schemes return £5 for every £1 spent.

Funding for flood protection was immediately slashed by a quarter in 2010 (Carrington, 2014d; see Unison, 2015). This left the government looking both heartless and inept when flooding became a political issue in 2012-13. But although some of the cuts were restored, over the last 5 years average yearly spending on flooding has been 10% lower than during the last Labour spending review period (Friends of the Earth, 2014). Hundreds of projects have been on hold and three-quarters of defences have not been adequately maintained. In 2014 it was announced that £2.3bn in total would be available until 2020 to improve defences, though more than 20% of this is expected to come from local councils, businesses and individuals (Carrington, 2014d). Annual flood damage already costs about £1.1bn and could rise to as much as £27bn by 2080; and even maintaining existing levels of flood defence requires spending to increase to over £1bn per year by 2035 (Bennett and Hartwell-Naguib, 2014; cf Committee on Climate Change, 2014: 37). (However, a new flood insurance scheme for the 350,000 most at risk properties is due to start in the summer of 2015.)

Similarly, the government has wanted a revived housing market to drive economic growth. But the 100,000 new homes announced in 2014 will be exempt from energy efficiency standards – precisely the wrong direction in which to move.

There is, then, little evidence of convergence between the social policy and environmental policies agendas, though it is only through a synthesis of the two that preventative strategies can be fully developed (Fitzpatrick, 2014). Much more government action needs to occur with respect to health and healthcare, housing retrofit, energy efficiencies (especially in relation to fuel poverty), public transport and air pollution. For instance, fuel and food poverties are ecological problems, not just social ones. From 2008-14 energy costs rose by 60% (Adams et al., 2014: 136) and,

> 'All food groups have risen in price since 2007...with rises ranging from 22% to 57%' (DEFRA, 2014: 21).

The poorest fifth spend 8% of their budgets on energy and 20% on food, double what the richest fifth spend (Adams and Levell, 2014: 18). Though according to Jenkins (2014), the poorest tenth spend *five times* as much of their budget on energy compared to the richest tenth.

Conclusion

For conservatives, 'environmental issues' continues to imply countryside, conservation and green belts. Abstract issues of 'climate change' find it harder to gain a hearing, especially in an age of austerity economics. The Liberal Democrats have been a restraining influence on some of the climate change deniers who still cluster within elements of the Conservative Party. But, overall, the record of the 2010-15 administration is not one we are likely to revisit with any sense of pride.

References

Adams, A. and Levell, P. (2014) *Measuring poverty when inflation varies across households*, York: Joseph Rowntree Foundation.

Adams, A., Hood, A. and Levell, P. (2014) 'The squeeze on Incomes', in C. Emmerson, P. Johnson and H. Miller (eds) *The IFS Green Budget: February 2014*, Report no. 91, London: Institute for Fiscal Studies.

Bast, E., Makhijani, S., Pickard, S. and Whitley, S. (2014) *The fossil fuel bailout: G20 Subsidies for oil, gas and coal exploration*, London: ODI.

Bennett, B. and Hartwell-Naguib, S. (2014) *Flood defence spending in England*, London: House of Commons Library.

Cabinet Office (2010) *The Coalition: our programme for Government*, London: Cabinet Office.

Carrington, D. (2014a) 'George Osborne: burying the good news of the green economy', *Guardian*, 29th September. http://www.theguardian.com/environment/damian-carrington-blog/2014/sep/29/george-osborne-burying-the-good-news-of-the-green-economy [accessed December 29th 2014].

Carrington, D. (2014b) 'Onshore windfarm opposition risks UK Jobs, says Davey', *Guardian*, 12th November.

Carrington, D. (2014c) 'George Osborne oversees biggest fossil fuel boom since North Sea Oil discovery', *Guardian*, 6th December.

Carrington, D. (2014d) 'The £2.3bn for Flood Defences in England is good news but still not enough', *Guardian*, 2nd December. http://www.theguardian.com/environment/damian-carrington-blog/2014/dec/02/flood-defences-england-not-enough [accessed 29th December 2014].

Committee on Climate Change (2014) *Managing climate risks to well-being and the economy*, London: Committee on Climate Change.

Daily Mail (2013) 'Cut the green crap! Cameron reveals his private view of energy taxation and orders ministers to dump the eco-charges adding £110-a-year to bills', *Daily Mail*, 21st November.

DEFRA (2014) *Food Statistics Pocketbook 2014*, London: DEFRA.

Department for Transport (2014) *Value for money assessment for the Local Sustainable Transport Fund*, London: Department for Transport.

Fitzpatrick, T. (2014) *Climate change and poverty*, Bristol: Policy Press.

Friends of the Earth (2014) *government spending on flooding*, press release, London: Friends of the Earth.

Jenkins, C. (2014) 'What is Driving Energy Price Rises?', in C. Emmerson, P. Johnson and H. Miller (eds) *The IFS Green Budget: February 2014*, Report no. 91, London: Institute for Fiscal Studies.

Martin, D. (2014) 'As Britain's economy totters, Huhne hands £1bn in foreign aid to poor countries to help them 'cope with climate change'', *Daily Mail*, 7th December.

McGlade, C. and Ekins, P. (2015) 'The geographical distribution of fossil fuels unused when limiting global warming to 2°C', *Nature*, 517: 187-90.

Osborne, G. (2009) 'The Treasury should lead the fight against climate change', *Independent*, 24th November.

Unison (2015) *Cuts at the Environment Agency*, http://www.unison.org.uk/at-work/water-environment-and-transport/key-issues/cuts-at-the-environment-agency/the-facts/ [accessed 19th January 2015].

Vaughan, A. (2015) 'UK's shale gas revolution falls flat with just 11 new wells planned for 2015', *Guardian*, 19th January.

WELFARE BEYOND THE STATE

Big Society or welfare failure: how does food insecurity reflect future welfare trends?

Lee Gregory and Ricky Joseph, University of Birmingham
l.j.gregory@bham.ac.uk
@AcademicLee

Introduction

The use of food banks has become increasingly prominent during the Coalition governments term in office, prompting a concern that levels of hunger are increasing in the UK. This contribution explores the rise in the use of food banks as well as the underpinning causes of this rise. The latter point enters the political debate which surrounds this explanation before moving on to argue that food bank use is not simply a result of the recession and social security reform, but a symptom of a longer term crisis in welfare provision.

Use of food banks

Stevenson (2014: 5) draws upon Trussell Trust data to show how the number of people using food banks has increased since 2010 (figure 1). Explanations for this increase however are heavily debated in the political sphere. From the normative end of the spectrum, Michael Gove has argued that food bank use demonstrates a family's inability to manage their finances – a sentiment echoed by Edwina Currie who went further, to suggest provision fostered increased demand and dependency. Others have drawn upon investigations into reasons for referral and use of food banks to offer a stronger evidence base. For example, Perry et al. (2014) and Lambie-Mumford et al. (2014), suggest life-shocks (unemployment, bereavement, etc.), problems with benefits (delays and sanctions) and chronic low income lead people to rely on food bank provision.

Additionally the All-Party Parliamentary Inquiry into Hunger (2014) suggests that the cost of living (combined housing, food and fuel costs) has been steadily increasing as a proportion of household expenditure since 2004. Consequently for the bottom income decile their expenditure on these three items has increased from 31% of income to 40% between 2003 and 2012. Recent data on expenditure, *Family Food* (DEFRA, 2014: v), illustrates how 'on average, UK households purchased 6.1% less food in 2013 than in 2007 while spending 20% more. They saved 5.6% on their unit prices by "trading down" to cheaper products of the same type'; however 'Households in income decile 1 (lowest income group) spent 22% more on food in 2013 than in 2007 and purchased 6.7% less. Trading down saved these households 1.0%'. The context in which low income households can afford food is drastically changing. Not only are they less equipped to protect themselves against financial/life-shocks, they have lower incomes resulting from cycles of no-pay/low-pay and wage stagnation, an increased proportion of which needs to be spent on purchasing food.

The evidence base contradicts the normative claims of Currie and Gove, supply is not driving demand. Previously Lord Freud has claimed that no causal link between social security reforms and food bank use exists. The growing evidence illustrates that these reforms are part of a wider picture. It is the combination of insecure/low incomes, an inability to (financially) manage life-shocks and increased living costs alongside social security reforms which are at the root of driving up food bank use, which is symptomatic of increased levels of hunger in the UK.

Figure 1: Use of Food Banks

Period	2010/11	2011/12	2012/13	2013/14
Number of people given 3 Days Emergency food and support by the Trussell Trust	61,500	128,500	347,000	913,000
Year over Year Percentage Increase	N/A	109%	170%	163%

*Data contains rounding error

Source: Stevenson (2014)

Big Society or welfare failure

Isabel Hardman's article in the *Spectator* presents food banks as a sign of a strong moral fabric in Britain. There is some truth here charity ensures that people do not starve. Yet, despite this good work, here is the core of the argument: food banks, despite being an excellent example of non-state provision to meet welfare needs, are symptomatic of failed welfare and economic systems. Consequently it is possible to see that different parts of the political spectrum are highlighting a range of contradictory explanations for the use and expansion of food banks – symbolic of wider differences in explanations of current social problems and potential solutions.

Little mention is now given to the Big Society as we reach the end of the Coalition Governments' term in office, yet its shadow looms large. Seeking to re-imagine the role of the state, Cameron articulated a narrative of the Big Society which saw the state take a step-back in welfare provision to allow other sectors to step in and fill the void. Here the voluntary and community sector, referred to by Cameron as the 'first sector' was to lead the way in providing innovative, local welfare services. Dismantling the welfare state was a key part of this project, for, it was argued, the state monopoly of the provision of services diminished non-state actors, preventing them from fostering self-help at the local level.

Within such a narrative food banks illustrate the Big Society in action. Welfare needs are met by agents outside of the state, communities pulling together so that others can survive in these turbulent economic times. Yet Perry et al. (2014) illustrates how those turning to food banks are doing so because they are constrained by their circumstances. The state does not adequately support them, their incomes are too low or they lack the financial assets to protect them from shocks such as bereavement and unemployment. Households, churning in and out of low pay and no pay alongside increasing levels of in work poverty are indicators of fundamental problems with the current economic system as families lack the financial resources to meet their basic necessities. Welfare provision, which once sought to provide social protection against such hardship, is now a factor contributing to the use of food banks. This is not a symbol of a Big Society resolving social problems. Adequate food consumption is a fundamental and basic need which is going unmet. Food bank provision is a fundamental failure in welfare and economic systems in the UK.

Conclusion

The growing evidence-base, briefly outlined above, indicates that food banks are used as a last resort – when all other strategies for cutting back and social network support have been exhausted. The stigma and shame of having to rely on this provision is so great that families delay as much as possible. Unemployment, low wages, insufficient hours of work, precarious work – these are not under the control of individuals using food banks. Nor can these same individuals predict and protect themselves from bereavement, homelessness, and other unexpected life shocks. Increasingly the social security system which once helped citizens mange these turbulent events in their lives has been replaced by workfare initiatives which seek to drive people back in to the low paid precarious work which caused harm in the first place. Such reforms have recently become highly suspect as 6.6m households are in 'in-work poverty' (McInnes et al., 2014).

Linking briefly with the international literature we see support for this argument. In a comparative text, edited by Graham Riches (1996), the use of food banks in Canada, Australia, New Zealand, the UK and the USA are linked to prolonged unemployment and underemployment, growing inequalities in wealth, declining real value of wages and benefits, and the subsequent decline of purchasing power. Riches, talking about the Canadian experience, argues that food banks only 'nibble' at the problem whilst simultaneously propping up the causes of hunger.

The broader problem of poverty and social exclusion in the UK has reached a point whereby people are going hungry. The developing evidence base suggests that there is a need to look beyond 'food poverty' to focus instead on the wider economic and welfare context in which people live. In responding to the problem of hunger, food banks unintentionally maintain the social harms caused by economic and/or welfare systems. Rather, alongside this good will, there needs to be a stronger challenge to social security reforms and a continued campaign effort to tackle low, wages and insecure employment. Accepting food banks as part of the Big Society will maintain the status quo rather than seek to challenge the contextual causes of food bank use – poverty and social exclusion. The Canadian experience reflects, to a certain extent, the institutionalisation of food banks: the acceptance of their use when times are tough which consequently legitimises their place in the wider welfare tapestry. Such a development in the UK will not only indicate the final stages of welfare dismantlement, but the abandonment of collective provision to address social needs which formed the core of welfare provision set out in the 1940s by Beveridge.

References

DEFRA (2014) *Family Food 2013*. https://www.gov.uk/government/statistics/family-food-2013 [accessed 5th January 2015].

Lambie-Mumford, H., Crossley, D., Jensen, E., Verbeke, M. and Dowler, E. (2014) *Household food security in the UK: A review of Food Aid*. London: DEFRA.

McInnes, T., Aldridge, H., Bushe, S., Tinson, A. and Born, T.B. (2014) *Monitoring poverty and social exclusion*. JRF. http://www.jrf.org.uk/publications/monitoring-poverty-and-social-exclusion-2014 [accessed 5th January 2015].

Perry, J., Williams, M., Sefron, T. and Haddad, M. (2014) *Emergency use only*. Available at: http://policy-practice.oxfam.org.uk/publications/emergency-use-only-understanding-and-reducing-the-use-of-food-banks-in-the-uk-335731 [accessed 5th January 2015].

Riches, G. (ed.) (1996) *First World Hunger*. Hampshire: Palgrave Macmillan.

Stevenson, A. (2014) *UK household food security: a review of existing research*. CHASM Briefing Paper: http://www.birmingham.ac.uk/research/activity/social-policy/chasm/publications/briefing-papers.aspx [Accessed 5th January 2015].

The voluntary and faith sector: 'stepping up' or 'waving but drowning' in the era of austerity?

James Rees, Rob Macmillan and Heather Buckingham, University of Birmingham
j.e.rees@bham.ac.uk
@3rdsectorRC

Introduction

Voluntary, community and faith sector organisations have long been part of the welfare mix. They are relied upon by many citizens, both as providers of formal publicly funded services as well as through the many and varied informal channels of meeting different needs. Yet this role is often overlooked and poorly understood. Despite the Coalition's Big Society and Localism agendas, which together seemed to promise a supportive policy context for civil society, more recent indications suggest that a 'perfect storm' of welfare reforms, growing and increasingly complex needs, and the marginalisation of the most vulnerable could be overwhelming many of these systems.

Certainly, in broad terms the environment for the voluntary sector has become less favourable since the 2008 financial crisis and subsequent austerity measures. Government funding has fallen from a peak of £15bn in 2010-11, to £13.7bn in 2011-12. The sector's overall income has also fallen in this period and yet spending has been maintained, suggesting that voluntary organisations have been drawing on reserves and other resources to maintain activity. There is of course a question mark over how long this can be sustained.

Thus the indications are that the sector acts as important buffer in meeting welfare needs; but many of the organisations that comprise it do so with a strong sense of their independence, moral purpose and the need to speak truth to power. These characteristics perhaps explain growing strains behind the façade of the Big Society, as voluntary organisations increasingly speak about the impact of austerity on the most vulnerable citizens and communities. In response, government ministers have betrayed frustration with the sector, telling it to keep out of politics and 'stick to its knitting', motivations which partly underpin the introduction of the Transparency of Lobbying, Non-party Campaigning and Trade Union Administration Act 2014 (the 'Lobbying Act'). For the Conservatives in particular, 'social action' in the voluntary, community and faith sector tends to be seen more as independent service to the community rather than campaigning for broader social change.

This can be seen as part of a wider project to refashion the relationship between the state and the voluntary, community and faith sector. If New Labour attempted to invest in a deeper complementary 'partnership' with the sector, a partial 'de-coupling' between the state and the sector may now be underway. There is less overall direct public investment in the sector, Labour's dedicated strategic voice and capacity building programmes have been decommissioned, and there has been an intensified rhetorical commitment to an 'independent' and 'enterprising' voluntary sector, freed from the claimed bureaucracy of the state.

This approach has developed incrementally, and involves some continuity with the previous government. It does not mean the end of public financial support for the voluntary sector; rather, it has involved a tighter focus on promoting several key agendas – social investment and 'investment readiness', closer links with the private sector, and targeted support for social action in particular fields such as youth services and mentoring in criminal justice. A watchword for the Coalition's approach here has been 'transition': the availability of temporary financial and in-kind support in order to reconfigure specific fields of voluntary action, such as advice services and local voluntary sector infrastructure. The aim is to promote the sustainability of organisations by becoming more enterprising and competitive. As a result they would be expected to make less of a demand on public funding, other than through winning contracts or sub-contracts to deliver core public services.

A shock absorber in a time of need

It is difficult to point to robust evidence about increased need and the extent to which the sector is responding, and it is of course partly for this reason that claims about growing need and fractures in society have been so contested. Indeed, it is a reflection of stretched resources that evidence about impacts *is* so piecemeal. In the last two years there have been reports of local advice and mental health services being overwhelmed by growing demands from individuals facing the consequences of the wide-ranging welfare reforms, cuts, and the heavy-handed use of sanctions (Forrest, 2012; see Butler, various dates). In the course of our own research into the provision of community mental health services in Birmingham a number of respondents made clear that they felt many people with severe needs were falling through gaps in services, exacerbated by cutbacks and the closure of some organisations; and the failure to address needs at an early stage meant that individuals presented to accident and emergency and other acute services with much more severe (and expensive to treat) needs (Rees et al., 2014).

Research conducted by the Third Sector Research Centre (TSRC) during 2013 explored the influence that voluntary organisations sought to exert on public policy. Notably, participants in focus groups conducted at a local level drew attention to the fact that welfare reform was significantly increasing demand for organisations' services (such as benefits and debt advice), at the same time as resources from local government were being reduced. This meant that whilst they were very aware of the policy and political factors contributing to the needs that their clients had, resources were absorbed in responding to these at the front line, leaving little scope for campaigning on the underlying causes (Buckingham et al., 2014). This scenario, of course, does not seem out of keeping with the sentiment of the Lobbying Act, and raises significant concerns in terms of social justice and the development of well-informed long-term solutions to social problems.

One area where 'voice' of increasing volume and political purchase has emerged though is in relation to food poverty. The proliferation of food banks across the country has sparked vigorous debate about what is driving demand for emergency food aid. Food banks have been criticised on the one hand for generating demand by their very existence, and on the other for allowing the government to evade responsibility for welfare provision. The recent All-Party Parliamentary Inquiry into hunger, however, attributed their growth primarily to 'low pay, growing inequality, a harsh benefits sanctions regime and social breakdown' (Wintour and Butler, 2014). The inquiry also found that volunteers tended to see their participation in providing these services as an uncomfortable necessity, not as a long-term solution. Whatever the exact combination of drivers of food bank usage – and DWP officials and ministers have vigorously refuted the voices from the Church of England and civil society – it is difficult to escape the report's claim that they have become 'the new shock absorbers of society'.

The UK's food banks have two particularly interesting characteristics: firstly, many of those involved in providing them are people with a faith commitment and many have been set up by local churches, and secondly – unlike many voluntary sector interventions during the New Labour years – they tend to be voluntarily resourced and independent of government funding. Whilst these characteristics might in one sense make them ideal 'servants' of Cameron's 'Big Society' rhetoric, they also – and perhaps contradictorily – have a certain resilience and a degree of autonomy, as well as alternative sources of authority, wisdom, resources and morality. This is certainly evident in the contributions that Archbishop Justin Welby has made to public debate on the issues of food poverty and pay-day lending, for example. But the voluntary nature of these services and their connectedness to faith communities also have implications 'on the ground' in local communities.

Recent research on faith-based social engagement in Birmingham and nationally explored the involvement of different faiths and denominations in meeting social needs in their local communities. In deprived communities, churches, faith groups and sometimes other grassroots organisations were frequently seeking to provide for communities' social needs, after public and other voluntary sector organisations had withdrawn due to lack of funding or other challenges. The ability to draw on voluntary resources – and a theologically motivated commitment to loving and serving others – were central to the work that many of these groups were engaged in. However, expertise and financial resources did place limits on what could be achieved, and faith communities were not always well supplied with volunteers.

Another important theme that emerged from the Birmingham-based research was the significance of 'encounter' in the context of faith-based social engagement. Welby (2014) alludes to how important this can be for food bank clients, explaining that 'the gift of food, delivered with compassion and a listening ear, can begin a remarkable process'. However, the way in which such initiatives bring together people with different backgrounds and life experience but a common humanity can also be transformative for volunteers. As one respondent put it: 'if you bring individuals into an encounter, then actually that changes you as much as the person'. This raises a question of whether a key 'political' role for the voluntary sector is to broker encounters – whether actual, or via the media – between individuals of diverse backgrounds and experience in an increasingly atomized and individualized society, in the hope that such experiences will shape, in a constructive way, their own engagement in the social, political and economic spheres within which they have influence.

Conclusion

It seems difficult, if not impossible, to get a clear grasp of the manifold impacts of retrenchment of public spending, reductions in local government capacity, the withdrawal of welfare entitlements, and growing and new forms of need. Nevertheless there are clear indications of growing stresses, fractures and inequalities within society – as voices from civil society testify (O'Hara, 2014). At the same time it also seems impossible to accurately gauge how the voluntary and faith sector is responding, other than to say that it is, as best it can and perhaps imperfectly, acting as an important 'shock absorber' within society. In many ways then this demonstrates a paradox at the heart of the idea of civil society stepping in where the state has withdrawn – and this is particularly well illustrated by the phenomenon of food banks: the necessity for them, and their very existence, is a shocking indictment, but they also offer spaces of hope and encounter within a colder cultural, political and financial environment. What remains to be seen, then, is whether the 'warmth' of such encounters will radiate outwards, bringing sustainable change at a more structural and strategic level, or whether we will continue to rely heavily on fragile, local and voluntary resources to support the most disadvantaged in our society.

References

Buckingham, H., Ellis-Paine, A., Alcock, P., Kendall, J. and Macmillan, R. (2014) *Who's speaking for whom? Exploring issues of third sector leadership, leverage and legitimacy*, TSRC Working Paper 121, http://www.birmingham.ac.uk/generic/tsrc/documents/tsrc/working-papers/working-paper-121.pdf .

Butler, P. (various dates) 'Patrick Butler's cuts blog', *Guardian*, http://www.theguardian.com/society/patrick-butler-cuts-blog [accessed 28.01.15].

Forrest, A. (2012) 'Welfare Reform: the cutting edge', The Big Issue, http://www.bigissue.com/features/890/welfare-reform-cutting-edge [accessed 28.01.15].

O'Hara, M. (2014) *Austerity Bites*, Bristol: Policy Press.

Rees, J., Miller, R. and Buckingham, H. (2014) *Public sector commissioning of local mental health services from the third sector*, TSRC Working Paper 122, http://www.birmingham.ac.uk/generic/tsrc/documents/tsrc/working-papers/working-paper-122.pdf.

Welby, J. (2014) 'Archbishop of Canterbury on hunger in Britain', http://www.archbishopofcanterbury.org/articles.php/5459/archbishop-of-canterbury-on-hunger-in-britain [accessed 28.01.15].

Wintour, P. and Butler, P. (2014) Tories seek to avoid rift with Church of England over food bank report,' *Guardian*, http://www.theguardian.com/uk-news/2014/dec/08/tories-avert-rift-church-food-bank-report [accessed 28.01.15].

Food poverty, welfare reform and health inequalities

Kayleigh Garthwaite and Clare Bambra, Durham University
k.a.garthwaite@durham.ac.uk
@KA_Garthwaite

Introduction

Emergency food banks have become an increasingly prominent and controversial feature of austerity in the UK. Food poverty and insecurity has reached epidemic proportions with an estimated 4.7 million people in the UK now living in food poverty. This has led to warnings over food poverty as becoming 'the next public health emergency'. Food banks are filling the void created by austerity and welfare cuts where many people are now only 'one bill away from hunger'.

Food banks

In 2013, almost a million people in the UK received emergency food from a Trussell Trust food bank (Trussell Trust, 2014). The Trussell Trust is a large, national, Christian food bank franchise in the UK. It operates a voucher system for those seeking emergency food provisions. Vouchers are provided by referring care agencies such as General Practitioners (GPs) or social workers. Food bank users bring their 'red voucher' to a food bank where it can be redeemed for three days, emergency food provision, up to three times within one period of crisis (deemed by Trussell Trust to be a period of six months). The food parcel contains 'a minimum of three days, nutritionally balanced, non-perishable food' such as cereal, tinned soup, tinned vegetables, pasta sauce, long life milk, tea or coffee, pasta, rice, juice, and other basic staple items.

In the UK, there are currently 423 Trussell Trust food banks. In its most recent press release in April 2014, the Trust say that there has been an incredible 263% increase in people using food banks over the past year, from 346,922 people in 2012-13 to 913,138 people in 2013/14. This equates to over 20 million meals provided for people in food poverty. Increases in food bank use were even higher in more deprived areas such as the North East of England where food parcel receipt in 2013/14 was a staggering five times the 2012/13 level. Data from the Trussell Trust (2014) indicate that the main reasons why people are referred to food banks are a result of benefit delays, sanctions, and financial difficulties relating to the bedroom tax and abolition of council tax relief, highlighting the central role of welfare reform in growing food bank use.

Welfare reform v lifestyle choice

Food banks have proved to be politically controversial. There have been suggestions by Conservative MPs and commentators that food bank use is rising as there is a greater availability of food banks – however, the data does not support this, with the Trust reporting that despite the 263% rise in food bank use between 2012/13 and 2013/14, there has only been a 46% increase in food bank creation (Trussell Trust, 2014). The increase in food bank use also correlates strongly with increases in hospital admissions for malnutrition (Taylor Robinson et al., 2013). Initially the Coalition government appeared relaxed, even encouraging, about the growth of the food bank network. In 2012, David Cameron suggested food banks were 'part of what I call the Big Society' (UK Government House of Commons Hansard, 2012). This appeared to change when the Trussell Trust began to cite welfare reform as a key factor in rising food bank use. As a response, Work and Pensions Secretary Iain Duncan Smith accused the Trussell Trust of publicity-seeking and 'scaremongering'. Duncan Smith, having refused to meet the leaders of the Trussell Trust, denied claims that the controversial benefit reforms imposed by the Coalition government were responsible for the soaring number of people who rely weekly on emergency food delivered by food banks.

Yet the government has struggled to explain why food bank use has risen, and continue to dismiss the links between welfare reform and food bank use. The recent report from the All-Party Parliamentary Group (APPG) warns that many poor families are 'one bill away from hunger' (APPG, 2014: 10) , and urges the government to ensure faster payment of benefits, to revisit the harsh sanctions regime, and to implement a living wage to tackle food bank use. The report asks: 'do we blame those who have little or nothing or do we find ways to help them?' (APPG, 2014: 6). This question relates to how the lifestyle choices of food bank users have frequently been called into question by the government, harking back to the now all too familiar 'shirker and scrounger' rhetoric so tirelessly used when discussing benefits recipients. Education secretary Michael Gove suggested that food bank users were themselves to blame, guilty of making decisions that showed they were 'not best able to manage their finances', while Lord Freud, Conservative minister for welfare reform, said food banks were 'a free good, and by definition there is an almost infinite demand for a free good'. Using social media as a platform, West Oxfordshire Conservative Future chairman Liam Walker said on Twitter: 'I have seen some 'food bank users' in the pubs of Witney ... priorities.' Conservative councillor Julia Lepoidevin labelled some food bank users as 'selfish', suggesting they 'make a conscious decision not to pay their rent, their utilities or to provide food for their children because they choose alcohol, drugs and their own selfish needs?'.

Similar arguments were put forward about food poverty, soup kitchens and malnutrition by the 1930s Coalition government during the Great Depression (M'Gonigle, 1936). It is itself depressing that the idea that food banks are a crutch for those squandering their money on non-food luxuries such as alcohol, cigarettes and other poor lifestyle choices still lingers within government rhetoric around food bank use today. However, empirical evidence from the front-line and from academic research shows a strong and convincing consensus – that it is *need*, not lifestyle *choice*, that is driving food bank use as food poverty continues to increase in the UK. People are using food banks following problems with benefit sanctions, chronic ill health (especially mental health), poor housing, low waged, insecure work, fuel poverty, and job loss, highlighting the stark inequality present in the UK.

Food poverty and health inequality

Health inequalities in the UK persist despite various attempts at tackling them. Data from Office for National Statistics (ONS) in March 2014 show males in the most advantaged areas can expect to live 19.3 years longer in 'good' health than those in the least advantaged areas. For females this was 20.1 years. The most deprived households in the UK spent almost a quarter of their income (23.8%) on food in 2012 compared with an annual spend of around 4% by the most affluent households (Centre for Economic and Business Research, 2013). Healthy eating costs three times as much as junk food – in 2012, the average price for 1,000 calories of healthy food was £7.49, whilst the same amount of unhealthy food was just £2.50 (Jones et al., 2014). The rising inflation of food, fuel and living costs – much higher in the UK than in other parts of Europe – has therefore translated into people cutting back on fresh fruit and vegetables and instead buying cheap, sweet, fatty, salty, processed foods, leading to people living in poverty often having worse diets and contributing to the rising rates of obesity, diabetes, and other dietary-related diseases, thus worsening pre-existing inequalities.

Poverty leading to inadequate nutrition is one of the oldest and most serious global health problems. Dangerously poor diets are leading to the shocking return of rickets and gout – diseases of the Victorian age that affect bones and joints – according to the UK Faculty of Public Health. One in six family doctors has been asked to refer a patient to a food bank in the past year, with GPs reporting that benefits delays are leaving people without money for food for lengthy periods of time. There are even rare reported cases of people visiting their GP with 'sicknesses caused by not eating'. This dismal situation has been described as a 'public health emergency' by academics and evidence from GP surgeries is matched by hospital diagnoses of malnutrition, which have nearly doubled in the past five years (Taylor-Robinson et al., 2013).

Conclusions

There is a distinct danger that the normalisation of charitable food banks as an everyday response to austerity can mean there is scant motivation for policymakers to seek alternatives – such as developing a welfare state that actually combats 'want' which is one of Beveridge's famous five 'Giant Evils' in his 1942 report. We agree that 'we should not allow food poverty in the UK to be the next public health emergency'. Food banks should not become an acceptable alternative to a proper social security system. Whilst food bank provision can provide short term relief in terms of alleviating hunger, for people experiencing complex and often long-term factors for accessing a food bank, this support is not enough.

Food bank provision can be unsuitable even in the short term for people with certain health conditions. This relates to the supply-driven nature of food banking in terms of what kind of, and how much food, people can and cannot obtain. Insofar as food banks give the illusion of effectively responding to hunger, they unwittingly facilitate the further erosion of the social right to state support for those at the sharp end of austerity, leading to a cycle of increased poverty, income inequality and a continued need for charitable emergency food provision.

References

All-Party Parliamentary Inquiry into Hunger (2014) Feeding Britain: A strategy for zero hunger in England, Wales, Scotland and Northern Ireland. https://foodpovertyinquiry.files.wordpress.com/2014/12/food-poverty-feeding-britain-final.pdf [accessed on 8.12.14].

Centre for Economics and Business Research (2013) 'Hard to swallow: the facts about food poverty'. http://www.cebr.com/reports/food-poverty/ [accessed on 3.9.14].

M'Gonigle, G. C. M. and Kirkby, J. (1936) *Poverty and public health*, London: Victor Gollantz.

Jones, N. R.V., Conklin, A. I., Suhrcke, M. and Monsivais, P. (2014) 'The growing price gap between more and less healthy foods: analysis of a novel longitudinal UK Dataset', *PLoSone*.

Office for National Statistics (2014) 'Inequality in healthy life expectancy at birth by national deciles of area deprivation: England, 2009-11'. http://www.ons.gov.uk/ons/rel/disability-and-health-measurement/inequality-in-healthy-life-expectancy-at-birth-by-national-deciles-of-area-deprivation--england/2009-11/stb---inequality-in-hle.html [accessed on 3.12.14].

Taylor-Robinson, D., Rougeaux, E., Harrison, D., Whitehead, M., Barr, B., and Pearce, A. (2013) 'The rise of food poverty in the UK'. *BMJ*: British Medical Journal, 347.

Trussell Trust (2014) Food bank statistics 2013-2014. http://www.trusselltrust.org/stats [accessed on 3.9.14].

UK Faculty of Public Health (2014) 'National policy and living wage needed to tackle food poverty', Health and Social Care Information Centre. http://www.fph.org.uk/national_policy_and_living_wage_needed_to_tackle_food_poverty [accessed on 2.12.14].

UK Government House of Commons Hansard (2012) Engagements. http://www.publications.parliament.uk/pa/cm201213/cmhansrd/cm121219/debtext/121219-0001.htm [accessed on 3.12.14].

The Big Society and the third sector

Pete Alcock, University of Birmingham
p.c.alcock@bham.ac.uk

Introduction – The Big Society discourse

The Big Society was a central feature of Conservative Party policy planning in the run up to the 2010 election, and in particular was promoted by David Cameron himself, who first mentioned it in his Hugo Young speech in 2009, and repeated it in an election speech in 2010. In practice the idea received a mixed reception in the election campaign itself and it was not the centre piece of the Party's campaigning. Nevertheless, shortly after the election and the formation of the new Coalition Government, Cameron again took the lead in launching the Big Society as a policy initiative in the garden of No.10 Downing Street in May 2010, with the Deputy Prime Minister Nick Clegg. Here Cameron confirmed that the Big Society would be at the heart of public sector reform, and would be based on ideas coming from the ground up and not the top down. At the same time a policy paper, *Building the Big Society*, was published by the Cabinet Office outlining some of the priorities for policy reform, and was followed later by a string of other papers aimed at strengthening what the Government now called Civil Society.

Central to the new Government's early support for the Big Society was a broader political discourse on the nature of public life and the role of government. The Big Society was contrasted implicitly (and sometimes explicitly) with the 'big state' of post-war welfare reform, which had stifled individual and community initiative and responsibility, and had become politically, and economically, unaffordable. The replacement of top-down state control with bottom-up community innovation was championed in a later Cameron speech in July 2010, when he launched a 'Community Vanguards' initiative in four local areas (Liverpool, Windsor and Maidenhead, Sutton and Cumbria's Eden Valley) to provide support for local people to take control of their own services, such as shops, pubs or broadband delivery; and where he referred to the Big Society as his 'great passion'.

Although it was, and has remained, closely associated with David Cameron, the Big Society has had a range of other proponents and supporters both inside and outside Government. For instance, Nick Hurd was appointed as Minister for Civil Society within the Cabinet Office; and, shortly after the 2010 election, Cameron elevated Nat Wei to the House of Lords to be an unpaid advisor on the Big Society. Conservative MP Jesse Norman lent his support publishing a book on the subject, which sought to trace the idea back through traditional Conservative thinking over two centuries (Norman, 2010). Outside of government the Respublica think tank, led by Phillip Blond, supported the Big Society as an alternative political direction between (the failures of) the big state and the global financial market (Blond, 2009); and the Big Society Network was funded by the Government and the Big Lottery Fund to promote community based initiatives.

The Big Society discourse promised to extend beyond Cameron and the Cabinet Office therefore, and to champion a new approach to non-government collective action. It also coincided, of course, with the introduction of the massive cuts in public expenditure announced in the 2010 Spending Review; and this led critics, such as the New Economics Foundation, to suggest that in practice it was little more than a fig-leaf to cover the yawning gaps that would be appearing in public services (Coote, 2010). For Cameron in particular, however, the Big Society was not just about government cuts, it was about a new political rhetoric for smaller government, which a Conservative government ought to be promoting whatever the economic context.

However, it was within the political discourse in particular that the Big Society failed in practice to achieve traction, and over the course of the following four years was gradually removed from its high profile in political exchange. First, it is important to recognise that the Big Society was in practice only ever an English political initiative, with Cabinet Office responsibility for civil society now devolved to the separate administrations in Scotland, Wales and Northern Ireland; and in the 2011 elections in these countries the Big Society did not feature significantly, even in Conservative campaigning.

Over the following years its profile in England waned too. In 2010 it was mentioned four times by Cameron in his Party Conference speech. In 2013 it was not mentioned at all. Its supporters began to fall away. Nat Wei quit his role, claiming that he could no longer afford to dedicate his time to such voluntary activity. Jesse Norman fell from favour after twice voting against the Government in the Commons. Respublica lost financial support and political influence. And the Big Society Network was investigated by the Charity Commission and the National Audit Office for misuse of public funds. Key political commitments also failed to materialise. A Big Society Day, mentioned in early policy papers as a national focus for voluntary and community action, was dropped; and the Vanguard Communities were also quietly side-lined – although not before Liverpool had publicly withdrawn, claiming that cuts to local authority budgets meant that supporting local action was no longer really feasible.

Civil society and the third sector

That the Big Society should turn out to be something of a passing fad should not be much of a surprise – big ideas rarely last long in political discourse. More important perhaps, especially for social policy, is what happened to the policy changes initiated under it. Here the focus was primarily on the third sector, which might in practice be expected to deliver the bottom-up, non-government, collective action that would make the Big Society work. In fact the Coalition Government did not like the term third sector, preferring instead to use 'civil society' to refer to this – including retitling the Cabinet Office section led by Nick Hurd, the *Office for Civil Society* (OCS).

The Cabinet Office (2010) policy paper outlined key commitments here:

- Making it easier to run voluntary organisations
- Making it easier for organisations to work with the state
- Getting more resources into the sector.

These were, however, rather like 'motherhood and apple pie'; and they contrasted to some extent with the significant cuts to the support for the sector which had been developed under Labour. Indeed virtually all of the new programmes introduced by Labour (Alcock and Kendall, 2011) were curtailed and support for the 'strategic partners' within the sector was phased out. Although it has been the cuts to local authority budgets which has had the most far-reaching effects on third sector organisations more generally, with around two-thirds of public funding for the sector coming through local government.

Despite this there were some new policy initiatives led by OCS. A Red-tape Taskforce explored ways to remove barriers to local community action; and a Mutuals Taskforce sought to promote the floating-off of public services to independent organisations set up by former public workers, under what was called the 'Right to Provide'. Funding of around £2m was provided to kick-start the training of 5000 local community organisers; and £50m for community first grants was used to co-fund local endowments. The largest new programme run by OCS, however, was the National Citizen Service, which aimed to provide short term volunteering opportunities for 16 year olds in their summer vacations. These were fully funded and delivered by selected volunteer providers; but inevitably could only reach around 30,000 young people each year (out of an age cohort of around 750,000), and in practice did not even reach target numbers in the first few years.

Although the new government were keen to distance themselves from previous Labour policies, in fact some of the more important civil society policy developments continued ideas and trends developed under Labour. Big Society Capital, the social investment bank eventually established to seek to bring commercial investment income into third sector organisations, had been planned by Labour, as had the 'mutualisation' of public services under the Right to Provide (called the Right to Request under Labour). Most significantly the Coalition continued Labour's policies of extending the contracting-out of public services to third sector providers. In 2011 a White Paper proposing plans to *Open Public Services* was published, outlining commitments to increase the role of non-government providers across a range of public services. This was followed by new guidance on commissioning for public agencies and the passing of the Public Services (Social Value) Act 2012, which was supposed to promote the use of social value assessments in the commissioning of services.

Significant public service programmes have been contracted-out since 2010, most notably perhaps the *Work Programme* from the Department of Work and Pensions, and more recently probation services from the Ministry of Justice. However, in the Work Programme in particular it was private companies, rather than third sector organisations, who secured most of the major contracts, largely because only they had the financial capital and organisational scale to take on the risks of contracting. Despite the existence of the 'Social Value Act', there has been no attempt to define what this means or to use it to promote the role of third sector providers in public service commissioning; and more generally it has been market competition rather than voluntary and community action which has been at the forefront of the Government's public service reforms.

This exposes some of the serious contradictions that underlay the Big Society and third sector policies of the Coalition Government. Competition for public service contracts is inevitably going to be driven by market principles, in particular if the government is not prepared to intervene to steer or control commissioning practice. This was exposed in the debates surrounding the passing of the 'Social Value Act' (Teasdale et al., 2012), most notably by one of the Conservative members of the House of Lords (Lord Bates, 2010), who pointed out that: 'There is a paradox at the heart of the 'Big Society' message namely that it can be identified as desirable by legislators, but it cannot be legislated for. For if we legislate for the Big Society then it is no longer society which expands but the state'

This is a telling indictment of Big Society politics, and does much to explain why in practice it has been so difficult for the Government to deliver on the political rhetoric of non-government action. More significantly perhaps, it reveals a fatal flaw in the thinking behind the Government's strategy more generally. As Evers (2013) has argued, we cannot really separate the public and voluntary dimensions within civil society. They overlap in practice, with some independent providers becoming hybrid, quasi-public bodies; and they overlap in principle because many third sector organisations rely on support from, and collaboration with, public agencies. As result the response of much of the third sector to the declining role, and scale, of public support has not been to rush forward to create a new bottom-up Big Society, but rather to campaign against the cuts in public expenditure which in practice are hurting them and those they seek to support and protect.

References

Alcock, P. and Kendal, J. (2011) 'Constituting the third sector: processes of decontestation and contention under the UK Labour Governments in England', *Voluntas: International Journal of Voluntary and Nonprofit Organizations*, 22, 3, 450-69.

Bates, Lord (2010) *The essential ecology of the Big Society*, accessed at http://lordsoftheblog.net/2010/12/30/the-essential-ecology-of-the-big-society/.

Blond, P. (2009) *The Ownership State: Restoring excellence, innovation and ethos to the public services*, London: Respublica/NESTA.

Cabinet Office (2010) *Building the Big Society*, London: Cabinet Office.

Coote, A. (2010) *Cutting it: The 'Big Society' and the new austerity*, London: New Economics Foundation.
Evers, A. (2013) 'The concept of "civil society": different understandings and their implications for third sector policies', *Voluntary Sector Review*, 4, 2, 149-64.
Norman, J. (2010) *The Big Society*, Buckingham: University of Buckingham Press.
Teasdale, S., Alcock, P. and Smith, G. (2012) 'Legislating for the Big Society? The case of the Public Services (Social Value) Bill', *Public Money and Management*, 32, 3, 201-9.
White Paper (2011) *Open Public Services*, Cm 8145, London: The Stationery Office.

Food banks: the best kept secret of British social policy?

Rana Jawad, University of Bath
r.jawad@bath.ac.uk

Introduction

Food banks have existed for a long time in the UK but the work that they do and the populations they serve have fallen under the radar of mainstream academic and policy debates in British social policy. Some of the key reasons for this are that food banks have been mainly run by little known faith-based organisations and government policy in the 2000s has been hesitant to shed the spotlight on them. All this changed under the Coalition Government with the shocking claims that up to one million people have relied at one point or another on food packages from charities like The Trussell Trust.

The surge in media attention and the reluctant policy debate around food banks under the Coalition Government have highlighted the ever-closer realignment of the British welfare system to a two-tier system of employment-based social security and an officially sanctioned system of social safety nets populated in large part by charities – i.e the type of welfare system which exists in countries with weak or underdeveloped welfare states. This entry incorporates a desk review of available literature on food banks in the UK as well as published research conducted by the author among social welfare charities and voluntary organisations both in the UK and in the region of the Middle East and North Africa, with particular reference to organisations that have a faith-based or religious character.

Emergency food aid or food security?

Though not a new phenomenon in the UK, emergency food provision in the form of food banks has helped to standardise and formalise this provision on a national scale (Lambie-Mumford, 2013). The network of Food Banks led by The Trussell Trust has played a key role in this situation. In other parts of the English-speaking world charitable forms of welfare and social assistance types of programmes are more the norm, such as in the USA and Canada where emergency food aid has a more established history. Equally, readers will be most familiar with emergency food aid to populations affected by civil conflict or environmental crises further afield in regions such as the Middle East or Africa. Here too the more common configuration for social welfare provision privileges the smaller proportion of formally employed workers (usually able-bodied men or public sector workers) and leaves the larger proportion of vulnerable members of the population or informal workers more dependent on forms of social assistance, including food aid. The evidence of the last decade in the UK shows that the UK, though at a different level of welfare development, is moving in the direction of this two tier system.

The use of emergency food aid and recourse to food banks has indeed increased in the UK in the last decade, but the evidence base on the role of food banks, the profile of their users or the reasons why individuals and families use them remains scant (Oxfam et al., 2015). Food banks in the UK provide food aid to people in need based on a system of referral by a health or social care professional, or other front-line agencies (Lambie-Mumford, 2013). Food banks are run by a variety of voluntary and often faith-based organisations who themselves acquire the food donations from consumers, retailers and the food industry. The largest network of food banks in the UK is the franchise run by The Trussell Trust charity (Lambie-Mumford, 2013). The main source of data regarding food bank usage in the UK is The Trussell Trust Network since such data is not officially collected by the government. Food banks are only one example of a variety of community level food aid projects which have proliferated in the UK in the last decade (Dowler and Caraher, 2003).

A small number of reports discussing general trends were produced by Oxfam/Church Action on Poverty, namely *Walking the Breadline* (2013) and *Below the Breadline* (2014). These argued that the rise in food aid in the UK is not associated strictly with the growth of The Trussell Trust Network but that the number of meals provided by three of the main food aid providers (The Trussell Trust, Fareshare and Food Cycle) increased by over 50% between 2012/13 and 2013/14. A desk-review by the Department of the Environment, Food and Rural Affairs (DEFRA) argued that robust empirical evidence on UK food aid provision, and the reasons for its use, remained limited. The Department for Work and Pensions has also recently stated that there is 'no robust evidence' linking the effects of welfare reform policies to the rising use of food banks. But it is clearly not possible to separate discussion of food bank use in the UK from the current economic context which has become marked by higher food and fuel costs, stagnating or declining real wages and the continued effects of the economic recession.

In sum, food banks are an emergency resource which deals with the symptoms of poverty and not its causes. They are an expression of the good will of voluntary sector organisations who are able to step in at times of crisis to offer direct support to those in need. But their growth and formalisation in British society reflects not only the detrimental impact of economic recession but the tightening of social security laws which are pushing citizens out of the social protection umbrella of the state.

Key implications for social policy in the UK

The issue of food banks is deeply linked to broader debates about food security and human rights. Dowler and O'Connor (2012: 46) cite a recent UN rapporteur on food security as arguing that 'focusing on food experiences in the context of human rights, food poverty and food insecurity can be interpreted as symptoms of the failure of a system to ensure adequate income levels and the availability and affordability of healthy food. The dependence on food banks is 'symptomatic of a broken social protection system and the failure of the State to meet its obligations to its people'.

These issues are also made clear in a recent joint report by Oxfam, Child Poverty Action Group and The Church of England (2015) on the perspectives of users of food banks in the UK whereby by evidence clearly suggests that difficulties vulnerable groups experience with the benefits system in the UK increase their dependence on food banks like The Trussell Trust. Factors such as having to wait for benefits, dealing with the impact of sanctions, experiencing delays with disability benefit or tax credits were cited as key reasons for seeking recourse in food banks. These factors occur against a backdrop of difficult living circumstances such as geographical isolation, physical and mental illness, caring responsibilities, difficulty obtaining educational qualifications or skills and financial indebtedness. Hence some of the key policy recommendations made in the Oxfam et al. (2015) report include: (1) Improving access to short-term benefit advances; (2) Reforming sanctions policy and practice; (3) Improving the Employment and Support Allowance (ESA) regime so that help can be maintained when claimants are challenging a decision; (4) Sustaining and improving access to emergency financial support; (5) Ensuring Jobcentres provide an efficient and more supportive service; (6) Improving access of benefit-users to appropriate advice and support.

Food banks are an emergency measure but a clear sign that state social protection in the UK is increasingly unable or unwilling to address the challenges posed by an uncertain economic climate and a tough welfare reform agenda.

Conclusion

In conclusion, it has been argued that food banks have a long history in British social policy but their role has become more prominent in the last decade. Though they are underpinned by the good will of a vibrant charitable sector, acknowledging their role formally in the current political and economic climate confirms the new welfare settlement within which poverty alleviation is to take place in the UK.

References

Dowler, M. and Caraher, M. (2003) 'Local food projects: The new philanthropy?', *The Political Quarterly,* 74 , 1, 57-65.

Dowler, E. and O'Connor, D. (2012) 'Rights-based approaches to addressing food poverty and food insecurity in Ireland and the UK', *Social Science and Medicine*, 74, 44-51.

Lambie-Mumford, H. (2013) "Every town should have one": Emergency food-banking in the UK', *Journal of Social Policy*, 42, 1, 73 – 89.

Perry, J. (2015) *'Emergency use only': understanding and reducing the use of foodbanks in the UK*, A report by Oxfam, Child Poverty Action Group (CPAG) and the Church of England.

CHALLENGES TO WELFARE

Immigration, social class and politics

Anne Brunton, Royal Holloway University of London
anne.brunton@gmail.com
@CriminologyUK

Introduction

During the 2010 National Election campaign Gordon Brown, the then Prime Minister, bumped into Gillian Duffy, a member of the electorate, on a constituency visit to Rochdale. His subsequent comments were caught on a Sky News microphone on his lapel and made public. The two crucial phrases were as follows:

> Gillian Duffy 'You can't say anything about the immigrants because they're saying that you're a a a ... but all these Eastern Europeans coming in ...'
>
> Gordon Brown 'That was a disaster. You should've never put me with that woman ... She's just the sort of bigoted woman that said she used to be Labour ... it's just ridiculous' 28th April 2010.

Ignoring Gordon Brown's well noted lack of personal warmth when confronted with the electorate this particular, seemingly disastrous interaction highlights not just his but the mainstream political classes' apparent inability to discuss immigration. A more recent example shows an ongoing uneasiness with discussing this issue – Labour MPs were briefed to avoid discussing immigration on the doorstep during the 2015 campaign – practically an impossible task. This article hopes to shed some light on the impact this vacuum has had on the social and political context of the forthcoming election and, in particular, accusations of racism and the rise of the United Kingdom Independence Party (UKIP).

Post-imperial modernisation and immigration

As Haylett (2001) has suggested there was a fundamental shift in the parliamentary Labour Party from the party of the working classes to that of the middle classes under the leadership of Tony Blair. To some extent it was in response to the erosion of working class communities which had been decimated under Thatcher and a consequent fragmentation in the types of work done by the working class. However, it also reflected a move towards a metropolitan elite that was seen in the most senior roles held in the Labour Party and a desire to create a post-imperial, modernist and multi cultural society. As a consequence the old 'working class culture' became an embarrassment – culture-less. It was a culture which was increasingly seen to represent impoverishment – not just poverty, not being poor but 'a poverty of identity based on outdated ways of thinking and *being*' (Haylett 2001:352).

Whiteness as indicative of racial characteristics comes with its own burdens and impediments which have been created through socialisation, economic relationships and psychological processes. Therefore not all white groups are equal – this can be seen particularly when considering the Irish immigration of the 1930s -1960s and then more recently of Eastern Europeans. Indeed, the white working class has also been perceived as 'embarrassingly, excessively white' (Haylett, 2001: 355). As the culture of the white working class is divested and devalued their political value has also been ignored. They have been successfully rebranded as the underclass – stuck in the past, 'reliant on welfare', unable to accept change or move forward. In association, their experience of multiculturalism has been vastly different from that of the middle classes.

The working class have seen incursions into their communities and a seeming diminution in services and opportunities. Whereas '... middle class people are more likely to be observed performing "multiculturalism" in their tastes, manners and conversations. Not only does the dominant discourse of multiculturalism not threaten the economic basis of their own hegemonic citizenship it allows them to extend their cultural capital by cultivating liberal views on "ethnic" others and purchasing appropriate ethnic furnishings and foodstuffs as markers of how far they have come' (Haylett, 2001: 365). In contrast increasing insecurity and precariousness of working class lives has not left this option open to them.

As Blair noted in 2012 'I think most sensible people in Britain can see immigrants have made a great contribution to our country', (Winnett, 2012). Meaning those who do not see immigration as a 'great contribution' are not sensible.

The impact of immigration on the (unsensible) white working class

Broadly the impact of immigration seems largely positive for the host country due to the increase in flexible labour force, an increase in GDP and a positive impact on the dependency ratio (Pettinger, 2015). Indeed politicians and academics will highlight the contradictions inherent within the anti-immigration debate, noting that the UK has enjoyed the benefits of migration for decades – in particular the use of labour force in institutions such as the National Health Service – which would not function without medical professionals from across the world (Dorling, 2009).

Until relatively recently the debate around immigration has been largely polarised – either spoken of in glowing terms or negative stories which are then labelled racist and 'un-British' lacking both generosity and tolerance.

The problem with this is two-fold, firstly there is a negative impact on the working class population from immigration both directly and indirectly and secondly the 'problem' of immigration is being used as a scapegoat for other problems. This far more complicated and granular picture has left politicians at a loss as to how to respond to this issue with the electorate. Parties that largely wished to be seen as post-imperial and modern. Of course the white working class know about scapegoating having become a target for similar treatment within their own country as Haylett (2001) and Anderson (2014) note.

Blair said yes to immigration pre the world banking crisis of 2007/08. In 2004 when the first wave of Polish migrants came to UK there were more opportunities, and more services, however this was not unproblematic. A flexible labour force is a good thing for some (employers) but isn't if you are already a member of that labour force. An incursion of workers who are willing to work for fewer money, less rights, and more insecurity will have a detrimental impact on the host population. This is especially likely in areas with high unemployment or underemployment.

A direct impact on work and local housing markets has been the active recruitment from European job markets of employees who will work for the minimum wage. These workers are often housed by the employer at rents which are above the market value. Salaries are regulated although largely unenforced but the housing market is unregulated and so an employer can recoup large proportions of wages through housing costs, sometimes up to two thirds of monthly income. This is common amongst carers, farm workers and hotel workers. This means that UK workers become increasingly unattractive to UK employers with their expectations of set hours, liveable incomes and employment rights.

Moreover this has had an indirect impact on local housing markets where employers buy up accommodation for these new European workers to live in – a respondent interview suggests that a single room in a house in the south east can cost up to £600 for these workers whereas other European workers had lived in garages and converted cupboards in care homes.

In 2010 the Government's austerity regime led to stretched GP services, larger classes in schools, longer waits in hospitals, lack of housing provision, increase in fear of crime and cuts to welfare provision. The austerity programme occurred at a time of increased job insecurity and a growth in what is now known as the 'precariat', along with ongoing and increasing immigration. A combination of these issues has led to problems of austerity to be conflated with 'the problem of immigration'. Immigration has had an impact but that impact is diverse and complex.

Inability to discuss immigration

'It is notable that while class has largely disappeared from public discourse it has re-emerged in a critique of multiculturalism and immigration through the claim that there has been a prioritization of race over class ... While the whiteness of the middle class and policy makers is empty except in so far as it makes visible other ethnicities the whiteness of the working class is worthy of note. Their whiteness and the whiteness of Eastern Europeans is racialised' (Anderson, 2013:46).

During the 2010 election it became apparent that immigration was becoming an issue. During the leader debates David Cameron made a pledge to reduce immigration over the course of the parliament. At the time the leader of the Labour Party, Gordon Brown, noted that it was an impossible promise to meet because the majority of immigration into Britain was through the European Union's 'Free Movement of People' and as such not under domestic control and this has been proven to be the case. Immigration has continued to rise in association with swingeing cuts to public services.

As we saw from Gordon Brown's deeply uncomfortable reaction to Mrs Duffy's comments and the subsequent impact on the Labour Party it was clear that the electorate wanted to discuss immigration but felt accusations of racism would quickly follow. What if Mrs Duffy wasn't bigoted but had genuine concerns and fears over incursions into her community that had not been met with sufficient increases in infrastructure and that problems that were already there would only be exacerbated by more people regardless of their background or nationality? The inability to address these in a thoughtful and open manner has led to a political vacuum where more extreme interpretations can find a home.

Immigration uncomfortably foregrounded by mainstream political parties – too little too late?

Although we can acknowledge that the 'foreigner' has always been a convenient receptacle for national anxieties, it is apparent that immigration has become the catch all answer to all social problems that now face Britain. For the Conservative Party it was initially a stick to poke the Labour Party with, and it has increasingly become a bone of contention and a reminder within their party of the uneasy relationship they maintain with Europe. For the Labour Party it is a reminder of how out of touch they look, with Milliband recently admitting that the relaxation of immigration controls in 2004 was a mistake and had undermined living standards for some working class households. This discomfiture and hotchpotch of policies and talk has left room for the rise of UKIP. UKIP's policy seems simple and extreme: to close borders, encourage repatriation, leave Europe. However, regardless of the policy, their power surely lies in their ability to talk about immigration without fear or embarrassment and their refusal to accept that this talk is racist.

Nigel Horne (2014) notes that the rise of UKIP is down to Cameron, Milliband and Brown and their inability to respond to the electorate's fears around immigration which are according to Ipsos-mori (2014) and Katwala et al. (2014) far more nuanced than sound-bite politics allows. As 'British Future' highlights when talking about immigration there is a pattern of falling trust in every political party.

Conclusion

As Dorling (2009) and Brand (2014) would highlight, these issues are more complex than simply 'the problem of immigration' allows and by utilising this trope we allow for many others to get off lightly. As Dorling notes, there is enough housing for everyone, it is just in the wrong hands, for example rich overseas buyers who are buying London's mansion houses and turning them back into single dwellings from flats – meaning London is quickly losing housing capacity. Undoubtedly this is happening but it fails to address the day-to-day issues people face in employment, waiting times and classroom sizes – the total lack of investment in infrastructure. The deep problem here seems to be in the complete failure to communicate ideas and, as 'British Future' – a think tank – note, a concurrent problem of assuming that the working class is too 'thick' to understand (Katwala et al., 2014). This assumption stems from the categorisation of this class as cultureless and a political distancing from it. This has been a huge mistake, allowing UKIP to capitalise on what has almost become a caricature of working class culture, an extremist version of what it once was and now seems disregarded. Immigration needs to be openly discussed without embarrassment and our political leaders need to take note of the electorate including women like Mrs Duffy if we are to move forward.

References

Dorling, D. (2009) From Housing to Health – To Whom are the White Working Class Losing Out? Frequently Asked Questions in Páll Sveinsson, K (eds) '*Who cares about the White Working Class.*' Runneymede Trust http://www.runnymedetrust.org/uploads/publications/pdfs/WhoCaresAboutThe-WhiteWorkingClass-2009.pdf

Duffy, B. and Fere-Smith, T. (2014) 'Perceptions and Reality: Public Attitudes to Immigration' Ipsos-Mori https://www.ipsos-mori.com/Assets/Docs/Publications/sri-perceptions-and-reality-im-migration-report-2013.pdf

Haylett C, 2001, "Illegitimate subjects?: abject whites, neoliberal modernisation, and middle-class multiculturalism" *Environment and Planning D: Society and Space* 19 (3) 351 – 370

Horne, N. (2014) 'Rise of Ukip is Cameron's fault – and Miliband's and Brown's'. *The Week*. 1 February 2015 http://www.theweek.co.uk/politics/61412/rise-of-ukip-is-camerons-fault-and-milib-ands-and-browns

Katwala, S. Ballinger, S. and Rhodes, M. (2014) *How to talk about Immigration*. British Future. London. http://www.britishfuture.org/wp-content/uploads/2014/11/How-To-Talk-About-Immi-gration-FINAL.pdf

Pettinger, T. Impact of Immigration on the UK Economy. (accessed 30.1.2015) http://www.economicshelp.org/blog/6399/economics/impact-of-immigration-on-uk-economy/

Reily-Smith, B (2014) 'Ed Miliband's new election chief under fire over 'cack-handed' leaked strategy document' *The Telegraph*, 1 February 2015 http://www.telegraph.co.uk/news/uknews/immigration/11295382/Ed-Milibands-new-election-chief-under-fire-over-cack-handed-leaked-strategy-document.html

Winnett, R (2012) 'Tony Blair: I don't regret opening UK borders to European immigrants' *The Guardian*, 1 February 2015 http://www.telegraph.co.uk/news/uknews/immigration/9352335/Tony-Blair-I-dont-re-gret-opening-UK-borders-to-European-immi-grants html

Funerals and the state: an uneasy relationship

Kate Woodthorpe, University of Bath, and Liam Foster, University of Sheffield
l.foster@sheffield.ac.uk

Introduction

Although provision for the funeral and the disposal of a body was central to the establishment of the welfare state it has been systematically overlooked as a policy issue worthy of attention over the last 70 years. A lack of focus on funerals occurs despite the fact that at the conception of the welfare state it was recognised that 'death is a universal contingency. Each citizen will die, and the death of each will leave a many-sided problem' (Clarke, 1944: 3), of which the financial cost of the funeral is one.

Provision for a funeral was entrenched within the ethos of the UK welfare state at its inception through a universal death grant. No longer available in the form of a universal benefit, financial assistance for funerals is now dependent upon the availability of resources and family members through a centrally managed system of Social Fund Funeral Payments. This is provided alongside an alternative system of public health funerals administered by the local authority, which is intended to act as a means to ensure that there will be a funeral and body disposal for those who have no family members, or there are no means to pay. The viability of these respective systems is open to question given the projected rise in the death rate in the next two decades (Hatziandreu et al., 2008).

Overview of the Funeral Payment (FP)

The Social Fund Funeral Payment (FP) replaced the universal death grant in 1989, which had been allowed to wither in value since its inception. It was worth £30 prior to the universal death grant being abolished, which only represented about 5% of the cost of an average funeral at the time (Walker et al., 1992). The FP is available to assist individuals who are in receipt of particular benefits, including Income Support, Jobseeker's Allowance (income based), Universal Credit, Pension Credit and Working Tax Credit, to help pay for a funeral (see DWP, 2014 for further details). FPs are intended to be recovered from the estate of the deceased although, owing to an insufficient estate, the reality is that very little is ever recovered: in 2013/14 this figure was £0.3 million, against an expenditure of over £40 million (National Audit Office, 2014).

At the Social Fund's inception, the FP was initially intended to cover the cost of the funeral. Following a rise in demand in the early 1990s, in 1995 a cap of £500 towards the cost of a funeral (plus burial/cremation fees) was introduced and eligibility criteria changed. This cap on funeral costs was raised to £600 in 1997 and again in 2003 to £700. It has remained at this level ever since, despite the recommendation of the Social Security Select Committee (2001) that the FP should reflect the cost of a funeral and be reviewed annually.

With the average cost of a funeral (including burial/cremation) today around £3,500 (Sunlife, 2014), the FP has thus moved from a benefit that covered the cost of a funeral and burial/cremation towards a contributory award, open only to those people who fall into a particular category of family/friend and in receipt of specific benefits. From the latest figures available, in 2012/13 66,000 claims were made and 35,000 awards were provided (DWP, 2013). The average award was £1,225 for the burial/cremation and the funeral. This cost the state £43.1 million. Claims can be submitted to the DWP up to three months after the funeral and require a completed funeral director's invoice. The average time of assessment is 16 days.

Eligibility and the submission of a claim

It been argued previously (see Drakeford, 1998; Foster and Woodthorpe, 2013) that the provision of state support for funerals had been progressively eroded over the years meaning that particular individuals are no longer eligible for an FP. The DWP provides guidance as to which categories of individuals are eligible to claim an award and that their claim will be assessed according to whom else within their network may be able to pay for the funeral. The DWP bases part of their decision on whether to award an FP on the qualitative detail provided by the claimant in the 23 page claim form. If unsuccessful, it is assumed that the claimant can approach identified family member(s) to ask for a contribution towards the funeral, whether or not there is estrangement, or if they are in a position to pay for the funeral.

Drawing on research with FP claimants, Woodthorpe et al. (2013) have argued that addressing eligibility prior to submitting a claim would have one of the most significant effects on improving the efficiency of the FP. A further key consideration is who should be providing information about the FP, especially given poor levels of awareness around eligibility and availability. While the local Jobcentre is currently the designated source of guidance on the FP, complemented by DirectGov.uk, more often than not it is funeral directors who provide information and assistance to newly bereaved people about funding options available. This is potentially problematic given the dual role of the funeral director as both an advocate for bereaved people *and* a commercial enterprise. With approximately half of applications unsuccessful and a lack of clarity over who provides information, clearly the information provided by the DWP needs to be reconsidered.

Timing

At present FP claims require a completed invoice from the funeral director as evidence of the cost of the funeral. This means that the claimant is obliged to commit to funeral costs before their claim is assessed and before they are in a position to make an informed decision about how much to spend on the funeral. Claimants are under pressure to make these decisions quickly. The DWP's current average assessment period of 16 working days means that the funeral organiser may have to wait three weeks before they can know with confidence that they can afford the funeral. In a culture where the average time between death and the funeral is around 5-10 working days (and much less in some religions), the funeral organiser faces the choice of waiting to hold the funeral, or else hold the funeral before knowing what, if any, contribution they will receive from the state.

Speeding up the process of claiming would mean that those people tasked with organising the funeral would be able to make more informed decisions about how much to spend on the funeral and the financial consequences of committing to particular costs. A streamlined claim form may also simplify the process with complexity an important factor in people's decision not to claim from the Social Fund more generally.

Size of award

The gap between the FP and the average cost of a funeral has grown year on year. Thus, even if the claimant navigates the 23 page form and is successful in their claim, they will likely face a shortfall in meeting the cost of a funeral. This currently stands at approximately £2,000 compared to the average cost of a funeral. Woodthorpe et al. (2013) found claimants utilised a variety of means to make this up such as pawning items or agreeing ad hoc repayment terms with the funeral director. Others who had an established network of support turned to their peers, raising money through local community radio, social network websites and football matches. Borrowing money from others, taking out loans, or putting the funeral on a credit card were the most common ways of paying for the shortfall. Of course, loans can create long term debt problems for recipients. Even the extension of budgeting loans under the Coalition government to cover funeral payments in addition to the FP since 2012 can result in families being forced to live on extremely low incomes while they repay interest free loans. Thus the introduction of additional loans alongside the present setup has not alleviated the existing problems outlined in relation to the provision and administration of the FP.

Public Health Funerals

Operated separately from the FP, Public Health Funerals are provided by local authorities under the Public Health (Control of Disease) Act 1984. They are provided when there is no one able or willing to provide a funeral for a deceased person. Although far fewer in number than the FP, with the latest collated figures in England and Wales in 2011 showing 2,900 were organised, concerns have been raised that the inadequacy of the FP means that some individuals are bypassing the FP and turning immediately to the local authority (see LGA, 2011). As such public health funerals actually represent a small, but growing, amount of UK welfare expenditure. Furthermore, the same LGA (2011) report detailed that there are significant extra staff costs associated with administering a public health funeral, such as visiting/finding premises, searching for next of kin and attempting to recover the costs from the estate.

Conclusion

There are a number of issues with the operation of the FP and its knock-on impact on Public Health Funerals. However these issues have received limited attention from the Coalition government and its predecessors. With the increase in length of life has come complacency in addressing the cost of funerals and state provision for those in need. This complacency exists despite a predicted rise in the death rate. With no increase in the FP under the Coalition government, despite an increase in the cost of the average funeral during the time it has been in power, the expansion of budgeting loans to include funerals is unlikely to provide a long term solution.

The system is showing signs of failure when the death rate has been at a historical low. With the death rate predicted to rise around 17% over the next two decades (Hatziandreu et al., 2008), a coherent, easily accessible and fair method of providing support for those most in need is required. Indeed, given the number of issues identified here, it is arguable that on the cusp of a rising death rate an extensive review of state provision is required. At the same time, with much emphasis on end of life care in educational campaigns, such as that of the Dying Matters Coalition, further educational campaigns to raise public awareness about the cost of a funeral are required so that individuals and their families are better prepared prior to death.

References

Clarke, J. S. (1944) *Funeral reform*, London: Social Security League.

Drakeford, M. (1998) 'Last rights? Funerals, poverty and social exclusion', *Journal of Social Policy, 27, 4, 507-24.*

DWP (2013) *Annual Report by the Secretary of State for Work and Pensions on the Social Fund 2012/2013*, London: The Stationery Office.

DWP (2014) *Funeral Payments,* https://www.gov.uk/funeral-payments/eligibility, [accessed 15.11.2014].

Foster, L. and Woodthorpe, K. (2013) 'What cost the price of a good send off? The challenges for British state funeral policy', *Journal of Poverty and Social Justice*, 21, 1, 77-89.

Hatziandreu, E., Archontakis, F. and Daly, A. (2008) *The potential cost savings of greater use of home- and hospice-based end of life care in England*, London: National Audit Office.

LGA (2011) *Public Health Funerals.* http://www.local.gov.uk/c/document_library/get_file?uuid=59d4ed48-08a5-4f9b-80c3-00ce5fcd341bandgroupId=10180 [accessed 11.11.2014].

National Audit Office (2014) *Social Fund Account 2013-14,* http://www.nao.org.uk/wp-content/uploads/2014/06/Social-fund-white-paper-account-2013-14.pdf [accessed 12.12.2014].

Office for National Statistics (2014) Deaths Registered in England and Wales (Series DR), 2013. *Statistical Bulletin.*

Social Security Select Committee (2001) *Third report*, http://www.publications.parliament.uk/pa/cm200001/cmselect/cmsocsec/232/23204.htm [accessed 12.12.2011].

Sunlife (2014) *Cost of dying report,* https://www.sunlifedirect.co.uk/press-office/2014-cost-of-dying-soars/ [accessed 22.10.2014].

Walker, R., Dix, G. and Huby, M. (1992) *Working the Social Fund.* DSS Research Report 8. London: HMSO.

Woodthorpe, K., Rumble, H. and Valentine, C. (2013) 'Putting 'the grave' into social policy: state support for funerals in contemporary UK society', *Journal of Social Policy*, 42, 3, 605-22.

Devolving social policy: is Scotland a beacon for fairness?

Kirstein Rummery, University of Stirling and ESRC Centre on Constitutional Change
kirstein.rummery@stir.ac.uk

Background

Scotland has claimed always to be 'different' in social policy terms. Both in 1999, upon the first wave of devolution of policy making powers to the Scottish Parliament, and in 2012, when he was making a claim for Scottish independence, the respective First Ministers laid claim to 'social justice' and 'fairness' as the 'hallmark of Scottish Society' and proclaiming that 'an independent Scotland could be a beacon of progressive opinion – addressing policy challenges in ways which reflect the universal values of fairness'.

Scotland's 'difference' in social policy in some respects pre-dates devolution, due to different history, culture, legal and education systems, and some of the most marked policy divergence from the rest of the UK can be seen in areas where there was a different policy context prior to 1999, such as: a commitment to social housing and ending homelessness; free university education; and a resistance to marketisation in health care. However, health and social care, devolved in 1999, has not differed radically from the rest of the UK, apart from some key policies (such as free personal care, mental health legislation, and a different approach to children's criminal justice). Key writers argue that these differences are not that substantive in practice and are based on similar theoretical approaches as the rest of the UK. There has been no policy divergence at all in the area of social security policy which, until the Smith Commission's[1] recommendation to devolve some disability-related benefits is implemented, remains reserved.

Scotland's social policy distinctiveness: the example of social care

As in other areas of social policy, Scotland presents its social services as 'distinctive', as promoting social justice and the core values of social work in a way that differs from the rest of the UK, particularly in the post-devolution era. This is manifest in a rhetorical resistance to marketisation, and an assertion that the foundation of social services in Scotland under the 1968 Social Work (Scotland) Act created a framework and a set of principles to drive social work to tackle disadvantage and inequality.

However, this has arguably been a difference more rhetorical than substantive. The 1968 Act gave local authorities the power to make cash payments to tackle material deprivation, in a way that English local authorities were prohibited from doing. Nevertheless, the development of direct payments (whereby disabled people were given cash to manage their own support in lieu of directly provided care services) was a policy development that was instigated in England (where it was technically illegal), not Scotland (where it would technically have been legal). Despite a rhetoric of 'coproduction', user empowerment and social justice, social work in Scotland has resisted the development of user-directed services until relatively recently.

Scottish social services have not developed a more universal or fairer system of allocating resources and services to people who need support than the rest of the UK. Local authorities have the responsibility for providing social care services, which means that, just as in the rest of the UK, there are different service levels, eligibility and access arrangements. Moreover, council tax freezes have placed constraints on local authorities' ability to meet the growing demand for social care services from an ageing population. User-controlled services have been developed in the form of self-directed support, and there is substantial third sector and not-for-profit sector involvement in the provision of social care services; they follow patterns established in the rest of the UK and adopted (albeit in a refined way) by Scotland, rather than policy innovations developed in a uniquely 'Scottish' way.

Future fairness for disabled people in Scotland? The option of combining social care and benefits

Following the 'No' vote on independence, the Smith Commission recommended that social care remain devolved to Scotland, and that disability-related benefits also be devolved. The draft settlement on devolution which should be enacted after the 2015 general election specifically recommended that Scotland be given control over the likes of the Disability Living Allowance, the Attendance Allowance, the Carer's Allowance, Personal Independence Payments and Industrial Injuries Disablement Benefit. These represent the group of benefits that are related to personal care. Also devolved will be a significant amount of the work currently done by the Department of Work and Pensions to support disabled jobseekers – such as the Work Programme, which outsources the task of getting long-term unemployed people into work to various agencies and charities.

The ability to vary the operation of Universal Credit (currently being rolled out to replace out-of-work benefits such as Employment and Support Allowance) will also be devolved. But over two-thirds of disabled people are over working age, so the failure to devolve pensions leaves significant gaps in Scotland's ability to create universal joined-up benefits. This partial devolution of welfare reflects the fact that no overarching principles underpinned either the Smith Commission proposals or the draft settlement. Instead, powers have been devolved piecemeal based on the existing system. However, this could potentially offer significant scope for new policy developments.

Most working age disabled people want to work, but often face significant barriers in terms of accessing training and support, along with the poverty caused by the additional costs associated with their impairments. The lack of flexibility and joined-up policy in the work environment, the benefits system, transport, care costs, the inflexibility of health and social care systems, education, housing, leisure, and lack of formal and informal social networks to provide support all contribute to barriers faced by disabled people.[2]

There are over 650,000 unpaid carers in Scotland and over 100,000 young carers. Providing a significant amount of care for a disabled or older person increases the carers' risk of poverty and ill health, and if carers are providing more support than they (and the person they are caring for) are comfortable with due to lack of affordable alternatives, it can be harmful to the well-being and independence of both the carer and the cared-for.[3]

Giving disabled and older people the choice and control over their care and support services frees up unpaid carers to provide the additional support at a level they are comfortable with. This improves relationships, reduces the risk of poverty and ill health for carers (because carers are freed to engage in paid work if there are reliable services supporting the person they care for) and for those needing services and support (because they can 'purchase' the elements of care that they are comfortable with, which enables them to be parents, carers, workers, grandparents and spouses themselves) (Rummery and Fine, 2012).[4]

The following policy options could, theoretically, be possible in Scotland:

- The creation of a system of self-directed support that is universal and needs-led, and is not devolved to local authorities (i.e. disabled people would be able to access a system of self-directed support payments that was 'national', with the same criteria and levels of benefit);

- The removal of most of the funding for social care from local authorities and manage it at a central (Scotland-wide) level to enable this system to function;

- The retention of the role of social workers as support workers, service brokers, advocates and advisors for disabled and older people (i.e. maintain current levels of staffing in professional social work and allied professions);

- The removal of funding from the direct provision of services to enable a market for social care to develop where the 'disabled person' is the purchaser/commissioner of services;

- The diversion of funding to user-led organisations at a local authority level to provide advocacy, peer support and advice on commissioning and purchasing social care support;

- The integration of health, social care and other budgets to provide the full range of self-directed support.

- These policy options may offer improved efficiency and effectiveness and better outcomes than the present (complex) system of disability-and-caring related welfare benefits. However, the failure to devolve 'all' welfare benefits to Scotland misses a significant opportunity to develop a truly innovative and 'fair' system of welfare.

Scotland could have established a Citizens Basic Income (CBI)[5] (a policy option favoured by the Green party and currently being investigated by the SNP): a subsistence level non means-tested benefit that is universally available as a social right. CBI creates social cohesion, fairness, addresses poverty and inequality, and research indicates it would cost the same, or less, than the current benefits system to run, whilst being fairer. CBI removes the need for punitive 'welfare to work' programmes, and instead enables citizens to engage in paid work to supplement their income on the basis of their skills. This enables both disabled people and carers (and parents and other groups of society who would like to work but find engaging in full-time paid work difficult because of access, training, the costs of childcare and transport, skills and balancing caring and other commitments). CBI could also remove the need for the minimum wage, and enable the development of more creative enterprise activity, particularly in areas that would address youth unemployment, such as the creative industries, information technology and the provision of childcare and long-term care services. Because there would not be the need to make a 'living wage' entrepreneurs could take risks, provide more effective and targeted services (e.g. enabling disabled people to co-produce and run their own social care enterprises). CBI could also partially addresses carer's poverty and, given that the majority of carers who are unable to work due to caring commitments are women, would also help to address gender inequality.

Conclusions

It remains to be seen how innovative and fair Scotland opts to be: how much of its increased policy making capacity it chooses to use, and how. Certainly in political rhetoric both the Greens and the SNP are the only parties currently offering a credible alternative to 'austerity-driven' welfare cuts, pointing to the SNP's record in the Scottish Government since 2007 as balancing the books whilst continuing to invest in universal services such as free nursing care, free university education and free prescriptions. Scotland certainly has a different policy making style, due to its different governance systems and scale. However, when policy outcomes are examined (such as health, income and gender inequalities) much of the distinctiveness appears to be rhetorical rather than substantive. It needs to be bolder to be truly fairer.

Notes

1 https://www.smith-commission.scot/smith-commission-report/ accessed 29/11/2014

2 http://www.disability.co.uk/sites/default/files/resources/Barriers%20to%20Employment.pdf

3 http://www.york.ac.uk/inst/spru/pubs/pdf/HeartsandMinds.pdf

4 http://www.scotland.gov.uk/Resource/0038/00388624.pdf

5 http://www.citizensincome.org/resources/Newsletter20123.htm

References

Ferguson, I. (2008) *Reclaiming Social Work: Challenging neo-liberalism and promoting social justice*, London: Sage.

Rummery, K. and Fine, M. (2012) Care: A critical review of theory, policy and practice. *Social Policy and Administration*, 46: 321-43.

Young people and the predictability of precarious transitions

Hannah King, Durham University
hannah.king@durham.ac.uk

Introduction

Underemployment, insecurity and downward mobility have become the norm for young people in the UK today. Despite supplanting youth unemployment, unfortunately all of the political parties appear to be blissfully ignorant of the issue. A major underlying theme of Coalition policy has been to implement cuts that can save money immediately but which will almost certainly result in increased public expenditure in the future. The predictions made by Bob Coles in IDOW I have taken hold, including increasing youth unemployment and associated benefits costs. On the surface we do indeed appear to have returned to the 1980s where young people are concerned. Educational exclusion rates have consistently fallen under the Coalition and now so too, apparently, are NEET (not in education, employment or training) rates. After record levels of youth unemployment in the UK and globally during the first years of their government, 1 million young people remain unemployed, with almost a third looking for work for more than a year.

However, research into these issues paints a very different picture. Fundamentally, these statistics distract from the wider and deeper problem of youth underemployment and exclusion. The work of Shildrick et al. (2012b) demonstrates the complexity of the experiences of this burgeoning 'precariat'. The 'low-pay, no-pay' cycle is leading to newly predictable transitions of insecurity for large numbers of young people, from the top to the bottom of the qualifications hierarchy. The recession and austerity have not established new trends for young people, but accelerated existing trends in youth under and unemployment. A policy refocus from NEET to youth underemployment is needed. However, this must be premised on Byrne's (1999) approach to conceptualising social exclusion that focuses on changing social and economic conditions, instead of an individualising skills deficit discourse. Long-term public investment for addressing youth underemployment and rectifying the impact of Coalition cuts is proposed.

What policy?

Arguably the last five years has seen a complete abyss of youth policy. Whilst there were a number of well documented problems with this area of policy under New Labour, there was a clear focus and comprehensive attempt to address the main issues facing young people under their reign. Through, for example, Bridging the Gap, the development of Connexions and a whole raft of initiatives (e.g. Educational Maintenance Allowance, New Deal, Future Jobs Fund), a genuine effort was made at developing evidenced-based policy and practice to address the needs of young people. However, since 2010 a giant black hole has emerged in this area with little more than reactionary spurts of hot political air to the alarming youth unemployment statistics that periodically pop-up in the press. It is arguable that youth unemployment has now been significantly superseded by youth underemployment, with young people being sucked in and out of the precarious labour market. Worryingly, no political party has a handle on this. Instead, New Labour's ill-advised focus on NEET has prevailed and, on the surface, the Coalition appears to have simply turned the clock back to the 1980s in its attempts to tackle the NEET question. Youth policy 'by default' has occurred, with largely embarrassing piecemeal initiatives hitting the headlines, including the youth contract, work programme, workfare and the (not-so-) Positive for Youth. Along with reinstating the DfE and the return of the 'lost generation', obvious parallels can be drawn with Thatcher's approach to youth unemployment in the 1980s. However, the fundamental difference is that both Thatcher's YTS and Blair's New Deal, though flawed, represented major investments in this area. In comparison, the Coalition has overseen the largest de-investment in young people in living memory with the brunt of welfare cuts and austerity measures hitting this group the hardest. This will inevitably result in significantly increased public expenditure by future governments.

Not just the bottom 10%

A new global normality of underemployment has emerged for young people. They are almost four times more likely to be unemployed than adults and have been impacted the most by the increase in precarious work. Even with reductions, NEET figures remain persistently high at approximately 1 million 16-24 year olds (close to 15%). This cohort alone represent a lifetime cost to the economy of £160 billion (Coles et al., 2010). The experience of long-term churning between underemployment and economic marginality is a common experience into adulthood for many young people.

The Teesside studies (MacDonald and Shildrick), undertaken over the last 20 years, have demonstrated how disadvantaged young people's transitions to adulthood have become increasingly protracted and complex. For young people living in poverty and experiencing a whole raft of welfare problems, churning round a 'low-pay, no-pay cycle' has become normalised (Shildrick et al., 2012a). Their more recent research has challenged the unfounded current political rhetoric blaming young people for their unemployment, totally refuting the claims about 'generations of worklessness' and 'cultures of worklessness' within families. The evidence for this simply does not exist. Despite relentless searching in Glasgow and Teesside they could not find a single household with three generations who had never worked. Despite this, the condemnation of the 'undeserving poor' continues to feed contemporary prejudice against the working class and those in poverty. Even those experiencing the shame and stigma of poverty and unemployment, are drawn into the narrative of blaming 'the poor' for their poverty. Conveniently, the Coalition have steadfastly refused to acknowledge this research.

However, experiences of underemployment and churning are no longer the preserve of those at the 'bottom' of the skills hierarchy. For many young people in the 'middle', in a 'class structure gone pear shaped', the education system 'is like running up a downwards escalator where you have to go faster and faster simply to stand still' (Ainley and Allen, 2013). It can be argued that we have now simply pushed youth unemployment up the age range to 21 with the warehousing of young people in FE and HE. Consequently, this graduatisation of work has resulted in the convergence of experience for young people from the bottom to the top.

What's the problem and what can we do about it?

There has been virtually no policy attention paid to the issue of youth underemployment and the prevailing orthodox NEET myth preoccupies governments. NEET status and youth unemployment are often viewed as an educational deficit and fault of young people. This results in an assumption that simply up-skilling will solve the NEET issue in an increasingly high-skilled information economy. Deeper structural inequalities that have resulted in longer, riskier and less predictable transitions for young people from education to employment since the 1980s are masked by panic recession headline statistics. These inequalities are also further geographically compounded, e.g. with NEET rates of over 18% in the North East compared to 11% in London and the South East. The human capital approach of dealing with 'supply-side' problems, blaming and up-skilling young people clearly isn't working, as unemployment was increasing under New Labour before the recession and cuts. As Roberts' concluded even before the economic crash, 'underemployment is the 21st century global normality for youth in the labour market' (2009: 4). Along with others, he has argued that a 'new social generation' is emerging across Europe whose lives and prospects are now defined by insecurity. This is set to be the first generation to experience downward social mobility in comparison to their baby-booming parents. Others have argued that a new dangerous 'precariat' class is developing with young people at its core, defined by insecurity.

There are two fundamental issues that must at least be recognised politically by all parties, if not addressed, in order to have any chance of developing competent and creative policy in this area. Firstly, the issue of focusing on NEET as opposed to underemployment and secondly the basis for how we view young people, exclusion and employment. There are three main problems with maintaining a NEET focus – seeing unemployment as a static category ignores the dynamism and highly complex and insecure transitions of young people; it presumes that moving young people from NEET to EET solves unemployment and exclusion; and it ignores the problem and extent of underemployment. Various definitions of underemployment abound, but broadly this includes insecure and sporadic employment, over-qualification for jobs and involuntary part-time work.

Un-, under- and precarious employment have become a standard experience for young people across the classes and an inevitable consequence of neoliberal capitalist economies. The demands of such a flexible, casualised labour market fail to provide long-term or secure opportunities for young people. This has been reflected in 'supply-side' policies that try to educate and up-skill young people, with the intention of them going on to employment (Byrne, 1999). However, economic marginalisation and social exclusion is not simply a result of personal deficits. Responsibilising young people to take the blame for their personal characteristics completely fails to acknowledge the major structural inequalities within the UK economic system and wider institutions. Whilst some micro level policies that tinker with the systems in place could bring improvements, whole-scale macro reform is needed to address such a profound problem. For example, in 2011-12 94,000 people were trained for just 18,000 new hair and beauty jobs, while only 123,000 people were trained for 275,000 construction and engineering jobs (Gardiner, 2014). This represents just one area where micro level policy could have some impact, along with the revaluing of vocational qualifications, greater resourcing of apprenticeships, genuine work experience and careers guidance, greater employer engagement with the issues and a jobs guarantee. Ultimately, we are witnessing the accelerated growth of underemployment and precarious work, resulting in increasing inequality, a transference of risk to young people and the fuelling of social crisis, all of which young people are wrongly blamed for. Whether a new precarious class will emerge is yet to be seen, but as MacDonald (2013) suggests, underemployment, insecurity and downward mobility are the 'new condition of youth'. If we are to have any chance of avoiding successive 'lost generations', serious critique and fundamental macro-economic change are needed.

References

Ainley, P. and Allen, M. (2013) 'Running up a down-escalator in the middle of a class structure gone pear-shaped', *Sociological Research Online*, 18, 1, 8.

Byrne, D. (1999) *Social exclusion,* Milton Keynes: Open University Press.

Coles, B., Godfrey, C., Keung, A., Parrott, S. and Bradshaw, J. (2010) *Estimating the life-time cost of NEET: 16-18 year olds not in Education, Employment or Training,* research for the Audit Commission.

Gardiner, L. (2014) *Totalling the hidden talent: youth unemployment and underemployment in England and Wales*, London: Local Government Association.

MacDonald, R. (2013) 'Underemployment and precarité: The new condition of youth?', *Life-long Learning in Europe*, Issue 1.

Roberts, K. (2009) *Youth in transition: Eastern Europe and the West*, London: Palgrave.

Shildrick, T., MacDonald, R., Furlong, A., Roden, J. and Crow, R. (2012) *Are 'cultures of worklessness' passed down the generations?* York: JRF.

Shildrick, T., MacDonald, R., Webster, C., and Garthwaite, K. (2012) *Poverty and insecurity: life in low-pay, no-pay Britain*, Bristol: Policy Press.

The labour market before and after the recession

Stephen McKay and Rose Smith, University of Lincoln
smckay@lincoln.ac.uk
@socialpolicy

Introduction

The effects of the global recession and the austerity policies that followed have been felt quite strongly in the labour market. Whilst the total number of unemployed did not rise to historic levels, the job stability and job creation that followed was associated with a rather different employment pattern – with more part-time work, self-employment, zero-hours contracts (ZHCs) and under-employment.

Overall numbers in work – much higher than before

The adverse consequences of the great financial crash have not been felt in the labour market to the extent of past recessions, or at least not in terms of unemployment. The UK economy contracted by 6.2% (June 2008-June 2009), but the number of people in work fell by 'only' 2.6% from peak to trough (see Figure 1). By contrast, in the recession of the early 1990s a drop in output of 2.5% was associated with an employment drop of 3.4% (Faccini and Hackworth, 2010). A recession of the size experienced in 2008-09 might have led to much larger falls in employment. Moreover, job growth has been very strong in the most recent stage of the recovery. Since December 2012 the number of people in work has continued to grow, rising by some 1.7 million in the last two years or so, and now stands well above the level of employment before the recession (albeit less than might have been expected had past growth not been interrupted).

If it is less productive parts of the economy that cease trading in recessions we might expect a bigger employment drop than the drop in output. Because the level of employment held up relatively well in the 2008-09 crash, given the circumstances of a huge drop in output, economists have often referred to this time as presenting something of a 'productivity puzzle', as output per hour worked has declined and has been rather slow to recover. From a social policy perspective it is perhaps the 'pay puzzle' that is of greater salience. Whilst changes in rates of pay have tended to be relatively protected in past recessions, this time it has been the level of

Figure 1: Number of workforce jobs, and quarter-on-quarter changes in GDP.

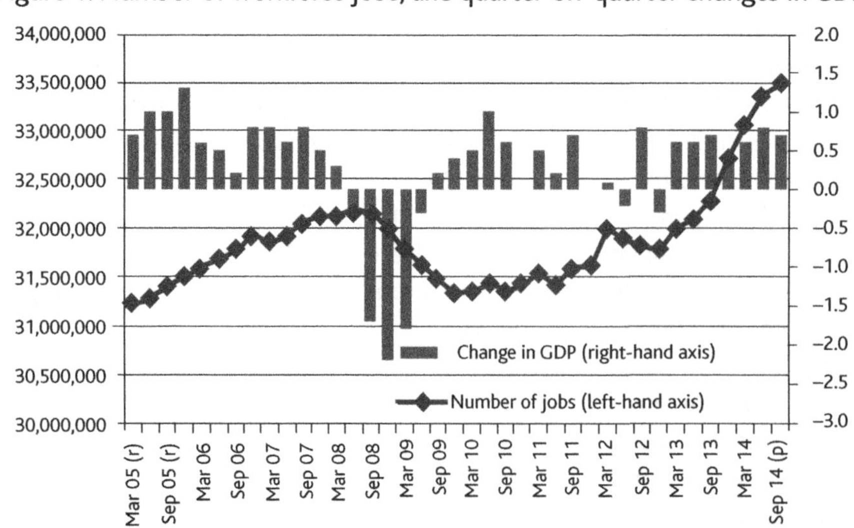

Source: ONS Workforce Jobs series, and National Accounts

pay that has been seen to be particularly sensitive to the economic conditions.

Levels of pay – unprecedented falls in real earnings

Whilst in past recessions earnings have tended to still rise, this recession has been characterised by a large fall in the real (after inflation) value of earnings. Real wages – whether per week or per hour – have dropped by around 9% compared with their peak levels (see Figure 2). Median hourly earnings in 2014 stood at £11.60. Had they grown at a modest 2% in real terms since 2005, they would now stand at £14.80 (even 1% annual real growth would have led to a figure of £13.40). With the benefit of the 2014 (provisional) data there is little sign of this turning around, even if one or two months' figures show tentative signs of growing real wages.

Since 2005, wages in cash terms have risen by around one-fifth. This compares with rises in gas and electricity bills of 120%, 50% for water charges, and rises in transport costs of around one-third. There have been reductions in the prices of other goods (such as clothing and footwear) but the rising costs of utilities and of travel have clearly had strong effects on household budgets and may be less discretionary spending than some of the items whose prices have fallen.

The record on employment must thus be put into context with the data on levels of earnings. There are more people in work, but this has been associated with gaping reductions in the real level of earnings, and particularly in the level that might have been expected in the absence of the recession. As has been widely appreciated, one consequence of this changing labour market is that most poor people are now living in households with someone in paid work.

Types of jobs

The precipitous drop in real earnings provides some kind of hint about the types of jobs being created as the recovery gains pace. Firms did not respond to the recession by large reductions in staffing, but instead seemed to have held on to existing staff. However, that has meant that some groups – such as the young and the long-term unemployed – have faced disproportionately harder conditions. Moreover the emphasis has been on having a job, perhaps any job, rather than on the quality of jobs. That pattern may also have been prompted by the steep rise in the

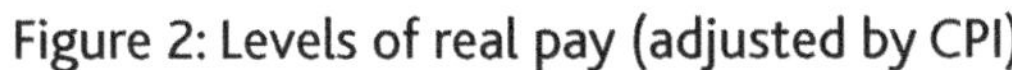
Figure 2: Levels of real pay (adjusted by CPI)

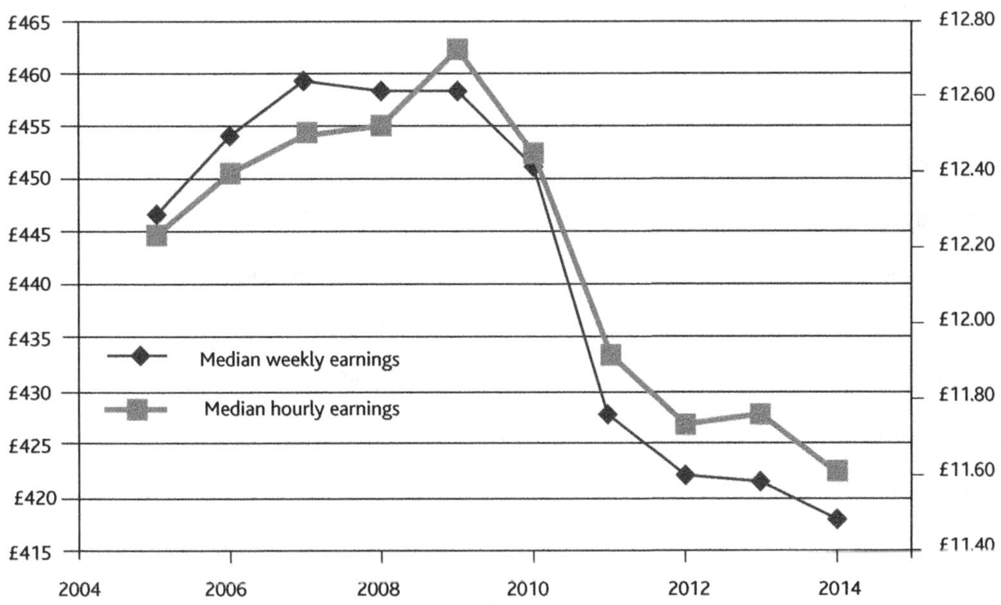

Source: ONS, CPI figures and Annual Survey of Hours and Earnings

number of sanctions taking place for those on Jobseeker's Allowance.

If we compare 2008 before the effect of the recession really hit, and recent data for 2014, we see that total employment has risen by over 900,000. However, accompanying this overall expansion has been significant increases in particular kinds of employment. The number being employed on zero-hours contracts expanded over the same period by close to 400,000. These have been the subject of political concern, with the Labour Party committed to ending any related exploitation from them, and the Conservatives seeking to stop any exclusivity clauses.

The largest changes have been in terms of those working but 'underemployed', and working as self-employed. The total number working as self-employed has risen by over 750,000. Whilst this is perhaps not a concern in and of itself, commentators on the labour market have noted that most of the rise in self-employed is at the lower-skilled end, rather than in terms of more professional roles (D'Arcy and Gardiner, 2014). The level of earnings of the self-employed over this period have dropped even more than for employees. This is also a group tending to have lower than average provision for retirement, and this research by the Resolution Foundation raises concerns about their apparent security and vulnerability.

Another significant development is the rise of 'under-employment', which is now close to 3m workers. In terms of the changes from 2008 to 2010, the number of people saying that they would want to work more hours at the same rate of pay exceeds 800,000. Alongside these may be placed the rise in part-time work of 760,000 with many of this group saying they are working part-time principally because full-time work was not available.

The profile of those in work has also become somewhat older. Over a six-year period when total employment has increased, the number of those aged 18-24 in paid work has fallen back by 300,000. To that extent, young people have been the most adversely affected by the recession. At the same time the number of those aged 60+ who are in paid work has increased by close to 400,000. This tends to support a picture of employees being retained, but with less hiring of new workers. This also happened against the backdrop of legislation removing compulsory retirement (in 2011), which may have assisted some older workers in remaining in employment for longer.

Figure 3: *Changes* in numbers of people in work 2008-2014 (Q2 for each year)

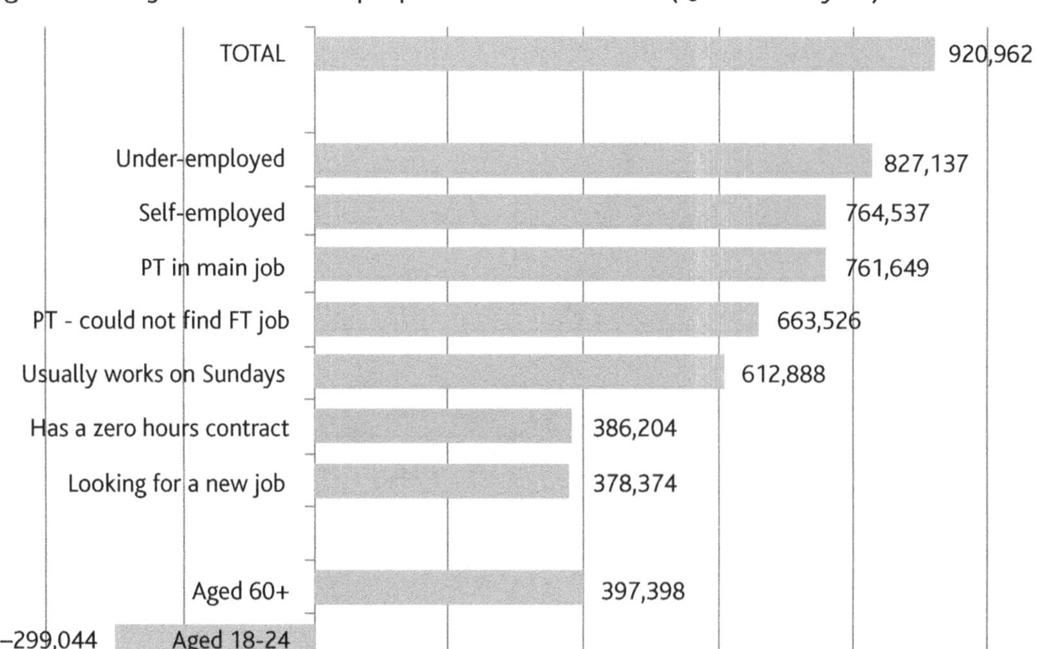

Source: analysis of quarterly Labour Force Surveys, 2008-2014

Private and public sectors

All of the increase in employment has come from the private sector (at least using the Labour Force Survey measurement of status). Between 2008 and 2014, employment in the public sector actually fell back (by around 150,000) with the private sector expanding by over a million. Most of the growth in zero-hours contracts has also occurred in the private sector, though that may also have been related to public sector contracting out of services. Because the public sector has fallen in size compared with the private sector, it is perhaps unsurprising that most of the overall changes have largely taken place within the private sector (and all of it, for self-employment). Nevertheless, a similar *proportion* of public sector workers as private sector workers say that they are under-employed (9% vs 10%), or that their part-time job is because they were unable to find full-time employment.

Policies that might help

A return to economic growth, at moderate levels, has helped to accelerate the number of jobs being created, and there is tentative evidence that the pressure on real wages may be falling. However, as shown above, job creation has not tended to be generating full-time jobs with secure conditions at high (or even average) rates of pay. Only time will tell if the current labour market trends associated with the recession and recovery are a temporary feature or instead will persist in the longer-term. Two areas that receive considerable attention are the regulation of earnings and the regulation of employment contracts.

The national minimum wage provides a floor to hourly earnings, but at £6.50 has not kept pace with inflation since 2008 (though neither have average wages), and more people are paid at the minimum level (Plunkett et al., 2014). Consideration might be given towards increases, and the Living Wage Campaign is seeking to encourage more firms to pay their workers and sub-contractors the living wage. It remains to be seen how far this figures in the election campaign, as prominent politicians from different political perspectives are interested in this concept. Another area that has received political attention is the sharp growth in the number of workers on zero-hours contracts. This could be regulated in different ways, and ideas of removing any exclusivity, or the duration of such contracts, have been discussed. The care sector employs a large number of workers on ZHCs, and often the underlying funding is from state sources, meaning the potential for quite clear state intervention. There has been lesser attention to how to deal with underemployment, except perhaps to note that Universal Credit is designed to be more responsive than existing transfers to fluctuations in earnings (which might also help those on ZHCs) and to avoid cliff edges at particular numbers of working hours (with currently 16 and 30 hours being crucial thresholds). Universal Credit is still a long way from implementation, but if it works as designed (a big if) it should match financial support to changing earnings, smoothing out variations in disposable income.

Conclusions

Over the course of the recession and the recovery the UK has, in effect, traded off lower wages for higher employment, and particularly so when compared with the experience of past recessions. Employment stayed higher than would have been expected, and has increased to an impressive degree. But real wages have dropped considerably. And many of the jobs created have been in a combination of insecure positions, with uncertain hours. Many more people are working part-time for the want of a full-time job. One of the clearest changes has been a rise in the extent of underemployment, with around 10% of workers wanting to work longer hours (at the same rate of pay) if they were able to.

References

D'Arcy, C. and Gardiner, L. (2014) *Just the job – or a working compromise? The changing nature of self-employment in the UK,* London: Resolution Foundation.

Faccini, R. and Hackworth, C. (2010) Changes in output, employment and wages during recessions in the United Kingdom. *Bank of England Quarterly Bulletin*, Q1, 43-50.

Plunkett, J., Hurrell, A. and D'Arcy, C. (2014) *More than a minimum. The Resolution Foundation Review of the Future of the National Minimum Wage: The Final Report*, London: Resolution Foundation.

Activating the (un)employed: embedded trajectories, embedded problems?

Eleanor Carter and Adam Whitworth, University of Sheffield
adam.whitworth@sheffield.ac.uk

Introduction

The Coalition administration has presided over considerable reconfiguration in labour market activation policies and the expectations placed on people in lower paying work. Two flagship programmes – Universal Credit and the Work Programme – have been rolled out with considerable fanfare but both have experienced significant, widely discussed and still largely unresolved problems. Our aim here is not to rehearse these debates but instead to focus on some of the key themes of these transformations and to consider the new messages, new directions and new problems that they create for any future government.

Since 2010 Coalition rhetoric has intensified around the stigmatisation of the poor and unemployed with the image of 'shirkers' and 'scroungers' now firmly seeded in hardening public attitudes to welfare. Accompanying this, new boundaries have been set in the reach of welfare conditionality with Universal Credit now, for the first time, applying conditionality to low-paid workers, redefining them by default no longer as hard working 'strivers' but rather as potential 'skivers' whose work efforts need to be constantly monitored. For the long-term unemployed Work Programme and, as a later addition, Help to Work have, despite their many problems, radically reshaped the activation landscape towards quasi-marketisation, outsourcing and payment by results.

Universal Credit: a quiet but radical expansion of conditionality

A wholesale rationalisation of the benefit system that has been beset with implementation problems, this typical depiction of Universal Credit (UC) neglects the more radical implication of the scheme which erases the longstanding clean binary distinction between 'in-work deserving' and 'out-of-work shirking' that Coalition (and prior) rhetoric has relied upon and consolidated as ideological justification for a series of reforms. This rhetorical device has stood firm despite shaky empirical foundations with, for example, other forms of productive labour besides paid work (caring and volunteering) and other ways of paying taxes (VAT, stamp duty and, increasingly, council tax) continually purged from discussion. Despite those empirical weaknesses this long-standing dichotomy has nevertheless provided a relatively crisp, 'safe' device for governments looking to strengthen conditions on the unemployed and for the broader public to buy into. Clearly there are implementation problems with the roll-out of UC but more fundamental in UC is the explicit fracture of this dichotomy and the repositioning of low-income workers receiving tax credits within a seemingly ever-expanding population of 'shirkers' in need of behavioural monitoring and reform.

This rebranding of the working-poor raises issues and risks/opportunities (depending on your perspective). Around 20% of working age households are currently in receipt of Working Tax Credit (WTC) due their low earned incomes and hence are now subject to UC's in-work conditionality. Children and single parents (the vast majority of whom are women) will be particularly affected by this expansion of in-work conditionality: around three quarters of families receiving WTC have children and of these most are single parent households. At a technical level it is questionable how effectively, and certainly how consistently, front-line advisor discretion will resolve decisions of what counts as enough work effort, how hard to push already working claimants, and when to sanction. More broadly UC crystallises the Conservative approach to labour markets and to the (now expanded and muddied) 'shirking poor' via policies that coerce the working poor to simply do more poor quality work (low paid and insecure) without having any reciprocal policies to change the nature of labour markets (improved job quality, security, pay or progression) or, even, to stimulate labour demand in sluggish labour markets. As such, UC distils a key micro/macro distinction and electoral battleground between the two main parties in the run-up to the general election: a Conservative Party committed to harrying the poor both in and out of work in their chase for larger *aggregate* numbers of workers, higher GDP and lower claimant counts without Labour's commensurate micro-level concerns for the quality of that work for *individuals* and *families* and the well-being and living standards of those in work. This presents risks to a Conservative Party who have previously worked so tirelessly to strengthen the work/non-work dichotomy and presents opportunities to an opposition Labour Party now gifted by the UC reforms vast swathes of low income workers now morally questioned and castigated for their efforts.

Welfare to work reform: big splash, lots to mop up

In the field of activation, following New Labour's smaller scale experimentations the Coalitions' flag ship Work Programme promised a revolution in back to work support through its universality across the long-term unemployed and the scale of its outsourcing, payment by results and provider flexibility. Since the outset major problems became almost immediately apparent and many still remain in need of remedy. Poor job outcomes in the early stages have improved for Jobseeker's Allowance (JSA) participants but still remain in-line with performance of previous schemes. Outcomes for Employment Support Allowance (ESA) claimants remain extremely disappointing with only around 10% achieving successful outcomes after 12 months on the programme. It would not be a surprise to see ESA claimants pulled out of the Work Programme model after recommissioning. The existing payment groups and differential payments system – intended to reduce 'parking' of relatively harder to help participants by varying payment levels across claimant groups – could be redesigned to work more effectively but is not currently functioning well. Its combination with light-touch oversight and weak and variable minimum service guarantees continues to leave participants vulnerable to poor quality and/or infrequent support. Despite the DWP's desires to tap into the stated creativity of the private sector, innovation within the programme seems scarce and most provision is of a fairly basic and generic type similar to that already received from Jobcentre Plus. Where innovations and successes do occur the 'black box' offers little hope of systemic learning or sharing of best practice amongst competitive providers or with the Department for Work and Pensions (DWP), stymying longer-term understanding, performance and value-for-money.

Work Programme is also a lesson in the importance of thinking carefully within a payment by results model about what 'success' means, how to sensibly measure it and what exactly one is paying for. The official performance metric was from the outset known to be poorly designed and has left the department liable for an estimated £44m over the course of the programme in unnecessary incentive payments to reward supposedly exceptional performance, even in cases where the DWP considers providers to be failing. Despite its stated objective to 'narrow the gap' between the performance of those with fewer and greater barriers to paid employment, the payment incentives and cost pressures in Work Programme all run counter-cyclically (and counter-intuitively) to what one actually wants in order to achieve this narrowing – rewarding providers more easily in economic booms rather than downturns and incentivising providers to shy away from investing energy and resources into claimants with more complex needs and geographical areas with weaker labour markets where job outcomes may be either unlikely or expensive (in terms of support costs) to achieve. It does not help that the scheme again pushes necessary issues of labour demand and more creative labour market interventions such as wage-subsidies, tailored voluntary work experience placements, job shadowing and work trials largely off the table.

On the results side of the payment by results equation, the focus on job outcomes is understandable but creates risks for those claimants in the programme with complex needs for whom a return to work may be a long-term project requiring considerable support and resources. Greater availability of resources to support such claimants would be one (possibly necessary) solution but so too would be the introduction of outcome payments for milestones relating to progressing claimants closer towards the labour market. Most basically, we know very little about the value-added of Work Programme provision and about how much precisely providers are contributing to the outcomes that they are being paid for. Most Work Programme payment volume, for example, is loaded within the monthly sustainment payments to providers for helping claimants stay in jobs if they secure them, yet only around half of those eligible noted receiving any in-work support and of those around two-thirds felt that the in-work support that they did receive had no impact on them staying in work.

The Coalition's WTW record: more change, less improvement, big questions to address

Surveying the Coalition's legacy across the newly formed welfare-to-work (WTW) policy landscape, two key overarching issues of systemic coherence and localisation emerge for the next government to tackle. Firstly, in terms of systemic coherence we are referring to a need to reorientate the disconnected and misaligned logics, sequencing and contents of the various key policies in existence – JCP, Work Programme, Work Choice and Help to Work. Why is Work Programme provision dominated by the type of generic support that claimants will have spent months receiving previously via Jobcentre Plus? Why are some disabled claimants referred to Work Programme and others to Work Choice? Why is it only in Help to Work, a post-hoc policy creation to deal with the unsuccessful outflows from Work Programme, that claimants are offered intensive coaching and community work placements? Our argument is not that the mandation within Help to Work is sensible or likely to be effective (daily signing-in at a Jobcentre isn't likely to boost job transitions for example). Rather, our point is to question why we have a system where people are unemployed for three years before they are able to access these rhetorical promises of 'more intensive support' via Help to Work. If tailored, intensive, relevant and meaningful skills courses, work placements and advisor coaching were offered far sooner in claimants' journeys back to work then all academic evidence suggests those interventions would be gladly taken up voluntarily by unemployed individuals who overwhelmingly want to get back to work. We need to fundamentally rethink the function and interactions of these schemes putting the claimants needs and perspectives at heart so that all receive the most suitable type and intensity of support at the most appropriate time point.

Secondly, Help to Work in particular appears to have opened the door to localised procurement of quasi-marketised WTW schemes and there seems increasing appetite for such localisation. There are indeed real opportunities for more holistic, locally embedded and genuinely joined up multi-agency support from devolved WTW delivery. At the same time, cascading responsibilities for the design, contracting, monitoring and financing of such schemes brings with it significant risks for local authorities and city regions. Reflecting on the many difficulties that Work Programme design, commissioning and contracting has faced, and noting the DWP's relatively stronger size and experience in these activities, it is not clear that local authorities necessarily have the capacity or expertise to ensure well-designed contracts and high-performing programmes, particularly after several years of bruising cuts to their budgets and workforces. There is in this context significant risk around variability, market fragmentation, over-payment, poor provision and financial risk to authorities and ultimately claimants.

Conclusion

Regardless of the colour of the next government the enormity of these reforms makes any significant policy paddle-back almost unthinkable, with the exception perhaps of in-work conditionality within UC should this element prove to be unworkable on the ground or publicly unpalatable. Yet at the same time the path left by the

Coalition across these reforms remains both littered with cracks and flaws for the next administration to work through. So whilst the broad direction over the next administration seems secure the fine details of how, for whom and at what spatial scale these will be implemented remains somewhat up in the air.

Towards a rights-based framework in UK welfare-to-work services

Dan Heap, University of Edinburgh
dan.heap@ed.ac.uk

Introduction

Given its expansion of employment support to a wider pool of claimants than previous programmes, merging of separate programmes into a single scheme and the large scale use of for-profit providers and payment-by-results contracts, the Work Programme is a step-change in the UK's welfare-to-work policy. As such, the design, implementation and functioning of the programme has been of great interest to policy scholars, and one of the key emergent themes has been the extent to which the programme offers good quality employment support to claimants most in need of help to return to work. Concerns have been raised that employment programmes which emphasise rapid entry into employment and structure provider incentives accordingly – as the Work Programme does – will poorly serve claimants with complex and/or multiple employment barriers, with evidence of this coming from previous UK programmes and schemes in the USA, Australia and elsewhere in Europe. Organisations representing people with physical disabilities, learning difficulties, mental health issues and other people experiencing labour market disadvantage report poor claimant experiences of the Work Programme and there is evidence of routine 'parking' of such claimants, in favour of 'creaming' of easier-to-help people.

Participant rights in the Work Programme

Such concerns draw attention to a number of problematic features of the Work Programme, including the ineffectiveness of incentives for providers to give longer-term and specialist support and the under-participation of third sector providers. Whilst such factors are important, the argument here is that many of the reported problems of the Work Programme can be traced back to a more fundamental weakness: that it is not underpinned by a concept of a right to employment-related support. Until participants have an enshrined and enforceable right to a clear package of services, it is argued here that the Work Programme will continue to fail claimants with greater needs.

Crucially, the Work Programme does not offer a service guarantee to participants. There are no central minimum standards – either in terms of the types of services offered, or the frequency and duration of contact with the provider that the claimant is entitled to. Individual prime providers do issue their own statements of the support they offer, but these vary significantly in the extent to which they specify what types of support are available, and few make clear what specialist support can be accessed by claimants with multiple and/or complex employment barriers, for example, claimants with health conditions or disability who are now accessing the programme in far greater numbers that previously. That the absence of a support guarantee makes it possible for providers to 'park' claimants with greater support needs was a concern voiced in some recent fieldwork I did speaking to policymakers involved in employment programme design:

'I think a critical point is that there are no centralised minimum standards attached to the Work Programme so it entirely depends on what the providers offer. They have to set their own minimum standards and those vary quite widely. It's entirely conceivable that somebody could go through two years of the Work Programme and not really receive the meaningful intervention that addresses their barriers to work ... In employment programmes *there are no rights: just responsibilities'* (DWP Official, quoted in Heap, 2015: 12).

Claimants are not in a strong position should they feel the need to complain due to having received poor support from their provider. The only option open to them once they have exhausted their provider's complaints procedure is to take their case to the Independent Case

Examiner (ICE), the ombudsman for the DWP, its agencies and contracted providers. Given that only 277 cases were received and 55 investigated in 2013/14 – out of 1.5m participants – this does not appear to be a well-used route for claimants to complain about insufficient support. (This figure relates to complaints received by ICE regarding all DWP contracted provision. Separate figures for the employment programmes and the Work Programme in particular are not available.) This makes the relationship between claimant and provider extremely unequal, as providers can request that the DWP sanction a participant's benefit if they are deemed not to be fulfilling their responsibilities. Furthermore, providers are responsible to the DWP primarily on a *contract-wide* basis for their *performance* in getting claimants into work, rather than for what they provide. DWP does inspect providers for their adherence to their minimum delivery standards, but some have proved too vague to be monitored adequately.

When put in historical and international context, the absence of central minimum levels of support and an enforceable right to employment support appears highly unusual. Previous employment programmes, such as Pathways to Work and the New Deals, specified the delivery of certain intervention at given times, and offered claimants menus of services they could access. A number of countries have a *de facto* or *de jure* right to employment support. Denmark, for example, has a long-established notion of a claimant's 'right and duty' to access activation services. As in the UK, claimants can face benefit sanction should they be deemed not to be making sufficient efforts to return to work, but this is balanced by a legal responsibility on the part of local social welfare authorities to help them do so. They must make a comprehensive assessment of the needs of the claimant and develop a plan to help them move into employment and, depending on their age and type of benefit, claimants are entitled to be enrolled in an activation programme for a guaranteed number of hours per week and for a minimum number of weeks. The local authority is fined if they fail to offer the right support in the amount owed to the claimant. To maintain a minimum standard of quality legislation lays down what kinds of activity that can be publicly funded and guarantees a claimant's access to one or more of subsidised employment, workplace training or skills and qualification upgrading. Specialist services for people with reduced work capacity are available and some are offered by right: claimants able to demonstrate significant incapacity have a right to an employment position with reduced hours and/or adjustments with a subsidy paid to the employer. Claimants who lose entitlement to benefits because they have not been provided with sufficient activation are entitled to compensation. Also important is the 'dialogue principle' – legislation gives claimants a right to influence the decision-making process related to their move back to employment and imposes a duty on the local authorities to ascertain if and how the claimants want to do this. The principle emphasises that the claimant is an active agent with rights, rather than the passive object of administrative action.

Features of a rights-based employment service programme

Whilst policy choices from countries with an established right to activation cannot simply be imported into the Work Programme, some changes to the rules and functioning of the programme could be made to make the claimant's access to the service less dependent on provider discretion and foster the concept of a participant's right to support:

- While providers should continue to have the flexibility to create innovative employment services, government should establish a minimum level of support – in terms of type and quantity – that the claimant can expect during the several phases of the return-to-work process: needs assessment, movement towards work, seeking work and in-work support. These minimum standards could form the basis of a charter of employment service user rights.

- There is also a case for having further guarantees for claimant groups with complex and multiple employment barriers. By creating different payment groups and paying more for supporting certain groups – for example, ESA claimants the Work Programme explicitly acknowledges that some claimants require more extensive support, and so it is questionable for government only to require a general minimum service statement and not one for each payment group.

- Providers should be responsible for the type and quantity of support – and not simply for a given number of employment outcomes -on both a contract-wide and *individual* basis. DWP inspectors should have the power to deduct from payments to the provider in the case of poor service provision.

- There should be an ombudsman specifically for the DWP's contracted employment programmes to which claimants who feel they have received a sub-par service can turn.

- A reformulated Work Programme should enshrine the participant's right as a co-decision maker in their return-to-work process. More radically, as has been trialled in a number of countries, including the Netherlands, the participant could have their own personal budget to spend on additional services at their discretion.

It should be obvious that such recommendations fly in the face of the thrust of recent welfare-to-work policy, which assumes that providers working on a 'black box' and payment-by-results will yield positive employment outcomes for participants. The experience of the Work Programme so far – in addition to evidence from similar programmes elsewhere – shows that it is difficult to use market incentives to drive desirable and discourage undesirable provider behaviour, and that relying on them to do so deepens the labour market disadvantage of already disadvantaged people. At a minimum, for the sake of social justice, some level of service prescription and greater monitoring of employment service provision will be required. Taken further, this could form the basis of an emergent right to employment support, whereby people out of work can lay claim not just to a minimum income through benefit payments but also a realistic chance to find and progress in employment through a package of quality services, and one that is not dependent on the discretion of profit-driven providers.

References

Heap, D. 2015 (forthcoming) 'Disabled people, welfare reform and the balance of rights and responsibilities', in L. Piggott and D. Grover (eds) *Work, welfare and disabled people: UK and international perspectives*, Bristol: Policy Press.

'Digital-by-default': reinforcing exclusion through technology

Simeon J. Yates, University of Liverpool, John Kirby, Sheffield Hallam University, and Eleanor Lockley, Sheffield Hallam University
simeon.yates@liverpool.ac.uk
@iccliverpool

Introduction

In the UK, the majority of welfare service users are members of those communities most likely to be digitally excluded. Yet, despite this, current UK government welfare policies are based upon a 'digital-by-default' approach to service delivery, wherein face-to-face, telephone and paper-based interactions are replaced by the use of web-based services or mobile 'apps'. In this piece, we consider the implications of this 'digital-by-default' agenda for welfare service users and the impact that the policy is having on statutory and non-statutory service providers. Our comments are informed by over eight years of collaboration with South Yorkshire city councils, social housing groups, government bodies and third sector digital inclusion organisations. Data supporting these comments is sourced from local and national survey work, service user and provider interviews, action-research and community interventions. This work has been funded by the ESRC and South Yorkshire city councils (see Coleman et al., 2010; Gorayah et al., 2011; Yates et. al., 2013).

'Digital-by-default'

In considering the roots of the 'digital-by-default' policy, it is important to remember that technology-based policies are as much imbued with political and ideological goals as policies in any other area. So, although initial rhetoric surrounding 'digital-by-default' appealed to the need to bring government services 'up to date' (that is, to match banks, insurers and holiday firms in their use of digital media), a more likely explanation for its adoption lies in anticipated 'efficiency savings'. The government's Digital Strategy (2013), for instance, 'estimate[d] that moving services from offline to digital channels will save between £1.7 and £1.8 billion a year', a figure that is equivalent to 5% of the reductions in the UK benefits spend proposed in the 2014 budget. The use of technology also supports the moral imperative of the government's welfare reforms to individualise welfare and make clients 'responsible' for their benefit expenditure, in theory making it easier to identify benefit fraud and administer sanctions.

It is important to remember that many DWP back-office services have been computerised for decades. Digital-by-default, in contrast, focuses on the clients' interaction with government. The web sites and apps to deliver this are predominantly developed and supported by the private sector. So, for example, the council run housing office becomes a private sector maintained, if council run, web site. It adds a layer of privatisation to welfare access.

The question is where do these savings come from and who do they affect? Arguments for savings through digital 'channel shift' are based, in all sectors, on assumptions about transaction costs. For example, it is typically argued (using a whole range of poorly verified figures) that digital transactions cost anything from 10 to 100 times less than face-to-face transactions. For instance, filling in your car insurance on-line can save the company on staffing costs and therefore potentially lowers your premium (or raises profits for the company). However, it is important to remember that the 'savings' lie in shifting the costs of processing transactions onto the customer and the IT system. As consumers, we therefore carry these costs in our ownership of technology (e.g. the cost of a laptop with internet access) and the use of our time, in addition to taking on responsibility for the veracity of the data we supply.

The same logic that underpins the above example is now being applied to government services, from tax to benefits. We will leave aside the issue of whether or not the 'savings' achieved go back into the benefits system, reduce the budget deficit or pay for tax cuts. There is, of course, a key difference between online customers for banks, insurance companies or holiday companies and the clients of government services: commercial organisations can choose to ignore expensive potential customers. A company such as Lastminute.com does not *have* to provide services to a disabled person on a low income with no access to the Internet. They can choose the low cost online customers. Government services cannot do this; they have to be available to all potential clients. They cannot ignore those who are disconnected from, or have limited access to digital media. Herein lies the fundamental challenge for 'digital-by-default', as extensive users of welfare services are considerably more likely to be digitally excluded.

So who are the digitally excluded? First, there are those who have no access to the Internet whatsoever. Government and Ofcom figures for 2014 place access to the Internet at around 80% of the UK population. This includes all forms of access from home broadband, access at school, work or community location, and access via mobile devices such as smart phones and tablets. It is this broad definition of Internet access that we use throughout the essay. A more detailed look at these measures indicates that good quality, regular access at home, at work or via a mobile device is lower than this – closer to 70%. Analyses of Ofcom and Oxford Internet Surveys indicate that the majority of those without Internet access:

- Are older (over 55)
- Live in social housing
- Score much higher on indices of deprivation
- Are more likely to be unemployed
- Are more likely to be disabled or have long-term health issues
- Are more likely to be from social class groups C2, D and E
- Have lower educational attainment

The second group of people considered to be digitally excluded – the less frequent and less varied users of the internet – fit the same profile as those without access. We have found social class to be one of the most reliable predictors of access and use, with social class groups C2, D and E all found to undertake banking, government service use, information-seeking and political engagement activities far less frequently than the national average. However, age remains the most significant predictor of access and use. This has led some, especially a number of right-wing think tanks, to argue that issues of access are 'temporary'. It is crudely argued that, as the population ages and older non-users pass away, a greater proportion of citizens will be online (see Policy Exchange, 2013). Yet, whatever one thinks of such arguments, they are logically flawed in two ways. First, many of the older citizens who now find themselves excluded are former IT users who had access at earlier points in their lives. Second, the issue is not just about access but inequalities in use.

By failing to recognise or appreciate the intimate relationship that exists between digital exclusion and social exclusion, the 'digital-by-default' policy has arguably exacerbated existing problems with social exclusion and over-burdened service providers in other areas of the welfare system – particularly in the charitable sector. As one of the social housing leads we interviewed noted, 'digital-by-default pushes down the balloon in government and it springs up elsewhere'. Our research has found that benefit clients are becoming reliant upon Citizens Advice, UK Online centres and local action groups to support their access to and use of services – for example, to complete online claims for Universal Credit or to use Job Centre systems. There is also evidence that the digital 'channel shift' has added demands onto the long-standing digital inclusion work by mostly third sector organisations such as the Tinder Foundation (formerly UK Online) and the GO ON programme.

Other service providers, such as social housing providers, have also had to plan for the impacts that 'digital-by-default' may have. If their clients lack digital access or skills and fail to engage with digital services their benefits will be affected, and this will impact the revenue streams to service providers, putting them at financial risk. Social housing providers are therefore actively addressing issues of digital inclusion by providing free or low cost Internet access and skills training. Elsewhere, government, both local and national, has engaged in 'forced channel shift' where non-digital options are simply removed or made second tier. For example, Job Centres are effectively becoming small IT centres with dedicated terminals. However, to address the fact that many clients lack access and skills, 'Assisted Digital' services have had to be offered, such as staff to help you fill in the online form in the Job Centre or a call centre that fills in 'your webpage' over the phone. We have noted such services being overwhelmed at times of 'channel shift', thus negating planned savings.

There are therefore three fundamental problems with the 'digital-by-default' approach. First, it has assumed that the majority of government services, no matter what their context, can easily adopt a model from consumer services. Second, it has failed to include, or chosen to ignore, the hidden costs of supporting this new system, which in practice tend to be pushed onto service users themselves or other service providers. Third, it has underestimated issues of usability across a varied and challenged user population. Though the government Digital Strategy emphasises usability, ensuring a high level of usability with all potential clients is very expensive and time consuming especially when the purchasers and users of the new systems, such as councils and their clients, have little if any input into system design. Yet where failure to properly use systems could lead to benefits being cut, services being lost or even fines, it is incumbent on government to ensure usability. It is not banal to argue that poor interface design overtly acts to further social exclusion and inequality.

Conclusion

We believe that in order to defend access to welfare services, current policy needs to accept that:

- The cost savings to government offered by 'digital-by-default' are often additional costs to welfare clients or other organisations
- Systems need to be far easier to use
- 'Assisted digital' support is likely to be needed both long-term and in greater amounts than currently planned
- Support for the third sector in providing skills support and internet access needs to be increased
- Further roll-out of 'digital-by-default' should be aimed at those groups with the greatest levels of internet access (e.g. social class groups A, B and C1)

We would also ask our academic colleagues working on issues of inclusion, exclusion and welfare to take heed of the policies and practices that can be implemented through technology solutions. These are not just neutral technical fixes or replacements for other media but a means to enact policy and to change the relationship between clients and welfare services.

References

Coleman, S., Morrison, D., and Yates, S.J. (2010) 'The mediation of political disconnection', in K. Brants and K. Voltmer (eds.), Political communication in postmodern democracy: challenging the primacy of politics, Buckingham: Palgrave.

Goraya, H., Light, A. and Yates, S. J. (2012) 'Contact networks and the digital inclusion of isolated community members', in E. Vartanova and O. Smirnova (eds), *Digital Divide Yearbook 2011*, IAMCR: MediaMir.

Government Digital Strategy (2013) https://www.gov.uk/government/publications/government-digital-strategy/government-digital-strategy.

Policy Exchange (2013) *Smaller, better, faster, stronger: Remaking government for the digital age.*

Yates, S. J., Kirby, J. and Lockley, E. (2014) Supporting digital engagement: Final Report to Sheffield City Council, http://iccliverpool.ac.uk/publications/.

Yates, S. J., Kirby, J. and Lockley, E. (in press) *Digital inclusion and exclusion: The social challenges of a networked society*, Oxford: Chandos-Elsevier.

LOOKING AHEAD

Why nationalisation or privatisation of public services might not be the only options

Zoe Williams, *The Guardian*
zoe@zoe-williams.com
@zoesqwilliams

Introduction

Move beyond left and right, urges the Social Economy Alliance manifesto. Ditch your traditional notions of public versus private, society versus business; take the best ideas from both, and see where that leads you. What follows is a deeply personal, impressionistic, doubtless flawed account of social enterprise; why I am not on the side that I always thought I would be on.

What I'm trying to move past is a sinking feeling. People of one stripe or another have been telling us to move beyond left and right for as long as I can remember. What it tends to mean is: 'Lefties, butt out. It's over for you.' When they say 'forget public and private' they mean 'give your public services to the private sector, yet still, if you please, continue to pay for them from the public purse'. When they say 'forget business versus society', they mean 'stop yammering on about human beings and get back to economic verities'. It is very hard, having lived through the privatisation of almost everything, from housing to energy to transport to children's homes, to welcome this kind of talk with an open mind, let alone open arms.

Public services – what to do?

Briefly, there are three schools of thought on public services: one, which we are living through right now, is that it should all be privatised. The problems that have been thrown up by this are extensive, and cannot be covered exhaustively here: briefly, companies attracted by the perpetual income streams of public services like adult social care and children's care do not, recent history tells us, seem to have the interests of the users at heart. Take, for example, adult social care. It used to be carried out by the public sector. Councils started to outsource. Private companies put in bids for the contracts that sometimes, if you assumed they were paying minimum wage, national insurance contributions and statutory benefits, were mathematically impossible. Councils awarded the contracts regardless, because they were so cheap. Conditions within the sector deteriorated. Minimum wage transgressions – care workers doing 16-hour days to get seven hours' pay, because they weren't paid travel time – are routine in this sector. You get care workers with 20 years' experience recast as apprentices for the lower hourly rate.

I interviewed someone recently whose pay hasn't gone up for 21 years.

The companies flounder anyway, because pay and conditions are so poor that their turnover is very high, and this inhibits quality; also, they're pulling out too much in profit. They end up in debt, and a private equity firm takes over; immediately, stocks rise, but only for two reasons. The first is the expectation that pay and conditions will be cranked down still further. The second is the understanding that there's money to be made from an 'opco-propco' deal, where you separate the property company from the operating company. Every care home scandal you read about – from Southern Cross nearing bankruptcy in 2011 to Care UK workers going on strike last year – springs from the attempt to wring profit out of this business at the expense of the lowest paid within it. The companionship of care work, the longevity of the relationship between the care worker and the cared-for, the living standards and career progressions of the workers – it is all hollowed out or tainted.

The document this submission is in highlights many of the other problems public services have faced under the previous 5 years being subject to this process. The business model is to reduce wages and ensure as little pay progression as possible. The cannibalistic corporate ethos tends towards two or three companies holding a vast amount of contracts, without necessarily having any specific relevant expertise. Local and central government appears not to have the wherewithal to negotiate effectively in its own interests and those of the people it represents. This issue, though very well illustrated by cases in the UK, is demonstrable across the developed world and in countries as politically diverse as Norway and the US, there is a big insourcing movement to redesign state services that can actually respond to and consider deeply the people who use them.

Understanding the alternative

The word 'insourcing' carries the assumption that services are better run by state bodies, because they are elected, accountable and there is no layer – of profit or ideally of unnecessary management – between the provider and the purchaser of the service. And then there is a third option, which is the social enterprise. Many proponents of insourcing see social enterprise as, if anything, not privatisation-lite but actually worse than classic privatisation. The businesses bidding for the work, having the fig-leaf of being pro-social, are by this view considered even more dangerous than classic profit-driven companies, side-stepping accountability by being even less transparent. It doesn't help, of course, that a number of companies operating plainly for profit – A4E, Circle Healthcare – have styled themselves 'social enterprises', deeply sullying the idea.

However, even having seen the way the idea has been abused, and the way any outfit not subject to democratic oversight can disappoint, I cleave to the idea that it can work, for these reasons.

To assume that everything has to come from within a local or central authority structure is, I think, to underestimate and under-use the creativity that almost certainly exists locally. In the end, if you want a local democracy that is genuinely participatory, that takes more than transparency and the ability to vote every so often; we can have all the Freedom of Information rights a (later regretful) government might throw at us, but an inclusive attitude to the delivery of services seems like a more sincere and meaningful statement of trust in, and partnership with, people outside the bureaucratic structures.

I'm thinking in particular of the Sandwell Community Care Trust, an asset-locked social enterprise delivering elder care to a number of different local authorities. Actually, as it grows, it does not draw all its contracts from its direct locale, but the unifying ethos has been kept: that there is no point making promises about the dignity of the cared-for, unless you also prize the dignity and fulfilment of the people caring for them. This means a proper career path, pay progression, but also, the freedom to self-manage within teams, a belief that contributions are valued and expertise trusted. There's nothing stopping any local authority doing any of this, but to assume that only a local authority can do it, or that local authorities naturally will do it, would be to be ignore great practice going on elsewhere.

There are often situations – the prison service is the example that stands out for me – where the best ideas come at a granular level, and are then disseminated around the service (rather than decided centrally, then enforced by targets). Naturally, this can come from within the prison estate and usually does, but that's often in collaboration with outside organisations, social enterprises or third sector; prisons are extremely agile in the way they change and develop, being paradoxically freer than other public services because they are less contested. A good example of this is the prisoner listening scheme, in which prisoners were trained to act as counsellors for one another in times of crisis. That system – which led to a radical reduction in suicides, as well as a new era of collaboration between staff and inmates – was developed by one prison service employee – Joyce Cole, in Swansea prison, in the 1990s – working in concert with the Samaritans. It then spread throughout the service; change can come from the top, but it just as often trickles up, and all individuals gain support, ambition and insight from collaboration with organisations beyond their own.

Conclusion

If you believe in transparency, accountability and sheer decency – that the economy is there to serve people, people aren't there to serve the economy – surely the answer is to in-source? Why can't we reclaim public services for the public sector, run it as it was always run? Well we can: social enterprises have not set themselves up in opposition to state-run services. But at present, we are already in a landscape of mass-scale outsourcing: we have to stop accepting business as antisocial in its essence. It seems we hand the market a lot of ground when we just expect it to be amoral.

In the end, we cannot move forward with mixed provision, and we probably cannot move forward with challenging corporate dominance and bringing services back in house, *until* we take as fundamental the idea that most people who are not driven by profit are instead driven by the desire to improve things. Sometimes that will be wrong, but surely it's a risk worth taking for the times when it is borne out.

Note

A version of this article is available as: Zoe Williams, Moving beyond left and right could save the public sector (http://www.theguardian.com/commentisfree/2014/sep/08/beyond-left-right-save-public-sector-enterprises-private-services). This version is expanded and updated.

References

http://www.theguardian.com/business/2011/dec/02/southern-cross-debt-barclays-lloyds.

http://www.theguardian.com/society/2014/aug/09/former-nhs-carers-intensify-strike-over-pay.

The Big Society five years on

Steve Corbett, University of Sheffield
s.corbett@sheffield.ac.uk
@StevenCorbett

> 'We need a social recovery to mend the broken society. To me, that's what the big society is all about' (David Cameron, 2011).

Introduction: The Big Society idea

The big society's origins lay with Philip Blond's Red Toryism, which proclaimed that over the previous three decades both the New Labour Left and the Thatcherite Right embraced a form of liberalism that disintegrated the communitarian basis of society, producing 'an authoritarian state and an atomised society'. Blond reserved extra opprobrium for the role of the state in the destruction of associative forms of community organisation (such as friendly societies, trades unions, mutuals), but he was also critical of the corrosive effects of extreme neoliberal individualism on community association.

In the concept's journey into a political project, via Jesse Norman's anti-'Fabian paternalism' take on the idea, David Cameron's Conservatives dropped the neoliberal market critique, focusing their ire in the slogan 'big society, not big government'. This was seen as a corrective for the notion of the 'broken society' and as a personal mission of David Cameron. It was a central theme in the Conservatives' 2010 election campaign, and also attempted to de-toxify the Tory brand by disassociating Cameron from Margaret Thatcher's infamous 'no such thing as society' legacy, by recognising a version of 'the social'.

A deeper examination of the concept revealed two strands to the project: Red Toryism and libertarian paternalism (Corbett and Walker, 2013). The Red Tory strand sought to reclaim an idealised conservative communitarian vision of organic solidarity, voluntarism, self-help and natural hierarchy, where the intermediate institutions of the family and 'little platoons' safeguard a Disraelian paternalist society. On the other hand, libertarian paternalism (associated with Thaler and Sunstein's 'nudge economics') was enthusiastically embraced by big society acolytes as 'compassionate economics'. This is a free market perspective which recognises the inability of people to act rationally in the market. The approach attempts rather awkwardly to marry the libertarianism of consumer choice with state paternalism in promoting welfare, by 'nudging' people towards desired ends.

The thesis of the big society is that people can be 'nudged' into retaining the public services that they most desire, using their 'freedom of choice' to become empowered by setting up public or voluntary sector mutuals, co-operatives and social enterprises. Otherwise, formerly publicly-provided services would be left to the market as 'big government' is downsized.

The Big Society in action

Once in power, Cameron occasionally repeated his commitment to the big society, despite the quiet downgrading of the concept as the Government focused its efforts primarily on the neoliberal austerity strategy of cutting public funding and reducing taxation. There was, however, early policy change on big society themes. The *Open Public Services* White Paper provided three key objectives: to improve public services while reducing expenditure; to devolve powers and autonomy to individuals and local communities; and to open up public services to new providers. Similarly, the *Localism Act* legislated for devolution of decision-making over services to communities and individuals. Further, the Behavioural Insights Team was set up to devise 'nudge' policies, and the Big Society Network was established as a consultancy-type organisation for the furtherance of the project.

Despite moderate success for the National Citizen Service, which seeks to instil the values of volunteerism amongst 16 and 17 year olds, the ambitious objectives for creating community co-operatives and increasing local control by voluntary organisations of functions previously performed by the state have been compromised by austerity. A key part of this was the capitalisation of the Big Society Capital social investment bank with around £200 million in order to harness social investors in big society projects. Big Society Capital commissions the wholesale of projects to organisations which expect to see financial returns, suggesting a social investment market from which profit can be extracted, extending the reach of private companies and increasing a reliance on loans, rather than the state, by voluntary and community organisations.

Perhaps unsurprisingly, in 2012, as the austerity agenda began to bite, Blond wrote in the *Observer* of the death of the big society ideal, citing the uncritical embrace of market solutions as part of the problem: 'Make no mistake: a radical Toryism has been abandoned, the once-in-a-generation chance to redefine conservatism on something other than a reductive market liberalism has been lost'.

The consequences of allowing private companies to compete with voluntary and community organisations (VCOs) and local communities for the provision of public services that have been offloaded from state responsibility are clear. The 2013 Big Society Audit produced by Civil Exchange remains positive about the efforts of VCOs, but points out that outsourcing public services is 'dominated by large private sector companies'. In 2012, Civil Exchange reported that 90% of prime big society contracts had been won by private companies. A tendency towards monopoly is emerging, as £4 billion of outsourced public sector contracts are with just four private companies; Atos, Capita, G4S and Serco, and concerns about a lack of choice, competition and transparency, and a 'race to the bottom' in both standards and working conditions have been raised.

According to Civil Exchange (2013), many VCOs are 'experiencing financial difficulty due to rising demand and falling income'. For example, in the North East in 2013, 56% of voluntary organisations relied on cash reserves to support their activities and nearly 25% had no reserves left. £6.6 billion is estimated as the cumulative loss of public funding by 2017/18 by Civil Exchange. In addition, the rise in food banks reflects an increasing reliance on VCOs to provide essential support to people in vulnerable circumstances, a deep and widely-held concern reflected by a cross-party parliamentary inquiry into hunger in Britain in 2014.

Even though volunteering has risen back to levels prior to the financial crisis, this is controversial given the 'increasing use of compulsory volunteering in welfare programmes'. Moreover, Civil Exchange also identifies a 'big society gap' along class lines and between geographical areas, along with disproportionate negative effects of cuts felt by disabled people, lower trust felt by ethnic minority people, and 'worrying' levels of political disengagement. This indicates that the potential benefits of the big society are weighted towards the more privileged, a reflection of the continued rise in inequality in Britain. Civil Exchange reflected in their final Big Society Audit in early 2015 that rather than uniting and improving society, these trends have produced a more divided society.

This suggests that the neoliberal ideology driving the Coalition Government's programme has won out, and while the big society concept at face value appears to address the sense of social dislocation, it actually creates 'a vocabulary for the promulgation of a neoliberal fantasy in which social equality is disregarded as a policy objective. It offers an idealised view of the community and ignores power and conflict' (Jacobs, 2014: 11). While community groups are elevated in the rhetoric, private businesses continue to profit from the dismantling of the functions of the public sector. The big society has provided a key justification for shrinking the public realm and putting formerly public concerns at the mercy of private interests.

Conclusion

The big society has been used to reassert the 'crowding out thesis' last employed in the 1980s by Thatcher. Where previously it was the market that was being crowded out by the state, this time it is civil society. However, all the evidence of the big society thus far suggests that 'society' has really served as a proxy for the neoliberal market and private profit. This indicates that, far from mending the 'broken society', the big society is contributing to increasing damage to the social fabric of Britain.

The bankruptcy of this ideological project has not been recognised by the largest political parties, with more of the same public sector cuts and welfare state outsourcing promised for the next parliament by the Conservatives under the guise of a 'long term economic plan', and Labour's 'Tory-lite' offer of slower deficit reduction, with some concessions to addressing rising inequality, such as minimum wage increases, 'mansion' taxes and freezing increases in utility bills. This suggests that mainstream right and left wing parties continue to operate within a neoliberal framework.

Piketty's (2014) analysis of inequality moves beyond neoliberalism and recognises the fundamental requirement for a significant redistribution of wealth and opportunity in society. This could become part of a political project to better promote community empowerment, local autonomy, social justice and sustainability. A democratic economy underpinned by worker-ownership, land-value taxation, strong legislation against corporate tax avoidance, nationalisation of utilities and public transportation, mutualisation of the housing market, significant green investment, supported by a citizens' basic income, can help to make the economy serve society, not the other way around (Sayer, 2015). This would be a better strategy to realise the big society's professed aims of community empowerment and localism.

These are amongst a raft of alternative proposals, notably present in some of the Green Party's proposed policies, which are being developed to counter the failed thinking of recent political projects. The task for those who are concerned with empowerment, sustainability and social justice is to develop a social policy and political programme, both nationally and internationally, that articulates these ideas.

References

Civil Exchange (2013) *The Big Society Audit 2013*, available from: http://www.civilexchange.org.uk/wp-content/uploads/2013/12/THE-BIG-SOCIETY-AUDIT-2013webversion.pdf.

Corbett, S. and Walker, A. (2013) 'The Big Society: Rediscovery of 'the social' or rhetorical fig-leaf for neo-liberalism?', *Critical Social Policy*, 33, 3, 451-72.

Jacobs, K. (2014) 'The Allure of the 'Big Society': Conveying authority in an era of uncertainty', *Housing, Theory and Society*, available from: http://dx.doi.org/10.1080/14036096.2014.947171.

Piketty, T. (2014) *Capital in the Twenty-First Century*, London: Harvard Belknap Press.

Sayer, A. (2015) *Why we can't afford the rich*, Bristol: Policy Press.

Towards an early action social security system

Liam Crosby and Luke Price, Community Links, London
luke.price@community-links.org
@Luke__Price

Introduction

At its best the social security system ameliorates and prevents socio-economic insecurity and promotes opportunity. However its current approach is too focused on short-term goals to do this successfully. It compensates for failures elsewhere without addressing underlying issues, and does not empower those who use it.

Our primary research shows how its short-term approach is passed on to people: undermining resilience and leaving many in a precarious 'survival mode', with significantly reduced capability to focus on the long-term and seize opportunities. These fundamental problems point to the need for a recapturing of the original purpose of the social security system.

Ultimately the system should take a longer-term approach, and should enable rather than constrict. It should focus on investment in people: in individuals, in communities, and in the whole of society. By both re-stating the principles of our social security system and changing the spending rules we can move towards this approach.

The social security system

The social security system as it currently stands is dysfunctional, though not in the way portrayed by popular narratives of 'scroungers' and 'waste'. It focuses excessively on the short-term, seeking solutions to immediate crises rather than addressing their underlying causal factors. The success of jobcentres is measured by benefit off-flow rates rather than getting people into quality work; insufficient levels of housing benefits force people to move away from supportive social networks and job opportunities; and the salami slicing of benefit eligibility – such as 1% uprating and increasing waiting times for benefits – ignores longer-term impacts in the name of immediate savings. The social security system acts too late, pays too little to live on, stigmatises receipt and erodes confidence (Horowitz, 2014), thus reducing people's ability to deal with setbacks and seize opportunities.

The system also compensates for failures elsewhere, applying sticking plasters rather than tackling underlying problems early. Tax credits under the Coalition Government are estimated to have been £5 billion higher than predicted in 2010, as endemic levels of low paying jobs have been left unaddressed. The housing benefit bill is set to double in less than a decade, a short-term and expensive response to the housing crisis.

Community Links' longitudinal research into the impacts of welfare reform in Newham, East London, illustrates how the short-termism of the current system and of the various recent benefit changes is forced upon, and reflected in, the behaviour of front-line staff and claimants. Sometimes this is explicit – for example the Benefit Cap incentivises movement into any job, regardless of its quality and sustainability. However much of it is also implicit. By narrowly focusing on short-term goals, welfare reform 'is forcing people into survival mode' leaving individuals and families 'to deal with incredibly stressful situations day-to-day and unable to focus on the longer-term' (Roberts et al., 2014).

Take Diana, for example, who 'used to love going to work' as a school cook and cleaner, but was forced to stop due to illness. Affected by multiple changes, her income fell drastically and she was pushed into £2,000 of rent arrears. Consequently she had to skip meals, exacerbating both her diabetes and depression:

> 'I know it sounds stupid but I'm past the stage of caring … I just don't feel secure at all … I feel like I'm just living here week-by-week … I can't see no hope, there's nothing to look forward to.'

This sense of despondency and inability to look forward to positive changes were common themes in our research. People come to fear, rather than hope for, change: 'I worry when the postman comes because I think, oh god, another letter is coming too'. Other respondents said they were 'just about surviving' day-by-day and 'robbing Peter to pay Paul' – moving costs around without being able to take longer-term steps to improve. The negative knock-on impacts on people's mental and physical health and more broadly on their social relations are clear: 'I'm in more stress ... I'm shouting too much at my wife because I just can't afford everything. It's very hard'.

Developments over the past few years follow a concerning trajectory. Firstly austerity, itself a quick fix to a long term problem, demands immediate cuts to both cash transfers and support services that are an integral part of social security. Secondly, increased conditionality – soon to be extended to people in work – further shifts responsibility from structures to individuals and is backed by harsh sanctions. Finally, reduced eligibility and increased means-testing result in much hardship, damaging well-being and putting additional costs on other services.

All of these trends continue to move costs around rather than addressing long-term problems. Perhaps the clearest example from the current reform programme are the Discretionary Housing Payments (DHP) offered to people affected by the bedroom tax or benefit cap. These do not offer a long term solution, even if for many they are the only way to survive. Many of our respondents relied on DHP to make up for shortfalls caused by drastic falls to their income, but a lack of understanding and support meant that few were enabled to make long-term changes to their situation.

The current approach is unsustainable. It erodes resilience and undermines readiness, preventing people from thriving and thus maintaining demand within the system. It also causes knock-on costs elsewhere in public services and reduces people's ability to contribute to society and the economy. Even in terms of cutting costs the reforms have failed, saving just £2.5 billion of an expected £19 billion (Hood, 2014).

Acting earlier for social security

We need to recapture an approach to social security that is not just about surviving, but about empowering people to thrive. One which makes people both able to deal with setbacks ('resilience') and ready to seize opportunities ('readiness').

Many – from diverse political perspectives – would support such a vision, but it has been lost from our current social security system. The continued focus on short-term thinking and the notion that social security is a 'bill' to be 'cut' act as barriers to realising it. The Early Action Task Force has set out principles that would underpin an *early action approach to social security* (Horowitz, 2014). Presuming the willingness of people in the system rather than starting from a point of suspicion should encourage people to want to engage early. Valuing relationships would enable the people who are best placed to understand their own situation have more say over how to improve it. Valuing ways in which people contribute to society beyond work can strengthen the supportive informal support that helps people to thrive.

These principles would be crucial to a social security system that acts early, preventing crises from escalating rather than dealing with consequences. Acting early means ensuring that support is available as soon problems begin to arise, rather than only when they become crises. More than that, it means breaking down the barriers that mean services support people with one issue – like finding work – without consideration of other issues, like their health or their ability to look after their children. Fundamentally, acting early in the social security system means investing in people, and seeing spending on people – on their housing, childcare, employment and public health – as just that: investment. This would improve outcomes for individuals, reduce demand on the social security system and therefore, in the long run, save public money.

Long-term investment in people

However, existing rules for spending within government entrench the bias towards short-term thinking and institutional silos. Short-term budgets and the split of Annually Managed Expenditure (AME, managed by the Treasury) and Departmental Expenditure Limits (DEL, managed by departments) mean there is nothing to incentivise departments to invest in programmes which reduce costs further down the line. This makes it very difficult to invest now in order to save money in the future, or to invest in one area of spend to make savings in another.

Fortunately there are a number of responses to these problems with the spending rules. Firstly, we can **plan for the longer term** by setting firm five year budgets that are reviewed on a rolling basis every three years and which include a further five year impact assessment so that the future costs of inaction and positive value of social investments are clear. In the realm of social security, the recently-passed welfare cap presents particular barriers to long-term investment – instead creating a crude incentive for governments to cut spending in the immediate term. Because the cap operates year-by-year on the DWP AME budget, the only policy response that brings spending within the cap is to cut the DWP's AME budget within that year (rather than invest upfront or elsewhere to bring down future costs). The welfare cap should be reformed so that it discourages counterproductive reductions in entitlements and incentivises action that reduces demand in the longer term.

Secondly, we could **treat early action spend like capital spending** to aid the transition towards more preventative services. Like capital spending, social spending should be seen as an investment in the future and classified as such on government balance sheets. This would involve a 'one-way' valve that allows acute spending to be redirected towards early action social investment, but not the other way around. Without this mechanism investment in prevention can only be sourced from cuts elsewhere, which is self-defeating.

Thirdly, we need to **better understand the impact on spending now and in the future.** DWP has large potential to achieve savings from investments in other sectors like health or education. Treasury should begin by mapping the major linkages between the AME and DEL budgets: areas where spending decisions in one area are likely to have a significant effect on another; this would act as a starting point from which to concentrate further analysis. The Treasury should also ensure guidance from its Green Book, which aims to ensure policies' future impacts are assessed, is followed: officials admit this process is currently given cursory attention in most cases.

Conclusion

The endemic short-termism of the current social security system traps us in a cycle in which heightened insecurity and undermined readiness result in poor individual and systemic outcomes, to which the response is the introduction of further insecurity. The role of the social security system – in preventing socio-economic insecurity and promoting opportunity – is too important to be lost to such an unsustainable cycle. As spending continues to rise, human potential continues to be wasted and as such contributions become limited; change is inevitable. It must be led by the question: how could the social security system act earlier?

References

Horowitz, W. (2014) *Secure and ready: An early action approach to social security,* London: Community Links.

Hood, A. (2014) *What is happening to spending on social security?* Available online at http://www.ifs.org.uk/publications/7447 [accessed 22.12.2014].

Public Accounts Committee [PAC] (2013) *Early action: Landscape review*, London: House of Commons.

Roberts, E., Price, L., Crosby, L. (2014) *Just about surviving: A qualitative study on the cumulative impact of welfare reform in the London Borough of Newham,* London: Community Link

Defending welfare and the Scottish independence debate

Gerry Mooney, the Open University in Scotland
gerry.mooney@open.ac.uk
@gerrymooney60

Introduction – 2014: A transformative year?

The year 2014 proved to be a momentous one with the UK state and the establishment facing a political crisis that had not been seen in generations. The event that provoked this crisis was the 2014 Scottish Independence Referendum, but the underlying factors have had a longer gestation, not least the rise of nationalism in Scotland over successive decades, culminating in the 2011 Scottish Election success of the Scottish National Party (SNP). Today, the political landscape of Scotland and the UK is shaped by the outcomes of the Scottish Independence Referendum of September 18 2014.

This landscape also reflects growing policy divergences between the different countries of the UK. The introduction of Devolution in 1999 led to a broad range of powers coming under the control of the Scottish Parliament, the majority of these in areas relating to social policy and it was around questions of the future of social welfare – and what might be broadly termed social justice issues – that the Independence debate was fought, and which both shaped the outcomes of the Referendum and the ongoing controversies that now characterise the post-Referendum landscape in the lead-in to the 2015 UK General Election.

The 2014 Scottish independence referendum: Key issues

Much has been written about the 2014 Referendum and the longer debate around Scotland's constitutional future, but the main factors driving support for Independence have often been misunderstood. There are many commentators who have viewed the growing popularity of Scottish Independence as a reflection of increasing national/ist identity. Scottish nationalists, of course, have long held to the goal of self-determination, founded on the claim that Scotland has historically been an oppressed nation, constrained by UK membership. However, to view the pro-Independence campaign as narrowly nationalist and driven primarily by issues of national identity is mistaken.

Nationalist aspirations when evident were almost entirely entangled with issues that cannot be interpreted as 'nationalist'. The Independence debate was not about a future Scottish state – or about the continuation of the UK state as such – but revolved around the future of the welfare state, within the context of Scotland either continuing in the UK, or of full Independence. The Referendum offered scope to both the *YES* (pro-Independence) and *NO/Better Together* (pro-UK membership) campaigns to highlight the potential for a Scottish political settlement that safeguarded welfare and public services, and which also generated proposals for a fully *Scottish* welfare state which would be markedly different from the social welfare landscape being forged by the UK Government.

In this debate the future of the NHS played a key role with arguments made by *YES* supporters that only Independence could prevent the kind of privatisation impacting on the NHS in England. Controversies around the NHS acted a vehicle for concerns about the future of public services more generally – as well as for opposition to the 'austerity' measures of the UK Government.

That these issues are intertwined with questions around national futures is not new. There is a powerful narrative that the historical development of the welfare state in post-1945 era, for instance, played an important role in forging the UK as a nation. One of the many ironies that have emerged in the Independence debate has been the readiness of SNP politicians to claim that an Independent Scotland would remain true to the founding principles of this 'classic' UK welfare state at the very time, they claim, when the UK Government is diverging more and more from those ideals – highlighted not only by privatisation but by austerity and wide-ranging 'welfare reform', including the 'bedroom' tax and so on.

That these issues were core to the arguments made by pro-Independence supporters also signals that support for Independence extended well beyond the SNP. The mobilisation in the *YES* campaign of tens of thousands of supporters including many who were politically energised for the first time was strongly led by opposition to austerity and by campaigning around a range of social justice issues. The SNP worked alongside the Scottish Greens and Scottish Socialist Party, but many other groups were formed during the course of the two year campaign, the *Radical Independence Campaign* and *Women for Independence* groups among the most notable. The *YES* campaign was in many respects a broad social movement (Mooney and Gourlay, 2014).

However, given that the wide appeal of Scottish Independence spanned many disparate groups, it would be mistaken to suggest that all shared a same commitment to social justice issues (Mooney, 2014). Some sections of the *YES* movement offered aspirations that went beyond the rather limited constitutional vision of Independence of the SNP and beyond defending existing services and provision; for example, arguments for a Nordic-type welfare regime or a welfare state that was organised on a radically different kind of economy from the neo-liberal social and economic policies dominating today. Other proposals included free childcare for all pre-school children and arguments that a living wage should be a feature of an Independent Scotland built upon principles of social justice. Conversely, the *NO* campaign argued that it was only through Scotland's continuing membership of the UK would welfare and public services be safeguarded.

The 2014 referendum result and consequences

The 2014 Referendum saw 55% of voters voting NO to Independence and 45% voting YES. However it was clear from the 45% who voted for Independence and of a significant number of the 55% voting NO, that considerable change was being sought. Change, not just in terms of additional devolved powers for Scotland, but in the direction of social and economic policy making more generally. The majority NO vote was not a vote against change, for the status quo. While this was expressed in terms of a particular constitutional future, nonetheless behind these choices were more fundamental demands for a different kind of society, for a fairer Scotland.

The Referendum results reflect the inequalities that characterise contemporary Scotland and diminish the falsehood of Scotland as a homogenous nation. Four of Scotland's 32 council areas returned a majority YES vote: Dundee, Glasgow and its two Clydeside neighbours, West Dunbartonshire and North Lanarkshire. But these contain the most deprived areas in Scotland (and two other Clydeside districts with a high incidence of deprivation were very marginal NO voting districts). The YES vote here reflected the desire for radical change amongst the poorest sections of Scotland's working class. It was a rejection of Westminster politics and, with enduring consequences today, of the Labour Party also. With the exception of Dundee, those areas voting YES in large numbers, including all 8 Scottish Parliament constituencies in Glasgow, have traditionally been Labour Party heartlands. In contrast all 5 of the constituencies in Edinburgh returned a NO vote.

The result reflects the divided and uneven geo-political landscape of Scotland. The poorer the area, the more likely it was to vote YES, and the more affluent and elderly the population of an area, the more likely it was to vote NO. The middle classes largely voted NO, while it was the more vulnerable working classes – often in the large urban housing estates – where the pro-Independence vote was strongest. More securely employed sections of the working class tended to vote NO, many of them encouraged to do so not only the Scottish Labour Party but also by many of the trades unions. In relation to gender, more women voted NO but this may in part be a reflection of the larger number of women in the more aged sections of the population.

Conclusion – The post-independence referendum landscape: Political and constitutional turmoil?

The Independence debate was not simply a matter of controversy over territorial justice or constitutional futures, but provided opportunity for new ways of thinking about welfare and measures to address disadvantage and inequality. These arguments now also shape the political climate that has emerged in Scotland since September 2014. Much of this has revolved around the proposals of the Smith Commission, set-up in the wake of the Referendum to produce proposals for additional powers to the Scottish Government (Smith, 2014). The controversy around Smith, that it contains too few powers for Scotland, especially in the key welfare areas that many in Scotland had anticipated, has also been linked with possible devolution in England, with huge consequences for the future of the UK.

It was claimed that the Scottish Independence Referendum would settle the constitutional future of Scotland 'for a generation'. In the early months of 2015, few if any would put money on this. Depending on the outcomes of the May 2015 General Election and of any Referendum on UK membership of the EU, demands are already being made for another Independence Referendum. The SNP are enjoying unprecedented popularity in terms of membership and are riding high in the Scottish opinion polls and look certain not only to be the party with most Scottish MPs, but could hold the balance of power in a hung UK Parliament. Opinion polls at the end of 2014 show that 60% of Scottish voters believe that the higher the number of SNP MPs, the better the deal for Scotland, including further additional powers that go beyond the Smith Commission recommendations (Gordon, 2014). SNP support at this time sits on 43% (more than double what it got in the 2010 General Election), while Labour sits on 26%. The 2010 UK Government partners, Tories and LibDems, score just 13% and 6% respectively (Clark and Severin, 2014).

As the 2015 General Election campaign begins to heat-up, social welfare, austerity and inequality will be key political issues. The majority of Scots are in favour of far reaching redistributive social justice. *In Defence of Welfare* in this regard, then, is once more entangled with and linked to the question of constitutional futures, not only for in Scotland – but also increasingly for the UK as a whole.

References

Clark, T. and Carrell, S. (2014) 'Labour faces Scotland bloodbath', *Guardian*, December 27.

Gordon, T. (2014) 'More than half of Scots believe SNP Surge in General Election would force Westminster to give more powers to Holyrood', *Sunday Herald*, December 28.

Mooney, G. (2014) 'Campaigns fight to define what Scottish social justice means', *The Conversation*, September 15: https://theconversation.com/campaigns-fight-to-define-what-scottish-social-justice-means-31699.

Mooney, G. and Gourlay, G. (2014) 'Social media and grassroots activism have taken scotland to the brink of independence', *The Conversation*, September 8: https://theconversation.com/social-media-and-grassroots-activism-have-taken-scotland-to-the-brink-of-independence-31389.

Smith Commission (2014) *Report of the Smith Commission for further devolution of powers to the Scottish Parliament*, Edinburgh: The Smith Commission.

No going back? Can the austerity politics of the Coalition be reversed?

Peter Taylor-Gooby, University of Kent
p.f.taylor-gooby@kent.ac.uk

Introduction

The social policies of the 2010-2015 Coalition government can be looked at in two ways. From one perspective the over-riding objective was that stated in the 2010 Emergency Budget: to eliminate the deficit by cutting public spending commitments. The government has not succeeded in this. The second perspective sees the policies as having two further implicit goals:

- To embed a major restructuring of state welfare so that an incoming government finds it hard to reverse the changes; and
- To undermine solidaristic support for the welfare state so that a new government cannot gain sufficient support for the task of re-establishing the previous settlement.

This paper considers how for these goals have been achieved and examines future prospects for change.

The main changes in social policy since 2010 are detailed in other essays in this book. Apart from the cut-backs in all areas of spending except health care, schools and overseas aid (and bearing most heavily on local government and on short-term benefits) the main changes in welfare policies achieved by the government have been four:

- A much greater role for market systems and for the private sector in service provision across the board, from higher education to local government, from the NHS to the Work Programme.
- The restructuring of cash benefits, including cuts to short-term and family benefits, constraints on uprating and the introduction of a harsher sanctions regime for JSA and ESA claimers; reforms to benefits for disabled people involving a sharp reduction in numbers entitled; and real increases in retirement pensions coupled with an acceleration of the raising of pension age.
- A shift from direct to indirect tax (see Figure 1), mainly as a result of the increase in VAT to 20%, the abolition of the 50% additional tax rate in 2014, successive uprating of the income tax threshold, the impact of declining earnings on national insurance revenues, the reduction of Corporation Tax from 27 to 20% and the introduction of the Controlled Foreign Company rules which sharply reduce UK tax liabilities for many multi-nationals. These changes constrain potential tax revenues and generally shift tax burdens downwards.
- Policies that reinforce market effects in holding down pay. These include the introduction of fees of up to £1,200 for industrial tribunal cases, the reforms to benefits noted above and the weak recovery of wages. The new fees regime appears to have produced a 79% fall in the number of cases in the first year (TUC, 2014). IFS estimates indicate that the average fall in gross earnings in excess of 8% between 2008 and 2013 is unlikely to be made up before the end of the next parliament, with a more severe impact and slower recovery at the bottom (Belfield et al., 2014, Table 2.3).

How do these developments relate to the objectives of embedding change and restructuring solidarity?

Embedding change

It is in principle possible to reverse many of the benefit cuts and the policies (such as the below-inflation limit on annual uprating) that imply future cut-backs. The same applies to

Figure 1: Taxation Revenues 2007-16 as % GDP

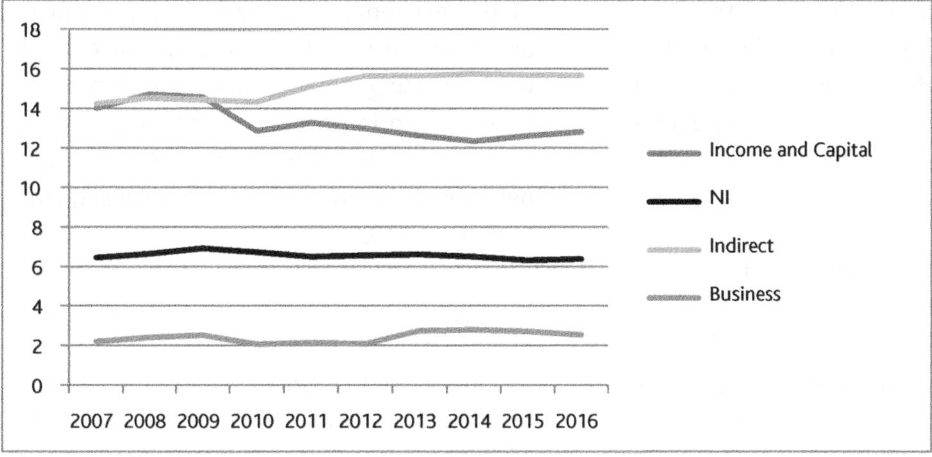

Source: ONS, 2014

changes in tax rates, and policies such as the industrial tribunal fees. Such a programme would require substantial extra tax revenue or higher borrowing, which would be unpopular.

The expansion of the private sector in areas such as NHS and local government service delivery and the Work Programme introduces further difficulties, due to the long time periods required to bring some contracts to an end.

The problem of low pay could be mitigated, provided government wished to do so, by strengthening work place rights. The raising of the minimum wage to living wage levels (roughly a 20% increase) might save government money as spending on wage top-ups fell. It would only be possible to make this transition without causing considerable disruption to the labour market by pursuing a sectoral approach and adjusting wage rates in areas with concentrations of low-paid staff, such as hospitality, catering, retail and tourism in a phased programme over time.

This brief review suggests that the great majority of the Coalition's reforms can only be seen as embedding change if they have also created a situation in which a new government is unable to raise the revenue to reverse them. This directs attention to the question of whether current policies have damaged solidarity in such a way that the case for higher taxes to finance higher welfare state spending can no longer be made.

Undermining Support for State Welfare

Much of the debate is about spending on cash benefits. Reforms since 2010 have widened the gap between benefit claimers who are pensioners and those of working age through, on the one hand, the 'triple lock', which has had the effect of raising state pensions faster than inflation, and, on the other, the cuts in short-term benefits mentioned earlier. This is reflected in the fact that the combined effect of all tax and benefit changes for pensioner households in the bottom third of the income distribution has been to increase incomes by about half of one per cent, while for working age households the impact has been a fall in real income of between 4% and 6% (Phillips, 2014).

A sustained campaign of seeking (counter-factually) to present the majority of claimers of working age as out of work households (in contrast to 'hard-working families') and to stigmatise benefits for them as 'welfare' rather than entitlement or social security, reinforced by the expansion of means-testing for this group, seeks to drive a wedge between them and other users of welfare state services.

If these changes have the effect of reducing the willingness of the mass of the population to finance provision for the poor, they may create a situation in which it is difficult for a new government to gain sufficient support for the tax and spending measures necessary to restore provision for this group. If the welfare state is understood to provide predominantly for the poor rather than for the mass of the population, solidaristic support for the whole welfare system is undermined.

Evidence on changing patterns of solidarity

There is no evidence of a decline in support for the welfare state, or for benefits for the poor since the crisis. On the basis of the most authoritative survey series, British Social Attitudes (Baumberg, 2014, Taylor-Gooby, 2015) four points may be made:

- First, while there has been a long-term tendency to view the poor, especially those of working-age, with greater suspicion, this trend seems to have come to an abrupt halt since the recession. The proportion believing that 'the unemployed could find a job if they really wanted to' rose from 27% in 1993 to 70% in 2005, but then fell back to 54% by 2010 and now stands at 59%.

- Secondly, there is established evidence of a division in public support between those welfare state services that have been relatively protected, and which meet the life-cycle-needs of most people (notably the NHS and education), and provision for specific poor minorities. However, there is no indication that this gap has grown wider since 2010. The percentage agreeing that 'cutting welfare benefits would damage too many people's 'lives' fell sharply from 59% in 2000 to 42% in 2010, but had recovered somewhat to 46% by 2014. Support for extra spending for the traditionally popular group of pensioners reached 80% in 2005 but has actually fallen since then to 67%. This may reflect the fact that benefits for this group are relatively well protected. Support for extra spending on the unemployed fell during the period of relative prosperity, between 1992 and the 2007 Great Recession from 32% to 7%, but has grown since then to 11%.

- Thirdly, people seem to be increasing aware of the existence of poverty and pessimistic about future trends. The proportion answering 'increasing' to a question about the perceived trend in poverty in Britain during the past decade, fell slightly from 36% to 32% between 2000 and 2006, but has subsequently risen to 64%.

- Fourth, while perceptions of one's own level of living bear on attitudes to the poor, there is no indication of a widening gap in perceptions between those who see themselves as better off and those who believe they are not, but rather the reverse. In 2010 some 14% of the sample described themselves as 'struggling' on their present income, while 50% said they were 'living comfortably'. By 2013 the statistics were 18% and 44%. The gap had fallen from 36% to 26%.

Both 'struggling' and 'comfortable' respondents were more likely to agree that the government 'should spend more on welfare benefits for the poor' in 2013 compared with 2010. The increase was from 42% to 51% among the first group and from 25% to 30% among the second. Similarly the proportion believing benefits for the unemployed are too low and cause hardship, which fell from 55% in 1993 to 19% by 2011, is now trending upwards and reached 27% in 2014.

The most striking findings are in relation to party support. Which Labour voters are rather less unsympathetic to spending on benefits for the poor of working age, this does not translate into a major political cleavage. The 2014 survey shows majorities of Conservative and Labour supporters endorsing the benefits cap (85% and 69%) and very substantial minorities believing that immigrants from outside the EU should never be able to claim UK benefits (48 against 33%).

Taken together these findings suggest that there is no evidence of a decline in solidarity or in support for welfare for the poor since 2010, and that more people across the income distribution recognise the existence of poverty and want government to spend money on unemployed people and on those in poverty. However there is also good evidence of a long-term established trend to greater social division in support for welfare and to willingness to accept the stereotype of the working age poor as primarily responsible for their own poverty.

Conclusion

Coalition policies have been highly divisive, but have failed to undermine solidarity in public support for the welfare state. The real question is whether an incoming government is willing to raise the taxes necessary to reverse the cuts.

References

TUC (2014) *At what price justice?* London: TUC.

Baumberg, B. (2014) 'Benefits and the Cost of Living' in A. Park, C. Bryson, and J. Curtice (eds.) *British Social Attitudes, 31st Report*, London: Natcen.

Belfield, C. et al. (2014) *Living standards, poverty and inequality in the UK*, London: IFS.

ONS: *PSF Supplementary Tables*, via http://www.ukpublicrevenue.co.uk/ [accessed 1.12.2014].

Phillips, D. (2014) *Personal tax and welfare measures,* http://www.ifs.org.uk/budgets/budget2014/personal_measures.pdf [accessed 2.12.2014].

Taylor-Gooby, P. and Taylor, E. (2015) 'Benefits and welfare' in A. Park, R. Ormston and J. Curtice (eds) *British Social Attitudes*, 32nd Report, London: Natcen.